SUNBURNT PENGUINS TOUR THE USA

SUNBURNT PENGUINS TOUR THE USA

America's East Coast and Midwest through the eyes of an Englishman

Jim Stanson

jimstansonauthor@gmail.com

ISBN 9798627828503

For Alison

Contents

Introduction

My wife's fiftieth birthday was looming on the horizon and I needed to get my skates on as I wanted to make sure she had a great one.

New York was somewhere she had been desperate to visit for an awfully long time, even though I could never understand quite why. Until we went there and experienced its magic.

Prior to that, a lot of big cities appeared the same to me and although New York is one of the world's great cities, so is London, in our own country. Indeed, given how many overseas travellers visit London, I honestly thought for the extra time, hassle and cost of travelling a few thousand miles to another continent, compared to the couple of hundred to London, we would be better travelling at home; spending the difference on better hotels, better restaurants and so on.

But, even if that's what I believed, it was her special day, so New York it had to be. Plus, she had put up with me for over thirty years and ensured our four children had grown up happily in a nice home and family environment. (Sadly, often on her own, due to my long hours at work). The least I could also do was try and ensure things would go as well as possible.

So, I spent an inordinate amount of time planning the trip. As well as using Tripadvisor for the usual reviews of hotels, restaurants, things to do, etc., I also read lots of trip reports people posted in the New York City forum. From these I gleaned ideas and tips and got a feel of what it was really like to visit NYC.

As others had helped me, so I wanted to do my bit in return and duly posted our trip report when we got back. Writing about our experiences was like nothing I had ever done before, as my career to that point as an accountant had been more about numbers than words. Even now I can see people shuddering, rolling their eyes and saying, "Accountants can't write. Everyone knows they're virtually illiterate – take their calculator away and they're practically bereft."

Well, that and, "I bet he used a spreadsheet when planning their trip."

So you can imagine my surprise when the responses to my trip report were not only polite, but positively appreciative. Initially, I thought my report would be succinct and that if I could help just a few people, in the way that I had garnered ideas from those I had read, that would be great. But the feedback was so overwhelmingly supportive, with people encouraging me to write more, I got somewhat carried away.

Comments like, "Perfection. Writes with such gusto that at times I felt like I was there with him… and I've not even been to New York yet!"

Or, "As an avid trip report reader, this is the best one I have ever read. Loved the insight, descriptions and sheer joy in the writing." meant that as well as being truly touched, I just kept going. A bit like Forrest Gump, I suppose.

I posted it day by day – it was as fast as I could write – and at the end, when some said they were genuinely sad that the last day was coming, it spurred me to extend our horizons in America and see where it took us. What started out as the holiday of a lifetime trip for Alison's fiftieth, ended up us visiting Graceland and knocking the single biggest item off her bucket list, with Florida, Boston, Michigan, Washington, North Carolina and Tennessee crammed in between.

At least you know who to blame now.

Whilst our initial trip was just over four years ago, we only hit Washington and Tennessee a few months ago, luckily before the coronavirus shutdown. I have, however, tried to update any relevant information to the time of writing – although of course these things constantly change.

Anyway, for those who first encouraged me, and to you dear reader, for buying and reading this, thank you. I hope you enjoy the journey as much as we did.

Oh, and just because some of the stories seem incredible, doesn't mean they didn't happen.

New York City

Game On!

Alison isn't the type for surprise parties. In fact, she had made it clear for some time that if I threw one, it would continue without her as she hates feeling the centre of attention. But, hey, where would life be without a little excitement from time to time?

An unintended benefit of me repeatedly exclaiming what a great city London was, every time she mentioned anything about New York, was she never considered for a moment this was somewhere we might go anytime soon. So, research and planning done, I procured ace tickets to a top Broadway show, and slipped them inside her birthday card. Then, over a quiet dinner at her favourite restaurant, I tried to be as nonchalant as possible as I handed her the envelope containing the card and tickets. All whilst trying to ensure the thing didn't catch fire as I passed it across the candlelit table. Sadly, as you'll see, it's often a fine line between cool and calamity where I am concerned.

Somehow though, this time, I managed it, and to see her face as she opened the card, saw the tickets and digested the address of the venue. Wow, it was like being 21 all over again. They do say that giving is better than receiving.

We had a few days between her birthday and flying off to allow her to pack. I may plan a bit and even be brave and risk a surprise present, but I'm not so stupid as to not let her pack her own case. It also allowed her time to plan anything particular she wanted from the trip.

This proved mighty handy as I had booked the flights, show tickets and hotel months earlier, forgetting that we were arriving on Halloween, and just how big that is in the United States. It turns out – even if we are largely unaware in the UK – the Big Apple is home to the world's largest Halloween parade, with sixty thousand participants and two million people watching it live in the streets. And we were heading right into the heart of it. GULP! Apparently a further one hundred million also watch it via TV, and they allow anyone suitably dressed to take part.

Hmmm. What to do? Well, what any self-respecting person who needs their head feeling for bumps would – we made some Halloween costumes and decided we'd join in. In homage to one of my musical heroes Dan Baird (ex-lead singer of the Georgia Satellites for those who have never heard of him), I went as a horror rocker, Dan Scared.

Clad in black trousers and jumper, onto which I painted some white bones; a horrible skeleton mask, with fake, bushy, ginger hair shooting from the sides; and topped with a huge Aerosmith style hat I'd bought years ago from Disney's Hollywood Studios in Florida, I thought it did the job. Even if my self-appointed fashion guide considered it an improvement on my normal looks. "Scaerosmith" she called me and said I ought to consider it as a new day-to-day style. Still, it'd make a change from what you'd usually wear to the office.

Alison grabbed a white Tinker Bell style dress, which she attacked with gusto – tearing at the material here and there and adding a few splodges of red food dye for extra effect. She applied some lipstick to her face in a haphazard, slovenly sort of way – as if she had tried to do her makeup after having had a couple of bottles of wine. Then, with a final twist of her tiara, she was done. My dear wife had turned into the bride of Frankenstein.

So there we were. Costumes sorted, bags packed. All set, revved up and ready to go.

The next morning, we caught the, sadly missed, Thomas Cook out of Manchester, England direct to New York's JFK airport. Despite not booking premium seats, we were amongst the first off the plane. Always a nice bonus. Then, without trying, amazingly we ended up being the first people to the immigration/passport control counters. Probably the only time that will ever happen to us.

Now, those who have travelled to the US will know how long those lines and that procedure can be, but we sailed straight through. Honestly, we've never been processed so speedily and I made the mistake of feeling this must be our lucky day.

When we got to the baggage reclaim and our first suitcase came off the conveyor belt super quick, we were now virtually in a state of shock. These kinds of things simply don't happen to us. Until – and why does this always happen? Until our second suitcase appeared on the conveyor...... only after the entire plane had picked up theirs.

From being first, now we were last. And now there was a big line to hand in your customs form for the final part of the arrival process. And we are talking *BIG* line.

Seriously, aside from the "why does this always happen to me?", how the heck can two cases that are checked in and go down the little conveyor belt to the plane *together,* end up coming out at the other end half an hour apart? Hmmm. Anyway, after the customs line eventually cleared, we headed for the AirTrain.

I'd debated the merits of getting a taxi over public transport and settled on the latter option. Including tips, the taxi to our hotel near Times Square would have been around $90 plus, compared to the AirTrain and subway at less than $20, for us both.

It's not that I'm a skinflint, bean counter or cheapskate, or other such words I have heard people use to describe accountants, but the journey time was similar for each option. Potentially worse for the taxi, depending on the traffic and lines to get one. Plus, taking the subway would allow us to get an early glimpse of the real New York. Granted lugging bags would be a bit of a pain, but only a bit – after all they have wheels these days – and we could easily put the seventy plus bucks saved to a good use.

It should have been straightforward enough to get from JFK to our hotel – Air Train to Jamaica, then subway line E to 42nd Street Port Authority, followed by a short walk to the hotel. That was until we got to the AirTrain station and they said no trains to Jamaica today due to works on the line or something. They said they would put a bus transfer on. I thought of the numbers of people going that way, all their luggage and us at the back of it all, and just thought, "Oh no. Why didn't I get a taxi, or the car transfer offered by the hotel?"

Then I remembered my planning and realised we could still go via Howard Beach and the C line to 42nd Street. A bit longer, but probably way quicker than queuing for the bus with all those people, not to mention everyone mounting then descending it. After double checking with a subway attendant that this worked, off we trundled. Now, by and large, I felt safe in NYC, but you still need to be sensible and remember you're in a big city – so keep your wits about you and don't draw attention to yourself.

Says he as he gets onto a subway train with two flipping large suitcases and a wife wearing a sweater emblazoned with "Go team GB." Something already noted by a customs officer who had asked us whether we were part of the official team. True. To be fair, he may simply have been trying to make Alison's day, and if so he did his job well, given the size of the smile he put on her face.

What is the relevance of this you might ask. Well, three stops after we caught the subway, a guy in his early thirties, about six foot two and reasonably athletic disposition gets on walking with crutches, but no obvious cast or broken leg. The look was complemented by wearing extremely low-slung jeans. Unhelpfully in his case, without the underpants that normally show with that style. Not a nice thought, I know, but it wasn't a nice sight either.

Having watched too many Eddie Murphy films when the bad guy walks into a bar in the middle of summer wearing a long coat, I didn't need to be Sherlock Holmes to know this didn't feel right. Particularly as he didn't seem to have too much trouble walking, other than he might have had a few sherbets/beers.

Anyway, the guy sits down – fortunately a few seats away from us. Handily, there were also quite a few other passengers in our carriage, but you could tell the atmosphere had changed. Dramatically. As most of the car had American accents and knew the score, I'm thinking this isn't a good sign. Well that, and why didn't I get the car transfer offered by the hotel?

Suddenly, a few stops later, the train shuddered as it rounded a bend and before you know it, this guy is flung forward (or maybe flings himself forward?) and lands on someone's lap with his jeans sliding off in the process. Sadly, confirming his lack of pants. Welcome to Brooklyn!

Apart from once again thinking, oh no (and why didn't I get the car transfer offered by the hotel?), when you're from out of town and there are quite a few locals around, you glance around and do your best to rapidly work out what you're supposed to do at this point. In

Manchester it would probably have kicked off at this point – which isn't good either – but at least when you're at home you know how to call the police, where the stations are, what's going to happen and so on.

Anyway, here in Brooklyn, the guy just goes back to his seat and everyone seems to carry on as though nothing has happened. Although people were now watching him even more closely. Fortunately, after a few more stops he got off and you could feel the train breathe again.

Perhaps it was all innocent and nothing had happened. Maybe it was a ruse to dip someone's pocket? Maybe he was just drunk. Whatever, it was certainly better when he got off.

Then, a couple of stops later, a guy gets on saying he's homeless and needs help and starts walking around the carriage asking for money. Now, I have every sympathy for the genuinely down at heel and often, rightly or wrongly, give money when I can see someone is in a bad way. Here, however, all I could observe was this guy seemed rather well dressed for the circumstances he was claiming.

Strangely enough, sensing out of towners, it's us he decides to approach first and ask for a donation. So glad we'd successfully blended in then. Thankfully, after politely declining, there was no bother and he got off a stop later, to work another train; leaving us to make the rest of our way uneventfully, if now a little nervously, to 42nd Street Port Authority.

I'm not sure I can fully describe my emotions as we surfaced at ground level, other than WOW!

The size of those skyscrapers.

The semi-permanent shade caused by their height; as you craned your neck to try and catch a glimpse of sky.

Dwarfed and surrounded by so many tall buildings. And so many people. In such a hurry. Like ants, buzzing from a scalded nest. So many smells. So many noises.

It was an assault on almost all your senses at once.

And boy, was I happy to be lugging two large suitcases and two carry-on bags through it all.

We crossed the madness of Times Square and, after a smooth check-in at our hotel, were straight out to the big city. Our first stop was back to Times Square where we tried to get a photo of us on the "Revlon Love is On" board – a huge selfie type screen where a camera beamed up street level images to one of Times Square's illuminated advertising panels.

Periodically, it would zoom in on a couple and encase them inside a pink heart. Kitsch, probably. Popular, certainly. Busier than a Black Friday bazaar, we figured we had about as much chance as Newcastle winning the league and so decided to return later. Instead, we scouted around the area and ended up in Bryant Park.

This hadn't been on our list, but it was great. It just had such a nice vibe. The ice rink was open for Winter and there were lots of craft stalls selling all kinds of knick-knacks. Even though they wouldn't be there all year round, you could tell the place had a positive feel. An enclave of greenery surrounded by all those high-rise buildings. And my goodness, they were tall.

Coming from Europe just does not prepare you for the height of those skyscrapers. Or the incredible beauty of some. In fact, I shall always remember that thrill of excitement on first seeing the Chrysler Building, as well as that on first glimpsing the Empire State. Walking around both Bryant Park and the surrounding area was almost otherworldly. To us, from the UK, it was like being on a film set.

Time was pressing on, however, and we had a parade to get to. So back to the hotel, change into our costumes and off to Greenwich village. Being European and still somewhat naïve as to how long it takes to cross roads in New York, we decided to walk to the parade's meeting point at Canal Street. Although, this wasn't as insane as might appear, as we wanted to break our journey in Madison Square Park, home of the original Shake Shack.

Shake Shack, for those who don't know, is a burger chain that sells very nice burgers along with beer, wine and some amazing, if sinful, desserts that I still don't fully understand. Desserts like concretes and frozen custards, but not custards in an English sense of the word.

Where I'm from, custard is something runny. It has the consistency of cream – pouring cream, as our American friends would say – and is almost always vanilla flavoured. Indeed, as far as I'm concerned should be vanilla flavoured.

In America though, as far as I understand things, custard is solid. They tell if a custard is good or not, by whether it stays in its container when you hold it upside down. Good ones remain in place. To me, that is something with the consistency of concrete. It is something we would lay roads with. Actually, given the amount of potholes we have on our highways these days, that might be an improvement.

Concretes, however, are where they take one of their solid custards (what you might be forgiven for thinking should be a concrete) and then blend things in. These can include pieces of toffee, marshmallows, jelly babies, chocolate chunks, honeycomb, fruit, even the kitchen sink it seems. Quite how they do this is beyond me – they must have seriously heavy duty machines – but the result is something we would probably use to insulate houses, instead of our stomachs. Even if they are rather nice. Dangerously nice.

Anyway, glad that's cleared up. Or not, as the case maybe. Shake Shack must make lovely burgers though, as they have grown from one food cart in 2001 to first conquering New York, and now to over 200 stores worldwide. Having heard so much about it, from people who had fallen under its spell, we knew we just had to try it.

What can I say? The evangelists were spot on. I chose a Smoke Shack (burger with smoky bacon and cheese), whilst Alison went for a special called the Road Shack, which was a burger with lots of mushrooms. We both had one of their beers. Brewed by Brooklyn brewery, it is a lager, unique to Shake Shack, tailored to partner the food*. It was all delicious, as anyone in our vicinity would have told you, given the way we fell upon our fare like a pack of wolves who hadn't eaten for a week.

Sitting there emitting squeals of pleasure, like Meg Ryan in the diner in *Harry Met Sally*, we slavishly devoured each successive mouthful. Sadly, I fear we may also have somewhat embarrassed ourselves, as burger juice dribbled down our faces whilst we remained oblivious; focussing intently on our meal, as though it might be our last on this planet. The house beer, the Shackmeister Ale, was also a perfect match for the burgers. Something that, regrettably, lead to yet more slurping, sighing, hooting, groaning and moaning in another unseemly way. Heaven only knows what our neighbouring tables thought of this

---

* As an aside, I know there are now a few Shake Shacks in the UK, but whether it's different water used in the production of the Shackmeister Ale in the US, or whether it's the ambience that is different, things are just not the same – a bit like the difference between fish and chips eaten out of a paper wrapper and eaten off a plate. Fine, if you have no alternative, but ultimately not the real deal.

grotesque couple in their midst, and that's before you factored in our Halloween costumes. We must have looked like something that had escaped from a chamber of horrors.

It also says a lot about the wonder that is New York City. Although you could tell people were looking at us rather strangely at first; although they were giving us a wider berth than usual as they walked past carrying their food – in reality, it was probably only to avoid projectiles of burger juice. In most cities, let alone small towns, we would have attracted quite a crowd, with people staring. Maybe even shouting abuse. In New York, however, once they'd assessed the situation and classified us as harmless, they merely shrugged their shoulders and continued conversing with their partner.

Replete, it was now time to go to the parade. It didn't start till seven p.m. but we had read that the Police would start closing side streets at six and it was now starting to get even busier. Sadly, our innocence was starting to haunt us. We got to 16th Street as things were closing down and roadblocks going up. If only we hadn't spent so long gorging at Shake Shack. Instead of staying at 16th though, where we had a good view, we compounded our errors by continuing to try and get down to the parade's start. We wanted to be in this damn procession after all!

As the crowds worsened, we adopted increasingly desperate tactics to make any kind of progress. Juking, spinning, jump cutting, we would have been good value for a running back slot in the NFL draft. Even if I drew the line at a stiff arm move for fear of starting a riot.

Going as fast as possible, we made it to Vandam Street by 6.30, but by this stage the crowds were huge. Indeed, we were now about eight deep from the road. With a clear run we were only five minutes away from our goal, but it wasn't clear. And with each step forward, the crowds got worse.

By now, with even fewer holes to squeeze through then the legendary 1985 Chicago Bears defence, we figured we no longer had a chance of making the procession and decided to stick rather than twist. To hold what we had, rather than risk an even worse situation. It was tragic. Just tragic. So near and yet so far.

Now, I realise it would have made for a perfect story if we could have made it through. If somehow I had thrown Alison over the crowds before somersaulting my way through, catching her, as I shouted

"Touch Down!". All with just a second left on the clock. But life isn't always perfect, and I can only write what happened.

Sadly, we didn't make it. Double sadly, the crowds were now so big and we were so far from the front, our view was also less than perfect. Indeed, apart from those on floats, or a few taller figures, such as ghosts on wire extensions which reached over the heads of the crowd, it proved next to impossible to see many of those walking in the parade. Maybe I shouldn't have drawn the line when it came to the stiff arming move.

Over the next couple of hours, as people left, we floated to the front. That improved our view, but sadly it didn't improve many of the participants. The parade was good, but it seemed plenty of people in it had hardly made an effort. Sure, many had dressed up, but there was also a large number who seemed happy simply to pile in and wander down the street without bothering. Despite the organisers website saying unless you come in costume, you can't join the procession. My cozzie wasn't fantastic, but I could easily have held my head high in there. Which, given I'm only five foot six, takes some effort. Still, it's not every day that you get to line the streets of a parade alongside two million other people.

When it eventually ended, and the adrenaline started to subside, we started to flag. Our bodies thought it was past 2 a.m. and, not being spring chickens anymore, we thought it best to retire and pace ourselves for the days ahead.

Before concluding the night though, I want to pay a tribute to the men and women of the NYPD. Sadly, the world we live in these days seems to get crazier and crazier at times, with all sorts of atrocities being committed, often targeting high profile locations or occasions. Following some awful incident, when people have been thinking about cancelling their long awaited holiday or trip, I've been asked many times what I thought. Although it's always easier to say than do, particularly where people are genuinely frightened, I always reply that you should go.

Firstly, you worked hard for that – why should you let the fear of something that may never happen, or someone take it off you? Secondly, we all have to carry on living our lives. Otherwise, the lunatics get what they want and win. Thirdly, due to the, often unseen and underappreciated, efforts of our security and police services, the chances of anything happening to you are remote.

On the night of the Halloween parade with so many people, a lot of whom were in masks, I was concerned that the event could become a nightmare. The NYPD responded magnificently though. They effectively flooded the city with law enforcement officers, who were literally on every street corner and more. Not only that, but as well as being constantly on alert and managing a potentially difficult situation really well, they were helpful and friendly when we talked to them. As a result, 99.9% of the millions of people out in Manhattan that night had a great time. Thank you.

Why Can't I Sleep?

One great thing about flying east to west is that you're up early and ahead of the crowds for the first few days. Sadly, in our case this was 3 a.m. (back home, it was 8 a.m.) and I woke to the sounds of sirens and cars.

Many people comment that New York is noisy, you can't sleep, you need rooms on high floors in your hotel, ear plugs and so on. Perhaps, but I honestly believe that it's probably jet lag – it wasn't the sirens that woke me, I woke because my body thought it was time to wake up. And then I heard the sirens. On all subsequent nights, we slept through. I also realised I had only just noticed a siren…… and we had been in New York fourteen hours. Normally you hear them within five minutes of arriving in London. Whether that's because London has more police chasing about, or New York has more distractions, who knows.

Anyway, after tossing and turning more times than a burger flipper at McDonald's, as I tried fitfully to get back to sleep, I thought to hell with it, got up and hit the shower. At least it provided the bonus of being first into breakfast. Actually, that's not true, we were only second into breakfast – another British family was there ahead of us.

After a good breakfast with some proper fresh New York Bagels, amongst a good deal of other ballast providing options, we were off to Hell's Kitchen Flea Market. (A car boot sale for my British readers).

I know you will be thinking this was an odd choice, and your face probably now looks something similar to my good wife's when I suggested over breakfast we go there. It certainly wasn't something we had planned beforehand. For some reason though, at three in the morning, as Alison lay sleeping, and I was searching for things to do nearby (that were clean), this was a recommendation that popped out of…… goodness knows where. Anyway, we thought well, we go to the odd car boot sale/flea market at home, it'll be interesting to see what they sell here.

Maybe it was its quirky name, but the more I think about this, the more I can't imagine what possessed me to conceive this might, even remotely, be a good idea in the first place. Other than it was the early hours of the morning and I was clearly jet lagged. I should have listened to the reviews which had said things like, "seems like each stall is required to sell old vehicle license plates before they get given a pitch." That pretty much summed the place up. Oh well, it was an experience and not too much of a diversion in terms of distance or time.

Then we caught the subway to Spring Street and wandered through the area we had been for the parade. We were heading towards Little Italy when Alison diverted us to a knish bakery. Knish not niche, although the latter might have been more appropriate.

Originating from Eastern Europe and brought to America with Jewish settlers, a knish is a thin dough dumpling. Traditionally stuffed with mashed potato before being baked, nowadays you can also get them with different fillings. Alison had read about it on Mumsnet back home and apparently this place made the best knishes in the world, and we had never had a knish, and blah blah we should go.

Entering the knishery was nothing our wildest imagination could have prepared us for. Proudly operating from the same premises where they started in 1890, understated and rustic, are some of the better thoughts that came to mind. Walking through its glass doors was like taking a step back in time. Not necessarily in a good way. A lot of the furniture and fittings even looked like they still dated back to when the business first opened.

Inside, the walls had lots of newspaper cuttings where such and such a visitor or celebrity attested that, in their opinion, these were the best knishes ever. Interestingly though, these too were faded from years of exposure to light. Perhaps that was more rustic charm, but you couldn't help wondering if it was still so.

Things weren't helped by the interesting sales technique of the waiter, who was also the owner and cook. We ordered a knish, of course, and I was interested in ordering the borsch as I'm quite partial to a nice beetroot soup. Amazingly though when I asked, "What's the borsch like?" (that's all I said, I promise), the owner retorted, "You won't like it, it's cold!" One sale less then.

Perhaps I'm doing him a disservice and as well as waiter, owner, cook and chief bottle washer, he was also a master of extrasensory perception. Hence he already knew that previously I'd always had it served hot, even though I hadn't mentioned this. Either that or, as part of the place's authenticity, this was still the original sales patter from 1890. Well, perhaps they do make the best knishes in the world, and it's just that knishes don't blow our socks off (or at the least the traditional potato ones that we ordered), but disappointingly this was another one we would have to chalk down as worth the experience.

Anyway, onto Little Italy which, as might be surmised from its name, is the area that became home to many of the Italian immigrants to New York. It was once even segmented into neighbourhoods based on which part of Italy people came from, as new arrivals clustered with others from a similar background. Infamous for its historic association with organised crime and mafia stories – and for those particularly interested you can now get walking tours that guide you around the scenes of its more notorious events – the district has slowly shrunk over the years as Chinatown and SoHo have expanded into it. Traditionalists will tell you it's nothing like it was, and indeed it now only runs a few blocks, along two or three key streets, with locals overrun by tourists. Nonetheless, it was still nice walking around, savouring the atmosphere and Italian delicacies. All whilst not being shot at.

We wandered into a tea shop (we are from England after all) that had a mind-boggling array of different teas. Honestly, shelves upon shelves of teas, many of which you couldn't pronounce, never mind had never heard of. Good, and definitely different, but rather like that cheap bottle of Retsina that tasted so sweet in the sunshine of Greece only to transform into something rank at home (especially after you have worked so hard to get a case of the damn stuff back), so too here. Something we tragically discovered to our cost, as exotic tea after exotic tea that we'd spent a small fortune on, still couldn't beat the good old English Breakfast blend when we returned home. Still, it was worth the experience.

Luckily, our next stop didn't let us down. Billed as New York's best cheesecake and New York's No 1 for dessert, our expectations had taken a bit of a battering from our earlier experiences. Perhaps understandably, we were now more than a little cautious as we opened the door to the unimposing premises of Eileen's Special Cheesecake. Particularly, with a shop not ten feet wide and space inside for less than twenty people (and only then if they were prepared to snuggle up close), it was hardly screaming best cheesecake to a city of eight and a half million people.

Having made the journey though, we decided to push on regardless, and boy am I glad we did. It was the best cheesecake that either of us has ever had in our lives. Thinking about it, I can still taste it, even now. It was creamy, but light, yet rich with a lasting depth of flavour. It was simply amazing. Even sitting here now writing about it takes me back there. Which is both good and sad. Good, because it brings back many happy memories and sad, because now I really want one of those gorgeous cakes and it will be a while before that can happen again.

They have a huge array of different flavours and sizes. You can even buy small cheesecakes designed for individuals, although given that these are American portions, two people could probably share. Actually, I should scratch that last comment, because unless you are on exceptionally good terms with the person you're sharing with, you would only end up fighting as the cakes are so good you wouldn't want to share even the tiniest morsel. Thirty years of marriage could evaporate in thirty minutes.

For those interested, I had a chocolate bourbon cheesecake and Alison the salted caramel. Impossible to say which was better – they were both so good. A small family business, they say their cheesecakes taste so good because they're made with love. Perhaps they're right, because there sure was a happy vibe that morning. From the friendly service we received, to the grins from ear to ear on the customers enjoying Eileen's delicacies.

Our next port of call was China Town and we headed for a restaurant on Mott Street, which had also been the subject of rave reviews. We'd been advised that the experience would be overwhelmingly authentic, with everything done in Chinese, from the waiters speaking little to no English, to the bill at the end. That it would be like going to China, without going to China. Even so, we weren't fully prepared for what we were about to experience.

When we arrived, which was still before noon, it was so rammed a sardine would have difficulty finding a spot to squeeze in. Whilst I was all for bailing as it was clear we would be waiting for ages, if not Alison's next birthday, my conscience in these matters wasn't as convinced.

"Always the sign of a good restaurant," she said, deciding for us both.

"The seafood will be fresh too," she added, pointing at large tanks that housed a variety of fish and crustaceans.

Inside the restaurant, it was somewhere between organised chaos and outright anarchy. It was like Times Square on speed. Full of big circular tables, each full of people shouting, chomping, slurping and generally having a whale of a time, it resembled an adult version of eating time at a children's birthday party. You know the part when they all sit around stuffing themselves with sandwiches, crisps and cake. Not always in the right order, and not necessarily into the right orifice. And why is there always one, in my experience usually called Billy, who decides to see whether peanuts are better in your ears rather than your mouth? Or as often as not, in someone else's ears. Which, of course, is when the mandatory food fight usually starts.

Whilst no one appeared to be putting anything into their ears, it wasn't clear that we wouldn't be eating them, judging by some of the food being shipped out. Goose feet certainly seemed a popular dish.

Nor, to be fair, did a food fight actually break out whilst we were there, but it seemed a close-run thing every time a loaded dim sum cart trundled past.

At this point, I should add that the staff here deserve special praise. Service was lightning quick and the waiters steering the dim sum carts did a great job. Not only in expertly passing through the small gaps between tables, but in accurately recording who from the baying crowd had grabbed what, and how much, from their cart. Not to mention those in the kitchen. The relentless speed at which food kept coming out would have driven even the most seasoned McDonald's crew to a nervous breakdown.

Yet still it didn't seem to satisfy the masses. For the poor sods working there, it must have been worse than the hardest level on space invaders. No sooner had they replenished a cart, then it was demolished. With a concerted effort, if they finished a table off and got them the bill, it was immediately repopulated with a fresh bunch of customers. At least you knew the food would be fresh. Whether you could stomach duck tongue, cold jelly fish or crispy fried pig intestine was another matter.

Time soon passed though, as you lapped up the scene and used it to try and decide which exotic food you might be safest trying. It was clear that once in the arena we wouldn't have time for these sorts of deliberations.

To make our wait pass even faster, one waiter considerately put on a show. Even if that hadn't been his intention. Rather like the stokers who used to constantly feed the boilers on steam locomotives, he'd been dispatched to get more fuel for the fire. Only in his case it was fish, not coal. Fine, except coal doesn't usually get any ideas. In his case, the fish did.

Deciding it wasn't yet ready to be sizzled, it wriggled out of his grasp as he scooped from the tank. Then, as it splashed onto the floor, it made a bid for freedom. At this point, you would have thought you should place all your money on the waiter in this contest. Fish aren't at their best on carpet after all. You would have been wrong though.

Wriggling and writhing like a 1970s disco queen, it was off. The poor waiter, fraught at the thought of having to explain to the chef why his prize piece was covered in fur and fluff, gamely set off after it. Those who have worked in busy kitchens, know this is something you wouldn't want to do lightly – stressed chefs aren't good at the best of times. Here he would probably be holding a meat cleaver as well.

Whether it was because half his mind was on how the chef was going to react, or whether he could see his paycheck disappearing out the same door the fish was heading towards, I don't know. What was clear though, is that the poor sod was struggling. The waiter, that is. Every time he caught up with the fish, it wriggled and again slipped from his grasp. He would pick it up, drop it, pick it up, drop it, pick it up, drop it. It was better than tennis at Wimbledon.

In an effort to improve his accuracy by reducing the distance of his lunges, he decided to bend over as he pursued the fish. Now almost bent double, as he scrabbled about in his white shirt and black trousers, he started to resemble Manuel, the hapless Spanish hotel assistant in that legendary UK sitcom *Fawlty Towers*. Rather like Manuel he also made a Horlicks of things, leant too far forward and over balanced. Maybe it was his version of a Chinese roll.

Shamefully, now on his fifth or sixth pass, he grabbed it again, only to see it slide away once more. As the audience strained for a better view, it was becoming hard to see who was the flounder here. I was just waiting to see if a hand stand might be his next trick. Eventually though, he got hold of his prey and sadly the show was over.

At this point we felt like clapping as it had been good value entertainment, but somehow it seemed wrong. It would have implied that we wanted him to win all along, which would not be in keeping with the British spirit of rooting for the underdog. Besides, I think he only won because the fish ran out of air. Which in my book means it wasn't a knockout, and the fish won on points.

Once sat down, we were too chicken to go for the more exotic dishes (I'll let you decide which one of us was sweet and which sour). So, somewhat conservatively, we chose prawn dumplings, Sui Mai, aromatic crispy duck and prawn cashew nut. All of which were good. And safe.

It wasn't easy though, as we were being constantly egged on by the Chinese diners on our table every time one of the carts containing the more unusual plates came round. Whether they thought we might now provide the entertainment – it's always hilarious to watch clueless, non-Chinese diners struggle with a bit of sauteed pork stomach, or house special boiled snail, after all. Or whether they thought we were just being polite, as we passed one esoteric dish after another. It was impossible to say.

"Please have some."

"No, no. I simply couldn't. All the more for you."

"Please, I insist."

"No, no. *Truly*, I couldn't."

Actually, that isn't the conversation that took place as the other guests on our table didn't speak a word of English and everything was conducted through a mixture of facial expressions, hand gestures and appropriate noises. Well, apart from one other guy, the only other non-Chinese customer in sight. A native New Yorker, who told us he ate there regularly because he loved Chinese food and here it was so good.

Lucky he was on our table. Not just because he became our lifeboat, but what were the odds? Although, thinking about it, I'm sure they deliberately sat us next to him so that we had someone who might look after us. It must have been the look of sheer bewilderment on our faces that did it.

Overall, the food was good, as were the prices for New York City. And anyway, before I get too hoity-toity about all these dishes that are an acquired taste, what really is the difference between eating a prawn, a lobster and a scorpion? Other than one can sting you.

Satiated, nutritionally and culturally, we headed for the Brooklyn Bridge.

Which was brilliant.

Just brilliant on so many levels. The scenery. The sense of occasion. The backdrop of the skyscrapers against the East River. The contrast between old and new, with the World Trade Centre and the Financial District on the left (as you looked back towards Manhattan) and the Empire State Building, Chrysler Building and Midtown on the right.

The sheer size and scale of what, at 5,989 feet (with a central span of 1,595 feet) was the longest suspension bridge in the world when it opened in 1883. The feeling of awe when you stand in its middle, nearly 150 feet above the water below you, as you feel the wind in your face*.

The majesty of the gigantic, Gothic, limestone and granite towers that rise 276 feet from the East River to take the weight of the bridge and everything travelling across it on their shoulders. The beauty of the bridge as a whole, because as well as its sheer grandeur and magnificence, it is a lovely thing to behold. And the icing on the cake, as we discovered, was that it was relatively uncrowded, as a lot of people were elsewhere watching the NYC marathon.

Taking appropriate stops to appreciate the scenery and our surroundings, we crossed the bridge and thought we would head towards Juliana's, the pizza parlour that had won awards for best pizza

---

* Those feelings of awe are heightened when you find out that because so many men were dying from decompression sickness due to the immense water pressure from digging foundations at that depth, the chief engineer, Washington Roebling, ordered a stop to further excavations on the Manhattan side, when that tower's foundations were still 30 feet above solid bedrock. Roebling calculated that the forces compressing the sand at that point should be sufficient to safely support the weight of the tower and bridge, and so further lives needn't be lost by continuing excavation. Still standing nearly 150 years later, his decision seems to have been vindicated, but it is still a rather odd sensation knowing that the bridge you are standing on is built on sand and not solid rock.

in the world. New York lays claim to an awful lot of bests in the world. But although full, who can't make space for a slice of the world's best pizza?

We had paused to check our bearings, when this guy asked us where we were going. We told him and said we were about to go such and such a way when he said, "well you can, but if you follow me, I'll take you the scenic route."

Now I know, in a strange city this is not always the best idea, but it wasn't as bad as it might sound. He seemed a regular guy; it was still daylight; there were people about etc. etc. and so we pottered off with him. Turned out he was a nice guy, did what he said on the tin and took us the scenic route.

We walked through Brooklyn Heights, with its tranquil streets and charming properties. Full of grand three and four story Brownstone houses, fronted by well-tended sandstone stairs on tree-lined streets, Brooklyn Heights felt every inch like the affluent neighbourhood it both is and was. Many of the homes still had their Halloween decorations up, something particularly noticeable to us from the UK – the Americans embrace the festival so much more enthusiastically than we do back home. It all added to the area's general warm glow.

Developed mainly in the nineteenth century, Brooklyn Heights boomed after the start of a regular steam ferry service to Manhattan to become one of the World's first commuter suburbs. It was much more than that, however, and also played a leading role in the abolitionist movement. Particularly through key figures such as Henry Ward Beecher, the first Pastor of Brooklyn's Plymouth Church.

Beecher, the subject of Debby Applegate's Pulitzer Prize winning biography *The Most Famous Man in America*, was a man who worked tirelessly for emancipation. He raised funds to buy freedom for individual slaves and sent rifles (as well as bibles) to abolitionists fighting in the pre-Civil War Kansas conflict. His passion for the cause, his persuasiveness, and his public speaking ability were so strong, that President Abraham Lincoln, no less, dispatched him to Europe during the Civil War. His mission was to influence European States of the righteous nature of the Union's fight and win their support. Something he did successfully, helping ensure no European Power recognised the legitimacy of the Confederacy. Nor intervened when Union forces blockaded confederate ports, cutting off supplies and funding to the rebel forces. (The South had thought Europe would come to their aid due to their dependency on cotton).

Towards the end of the war, Beecher was held in such high esteem that Lincoln even asked him to make the address when Fort Sumter, South Carolina – scene of the opening shots of the conflict – was recaptured. As Applegate notes, Lincoln believed Beecher had been crucial in winning the struggle.

I digress slightly, but Brooklyn Heights makes for a rewarding detour and those interested can tour the Plymouth Church, with public visits held most Sundays after service. Although, there was a moment of poignancy when we spoke to some local people in the church grounds. Not one had heard of him. The very grounds in which a statue exists in his honour. A man who had done so much for freedom and liberty in the United States. Once the most famous man in America. Yet none had heard of him. How times move on.

When we arrived at Juliana's it was bad news as they wouldn't serve pizzas by the slice – only whole – and even for the best pizza in the world, there are limits. Then we saw out of the corner of our eyes that unmistakable site...... Yooh hooh, it was a Shake Shack! Perfect for a small staging post and a quick snifter of that lovely Shackmeister Ale.

We weren't allowed outside with our beer, so we slurped as quickly as we could whilst still treating our pints with the respect and reverence they deserved (man that ale is tasty), before tottering out to Brooklyn Bridge Park and parking up on a bench. The sun had come out; it was a warm 21°C (70°F); and sitting down by the riverside, taking in the scene, with the bridge to our right and views out across the water to Manhattan, was serene.

After half an hour or so we decided we had better move or we would be in danger of taking root and so ambled along the park's boardwalk and around the chic, vibrant Dumbo area before hopping on the NYC Ferry at Pier 1.

The NYC Ferry is like a water taxi for much of the East River, with several stopping points across West Brooklyn, East Manhattan, Rockaway Beach, Roosevelt Island and Astoria in Queens. It even goes up to Soundview in the Bronx. For the cost of a regular subway ticket, as well as being another way of getting where you want to be, you also get a boat trip thrown in. In fact, it makes for a fantastic boat trip.

On that sunny day, it was the perfect way to get to East 34th Street. It was also the perfect way to see another side of the beautiful bridge. Having walked over it, then sat beside it, now we got to sail under it. After the Brooklyn Bridge comes the Manhattan Bridge and, although hard to believe, things went up another notch. As we sat on the top deck, our boat in the middle of the river between the two bridges, the sun setting over the skyscrapers on our left...... Well, for $2.75 things simply don't get much better. Although, if I am being a bit picky, a pint of Shakemeister at the same time might just have topped things off.

After alighting at the East 34th Street stop, a twenty-five-minute stroll took us to drinks at 230 Fifth. As the name implies, 230 Fifth is a cocktail bar located at 230 on Fifth Avenue, just north of Madison Square Park. Its beauty is a rooftop bar about twenty stories up that overlooks the Empire State Building. There is also a bar one floor down from the rooftop which has floor to ceiling windows, so you can look out from the warmth if it's a chilly night.

The views out over the city on that clear night were fantastic and, with relaxing music contributing to a chilled out vibe, we just sat there sipping away, looking at the Empire State Building lit up magically, thinking "wow, can't believe we're here."

"Can't believe we've only been here for thirty-two hours and how much we've already done," as we contrasted our experiences from the Flea Market to the Brooklyn Bridge. From the excitement on our subway from the airport, to the kindness of the stranger who showed us the scenic route in Brooklyn Heights. From our knishes to 230 Fifth. It was simply magical. After the perfect taxi, it was a perfect way to end the evening.

This Is a Marathon, Not a Sprint

Up early again and down for another filling American breakfast, hoping that yesterday's walking was balancing off the bagels, burgers, and beer. Today was the day for those brave souls who ran the official marathon – unlike our walked version around Little Italy, Chinatown and Brooklyn – to pick up their medals from Central Park. As the New York Marathon is the largest in the world and they would be in their tens of thousands, we thought it best to avoid that area once again and instead head out shopping.

I have to say at this point that my wife is incredible, not just having put up with me for the last thirty years, but at the way she can harness previously undiscovered energy reserves. Yesterday, she had mentioned on several occasions the amount of walking we were doing – and did we not need a staging post? Yet, dangle a few shops in front of her and suddenly she is haring around like a prize winning colt. Sadly, as the day wore on I was starting to resemble one of those ponies that get to carry all the bags up the Andes.

So we hit a number of shops. To put it mildly. I think I must still either be in denial, or suffering from post-traumatic stress, as it's all still a bit of a blur. Still, that's what usually happens to amateurs when they try and mix it with pros in a competitive sport.

In the interests of time, I won't list them all, but thought that with a couple of exceptions most of the shops were similar to those back home in the UK, with pricing not that different. Such are the effects of globalisation on the high street these days I suppose. Sure we don't have a Macy's and it was impressive and nice smelling, but at the end of the day it's just another, albeit huge, department store and you can get most of the stuff they sell pretty much anywhere. The shops that stood out were Aeropostale (good stuff at very reasonable prices), Loft and Abercrombie & Fitch (lovely stuff at not so good prices).

Although I'm not a seasoned shopper, the Abercrombie shop at 720 Fifth Avenue (5th & 56th West) is wonderful. It's the biggest I've seen of theirs, and that hypnotically sweet smell as you enter means you could stay there all day. Which is just as well, given its vast, four floors of merchandise. Perhaps it's all innocent, and it is only a nice smell, or maybe it's a more sinister, entrancing, subliminal thing, as I'm sure they use it as resuscitating salts to bring you around after you faint on seeing the cash register total.

Today also threw up another couple of thoughts/observations. By and large, the service we received during our stay (with exceptions such as Eileen's) was at best described as casual or perfunctory; certainly not friendly. We made sure we tipped following American guidelines and not what one would consider normal for Europeans (i.e., we were doing 18% plus and usually rounding up), but the waiters, whilst doing their job, weren't exactly friendly. I say this because in the Uniqlo shop (a mid-priced shop selling coats, jeans, thermal wear etc.), where they tailor jeans for free, the staff were super helpful and friendly. We tried to give them a tip, but they wouldn't, indeed said they couldn't, accept one. So I started talking to them.

"How does this work? You've given me a very personal service." (They measure & pin you up whilst you're standing in the jeans being tailored, which if you've ever had it done you will know can be a rather delicate matter). "You've been very helpful and friendly, yet I give you nothing. In the restaurants, cafes and bars we've been in though, they haven't been that friendly, have only bussed out a few plates or pulled a couple of pints, yet they expect eighteen percent plus. Not to mention you provide a skilled service."

"That's the way it is," was all they could say.

I appreciate that the wage per hour for the guys in the shops is probably more than for those in the hospitality sector, who rely on tips to make up their wage. In which case, wouldn't you have thought the latter would be more friendly? I then mentioned that when we had been to Florida, we had been overwhelmed by the friendliness of the people, particularly in restaurants and so on. They agreed (some of them had been down there), but just shrugged their shoulders and said, "That's New York!"

Another angle on this came when a local later explained that as people in NYC have small apartments, most socialising is done away from home. Restaurants and similar places become extensions of living spaces, and so the overtly friendly service customary in some places can appear intrusive here. With space at such a premium, we were told that people create psychological bubbles between themselves, neighbouring tables and the staff, and as long as you got what you wanted perfunctorily, a little professional distance wasn't considered bad. She also said that if we visited often enough, we wouldn't believe the intimate conversations people freely had at adjacent tables. There's something to look forward to.

Suddenly, a lot of the restaurant reviews I had read as part of our pre-trip planning made sense. Lots of comments for otherwise well regarded restaurants were simply variations of the theme 'food great, lose the attitude'. (As an aside whilst those reviewers might have been to Florida and experienced southern hospitality as a benchmark, I'm not sure they had yet had the pleasure of Boston). So where I had been avoiding restaurants based on those sorts of reviews, I decided I should think again.

For the record, I should add that it wasn't like that everywhere. Like anywhere you get good people and bad. We had great service in quite a few places (such as the Casablanca Hotel, Eileen's Cheesecake, Ample Hills Creamery, Shake Shack, Uniqlo, Abercrombie, Economy Candy, the Angel's Share, amongst others), but by and large waiters/bar staff were not friendly. They did their job, but in a transactional, functional way rather than in a happy to serve you way. At least now I understood why.

For lunch, sandwiched in between our rounds of shopping, we went to Xi'an Famous Foods, an Asian/Chinese noodle type place on 14 East 34th Street, near Macy's. Not having been anywhere like this before, it was initially rather alarming. You pick your dish from a picture menu on the wall, rather than a description of what it might actually be, before grabbing a berth anywhere you can in its tight, café style premises.

Having secured a spot, you then realise you have nothing to eat with and are grateful you came with a partner to protect your seat from others, also eagerly circling for anything that might resemble a spare space. You locate the communal trays where the cutlery lies scattered and sarcastically think to yourself, glad to see no expense spared here, as you examine your plastic knife and fork. Then, when you finally manage to do what you came in here to do, namely place a chunk of the mystery food in your mouth, everything suddenly makes sense. Why it was so busy with locals, and why money isn't wasted on accessories when it could be invested in ingredients. Mmm mmm. Man, it was good. So flavoursome, somehow combining sweet, sour, spicy and depth of flavour in each mouthful. All with the added excitement that comes from never being entirely sure what it was you ordered.

Late in the afternoon the Sherpa was allowed a cup of tea on condition he stopped bleating that he was dehydrated. He was also permitted to drop the shopping bags in our hotel room on condition he stopped moaning about his back. My wife is nothing if not generous. At the same time, I was also told in no uncertain terms not to get too comfortable as there was still much to do. No rest for the wicked. No rest for me. So after that quick pit stop, we shot out to the East Village and Economy Candy.

Although technically this still counts as shopping, I mention it separately because it was so different. Alison had read about it on Mumsnet or we would never have found it because it was off the beaten track, down a side street in the East Village. (108, Rivington St, for the record). Similar in size to an average corner shop, it was packed from floor to ceiling – and I mean *all the way* from floor to ceiling – with all kinds of chocolates, sweets and candies. You would have done well to slip an envelope between the boxes and jars. And, as you might imagine from somewhere full to the brim with such goodies, this lovely, sweet smell just hit you as soon as you entered the shop. A bit like the Abercrombie store, albeit less perfumed, you could have just stayed there all day without buying anything, taking in that lovely aroma. Although I suspect that if you actually did that, after a while the family that own the shop might have a discreet word.

A lot of the candies/sweets were the kind you used to see many years ago at your local sweet shop, but there was also modern stuff like jelly beans. Well, modern to us anyway. Pricing ranged from good value (for the jelly beans) to expensive (UK imported type chocolates) which of course depends on where you're from and the costs of having to get it there. It was different, and I'm glad we went as we ended up coming back with some unusual gifts for the family. Not to mention lots of jelly beans. Would we have made a separate trip? I don't know, but as we had other plans for the East Village that evening, it fitted in well.

Mercifully, it was also the end of our shopping. Perhaps that's why I enjoyed it so much. From there, it was onto cocktails at the Angel's Share and another amazing, if slightly surreal, experience.

I'd heard this described as a hidden away, speakeasy type of cocktail place, which did some lovely, but unusual creations. The term speakeasy being a throwback to the prohibition era when a lot of these bars were discretely located in hard to find places. The last sentence is a bit of an understatement.

The address was 8 Stuyvesant Street. The bar was called The Angel's Share. We are standing on Stuyvesant Street – yes at where no 8 should be – and I can promise you there is no bar called The Angel's Share, or anything remotely looking like it.

Fortunately, my prereading, had told me to go to the top of a Japanese restaurant called Yokocho, through there, and again through a secret door.

Well, there was a set of stairs between two restaurants going up, and looking hard I could see a sign pointing upwards to Yokocho. Off we go then, with Alison saying, "Are you sure this is right? I thought we were going to a cocktail bar. Are you sure know what you're doing?" etc. etc., to which I have often found "Trust me, I'm a doctor," (even though I'm not) goes a long way. Well, either that, or gets me into a lot of trouble.

So up the stairs we go and find ourselves surfacing in a fully functioning, busy Japanese restaurant.

"Table for two sir?" asks a waitress standing at the top when, quick as a flash, I saw to our left, across the side of the restaurant, an unmarked door. Hopefully, the one I had been told to look out for. Doing my best James Cagney impression, I looked at the waitress and glanced at the door and winked. Alright, gestured that we wanted to go that way – I've never been very good at James Cagney impressions. Or indeed many others, for that matter. Amazingly, she didn't call the police, but smiled and indicated we could pass.

So we wandered across the restaurant to the unmarked door, with Alison now increasingly firmly whispering in my ear "Are you *sure* you know what you're doing?" and me praying that it was going to fall the right side of one of my trust me I'm a doctor speeches. Crossing my fingers, I gave it a firm push.

Then, like *Alice Through the Looking-Glass*, we entered a completely different world. On the side we had just been was a brightly lit, even garish, Japanese restaurant. On the other was this cool, relaxed, even seductive, cocktail bar. I should also add that at no point on our journey down the rabbit hole (sorry I'm getting carried away), on our journey into this bar did it ever say Angel's Share. Not even at the last hurdle.

The cocktail menu was fairly extensive, but as indicated very unusual. Given how hard it was to find the place they certainly weren't going to get any walk in custom and so I figured the cocktails, although not cheap, must be good. Alison had something called a Cheek to Cheek which when it came resembled a dessert, like some form of raspberry trifle topped with whipped double cream. They even provided a spoon to drink (eat) it with. It was heavenly. Perhaps that's why they called the place the Angel's Share. Smooth, as fruity as it looked, and packed with layers of flavour. I know because I managed to beg a spoonful.

I, on the other hand didn't choose as well, opting for their signature drink called When Smoke Gets In Your Eyes. They burn tea leaves or cinnamon sticks or something like that (sorry I can't remember exactly) in your glass, before quickly turning it over. This snuffs out the flames and traps the smoke in your glass. In front of you they then turn the glass upright and add the cocktail liquid (some sort of whiskey combo).

All I can say is, sadly, it wasn't for me. Although not being one to needlessly waste precious drops – particularly at this price – I did my level best to finish it. It wasn't easy though. Rather like drinking a smouldering bonfire. On the plus side though, it's probably the best value cocktail I've ever had, as that smell and taste will stay with me for life. Something I was reminded of when we attended our home town's Guy Fawkes Night.

Nicely fortified, or kippered in my case, we set off for supper at a BBQ speciality restaurant called Mighty Quinn's about four blocks down. Just what I needed now, a blessed smoke house. The food was superb though, and great value for what you got.

I had thought before going it was like a full-service restaurant, but it turned out to be a mix between fast food and café service, which is probably how they kept the prices down. It also explains why they thought I was some kind of joker when I phoned beforehand to make a reservation. Sadly, they were also to end up thinking I was some kind of clown after we'd arrived.

Once inside the restaurant, you stand in a line and order your meat, which they place into a plastic carton for you. You then shuffle along to a different person/station and order your sides, which are also added to your carton, and continue shuffling until you get to the end when you order your drink, including draught beer if that's what you want. You pay and then find a table to sit at. Sounds simple when explained like that. Is simple, if that's what you were expecting. But, although this is embarrassing to admit, for some reason I couldn't get it.

Whether it's because I had it in my head that you placed your order at the counter and then they brought it to you like some restaurants I've been to. Or whether the cocktails were stronger than I thought (on an empty stomach in my defence). Or whether it was the jet lag...... or any combination of these, I don't know. What I do know though, is try as I might, I simply couldn't get it.

Tragically, I kept asking the wrong people for the wrong stuff in the wrong order. It was so bad, the staff would have been forgiven for thinking they were soon to star in a new run of *Candid Camera.* I managed to throw their whole system into confusion and ended up having to go back to the beginning of the line and start again. Oh, the disgrace of it. It was like being back at school with the walk of shame to the naughty corner. Oh well, at least it provided some entertainment, and a mild diversion for those there that night.

Halfway through my third lap, after having been sent back yet again for making another total mess of things, I selected a Brontosaurus Rib for my meat. Before unfortunately talking to a regular in the line, who recommended the brisket instead. After cogitating on this for some time, by which stage I had once again made it as far as the sides section, I belatedly decided to heed his advice...... and changed my order to brisket from the Brontosaurus Rib that I had previously requested. As you can imagine, this thrilled the serving staff even more. What did I say about keeping a low profile when new to a strange city?

To be fair, the staff were really patient and tried to help and humour the old fool (sadly that was me, not the guy I was talking to in the line) and everybody was happy in the end. Particularly the staff when I finally made it through to the end of what had started to resemble some horrible real-life version of a crazy video game. At least the guy in line was right – the brisket was fantastic.

We then thought you know where we haven't been in 24 hours...... Shake Shack!...... and Madison Square Park is kind of on the way home from the East Village. So we stopped off there to try one of their desserts. We shared one – sorry, I still don't understand the difference between their concretes and their custard – but it was plenty for us and made the perfect pudding to follow our BBQ feast. It also made it a hat trick as we had now visited them on Saturday, Sunday and Monday, which was every day since we had been in NYC.

As we toddled back from Madison Square Park to our hotel on West 43rd (well, by this stage teeter might be a better descriptor), we knocked another thing off the bucket list.

President Obama was visiting NYC that night to watch the show *Hamilton* and meet the audience afterwards in some sort of charity bash. The news that morning had said that it sold out months ago and he was expected around 10 p.m., but we had forgotten all about this, until we got to Bryant Park where the police had locked everything down. Not only traffic, but everything. You weren't even allowed to cross the road.

Then, after a few minutes waiting, a whole cavalcade of police cars, with a limo somewhere in the middle, came flying through. And we are talking *lots* of police cars. It was almost reminiscent of the final chase scene in the film *The Blues Brothers*. Then, as soon as they were done, a bit like at a railroad crossing after a giant American freight train has gone through, the roads were reopened and pedestrians were allowed across again. As we were crossing the road he had just come down, we heard two police officers talking to each other, "So did you see him? Did you get a good look?" It was nice and refreshing to see they were excited as we were.

Now alright, if I am honest here, must see a US president before we die hadn't been on our life bucket list – but it was still cool nonetheless. And so we retired to bed thinking not only have we packed a lot in to such a short time, but this town really is different. Amazing things do seem to happen here.

The Sun Shines On the Righteous

Every day we had been checking the weather forecast and tweaking our plans if appropriate. Monday had been warm but cloudy, so shopping was on the agenda. Or at least that was what Alison told me was the reason for us spending so much quality time together in those stores. She also told me that it was good for me to carry all those bags as it would save having to go to the gym.

The forecast for today was warm and sunny, so another switch saw us head for Staten Island and a boat trip. Rather than take the subway direct to the Ferry Terminal though, we decided to get off at Chamber's Street and walk to the Hudson River at Rockefeller Park. We could then enjoy a nice walk down the Esplanade, alongside the river, until we got to Battery Park itself. A charming stroll with greenery, marinas and sweeping river views, all made even lovelier by the warm sun that was now beating down.

As tickets are not required for the Ferry, we were pretty much straight on once we arrived at the Terminal. For those who don't know, the Staten Island Ferry is a 24 hour commuter service between Manhattan and, strangely enough, Staten Island, that goes straight pass the Statue of Liberty. Whilst it doesn't stop at the Statue, it does have the huge advantage of being completely FREE. If you only want good views of Lady Liberty, it's arguably way better and, being free, a good deal cheaper than the organised harbour tours.

On the way to Staten Island, the best views of Lady Liberty are to the right of the boat. Judging by the number of people that rushed to that side as we approached her, I initially wondered whether our ship would capsize. Or whether the seasoned travellers were now so attuned to this risk, they performed a coordinated move to the left to stabilise it. Either way, we were alive to this phenomenon, and had staked an early claim to the right-hand side railings of the upper deck. Liberty Enlightening the World (the statue's official name) rewarded our endeavour.

With the morning sun shining in her face, she gleamed. The flame of her torch, covered in 24 carat gold leaf, sparkled like a jewel in the sun. Especially with the angle of the sun's rays constantly altering, as the boat cut through the waves. It is a sight I shall never forget.

The green patina of her oxidised copper skin seemed to naturally offset the blues of the sky and water. She blended with her surroundings, whilst at the same time stood distinct. You couldn't miss her.

Reaching three hundred and five feet above the water, she was majestic. Radiant. She was proud and strong. She was captivating. Quite simply, she was beautiful. Even though she is small compared to the skyscrapers that now crowd Lower Manhattan's waterside, she is still not overshadowed. She has a serenity and elegance that is unmatched.

Guarding the entrance to the New World, one can only imagine what the sight of her was like, around the turn of the twentieth century, with no tall buildings as a backdrop. Particularly for those having endured an arduous ocean crossing to start a new life. In the Land of the Free.

We had wanted to visit more of Staten Island, as I had read about a secret garden in Snug Harbor on walkingoffthebigapple.com being a nice place to visit and pass some time. It was a glorious day though, and we thought the best place to spend it was Central Park. So, despite originally having planned to take time on Staten Island itself and visit the Snug, ashamedly we did what ninety-five percent plus of our ferry did as soon as it docked. We walked around the ferry terminal to get back on the next boat going out five minutes later.

On returning to Manhattan, we ambled around the financial district, walking down Wall Street, so we could say we'd been there, before going to see the statue of the bull as it was nearby. Crowded with people queuing up to have their photo taken, the bull is worth a diversion, but not a special trip. What was interesting though, was just how shiny the bull's balls were. Compared to the rest of the three and a half tonne bronze statue, they were nearly as shiny as gold. You'd be surprised how many of those queuing for their photo want to stroke and polish them. Although breathing on them before polishing seemed to be going a bit far.

We took in some of the other grand buildings in the vicinity, such as New York City Hall, the New York State Supreme Court Building and

Federal Hall. The latter being the site, if not the original building, where George Washington was sworn in as first President of the United States, in April 1789. It's hard to imagine now, but at that time Washington D.C. (then known as Georgetown) was no more than a village. Let alone the capital of the country. Even by 1800, the year in which the seat of federal government officially moved from Philadelphia, and almost ten years after its designation as the country's capital, Washington's population was still only 3,210.

In a city dominated by skyscrapers constructed in the last one hundred years, it was nice to see other grand buildings in classical styles. Aside from their timeless elegance, they also give glimpses into the early history of the United States. As well as early New York, before it became the king of commerce.

Little revealing details, such as the inscription carved above the columns that guard the entrance to the Supreme Court Building. Referencing a quote by George Washington, it reads, "The true administration of justice is the firmest pillar of good government". It provides an insight into the thinking, principles and morals of those who created the foundations for the fledgling nation. Even if the actual inscription is a misquote. Washington actually wrote "the *due* administration of justice is the firmest pillar of good government" in a letter to his Attorney General. A rather tragic typographical error, given it is now set in stone.

With the weather so good, we opted for another slight detour. Figuring that, with skies this clear, the view would be amazing, we checked our phones for ticket availability at the One World Observatory. As it was midweek and early November our luck was in, so off we swerved once again, after taking appropriate time to visit the reflecting pools of the National September 11 Memorial.

I am sorry, but my mere words are insufficient here. They cannot do justice to the memorial, appropriately convey the emotions involved, or adequately pay respect to all those who gave so much. From those who lost their lives directly through the horrific events of September 11, 2001 and the 1993 World Trade Center bombing, to those who subsequently died or became sick from inhaling toxins. Suffice to say, if you are in New York, you should go.

Once inside One World Trade Center, we passed efficiently and quickly through security. The elevator to the viewing deck is wondrous. As you whoosh up to the 102nd floor in 47 seconds, scenes of the surrounding skyline are beamed as a wraparound panorama onto its walls. These scenes evolve as time passes, so as you ascend, you perceive you are looking out on the landscape as it would have appeared from 1500 until today. From grasslands and rivers, through early settlement, to the metropolis that New York now is. Not only does the timeline advance as you gain height, but so too does the angle of your view. So where you start by looking at buildings and features, you end looking down at them. The detail is incredible and the overall effect impressive.

As is the view when you're presented with it. At 1,268 feet it is the tallest observatory deck in New York, at the time of writing. On a clear day you can see over forty miles, with the ability to walk around for full 360-degree views. Plus it's inside, so your hair isn't buffeted by a breeze.

Although, the wind still did strange things to us. The building can sway up to three feet. Something tall buildings are designed to do to prevent them cracking, much like when you bend a ruler. If the ruler couldn't flex, it would snap.

You couldn't feel or perceive the building moving, but as you walked around, things weren't quite right. As you put a foot down, the floor was never exactly where your brain expected it to be. Certainly not compared to walking around at street level. It might have only moved a few millimetres, possibly even only been a fraction of that out, but it was enough to make things feel a little odd. In some ways, it was akin to walking across the deck of a boat sailing a calm sea. Although we never felt worried for a moment, it was nevertheless a strange sensation.

The elevator down is also a spectacular ride. This time the sensation projected onto the panels is of you being in a lift that shoots out of the building and swoops around present day Lower Manhattan as it descends to earth. It felt like you were flying in the magic glass lift in *Charlie and the Chocolate Factory*.

By this time we needed to eat and so caught the subway to 42nd Street before walking the couple of blocks to Gotham West Market in Hell's kitchen, near the Intrepid Sea, Air & Space Museum. Filled with food vendors/stalls around a central eating area, it's like a food court in a mall, but classier with the stalls being smaller, non-chain, independent type places. We had various bits and pieces, but the highlight was dessert from Ample Hill's Creamery. I kid you not, it was the best ice cream we have ever had. Full stop. End of. Even now.

I had a chocolate and Guinness flavoured ice cream, mixed in with chilli spiced brownies and bits of toffee. Perhaps appropriately enough, it was called the Hell's Kitchen Sink. Sounds odd, but it worked well. Alison had the Salted Crack'd Caramel. That was the most amazing ice cream I have ever tasted. I was allowed one lick only. I suggested it was called crack caramel because this stuff was bound to be seriously addictive, but they said it was actually due to the large bits of solid toffee they put into it. All of which they hand made. Hmmm, I wonder.

The weather hit 23°C (73°F) that day. Yes, on the third of November. As we strolled along the Hudson river board munching away at our ice creams, it was like a summer's day. A bit of a walk to Central Park, but we didn't mind/were getting used to it. As we walked past the Intrepid, you couldn't help being awed at its size. It was like a floating city. Sadly though, we didn't have sufficient time to squeeze it in – a week just isn't long enough in New York. Still, at least we now had a couple of excuses to ensure we would return to this wonderful city at some point. Intrepid, and having seen the beauty of Lady Liberty from afar this morning, we also knew we would have to see her up close and ascend the crown. As that usually requires purchasing tickets four months in advance, it definitely had to go in the next time pile.

Eventually, we bowled up in Central Park, after body swerving more than one, if not one hundred and one, rent-a-bike salesmen. We had thought about renting bikes beforehand, but when it came to it were put off by the pushiness of the salesmen. Honestly, these guys could have given the traders in Wall Street's Bear Pit a run for their money. It all seemed more hassle than it was worth and you could just imagine the argument a few hours later, with them claiming pre-existing damage to the bikes had been done by you. But perhaps I'm being cynical.

That said, I'm not sure how much value they would have been anyway. Inside the park there are signs everywhere saying no cycling on the paths and if you're on them, you have to dismount and push. Admittedly, you can cycle off the paths, but that's across swathes of grassland. Plus some of the off path bits were roped to protect them and allow the vegetation to recover. Nor do the bikes allow you to get anywhere you wouldn't otherwise be able to, as the paths appear to go virtually everywhere. All said and done, it looked like the right call to give the bike peddling salesmen the push.

The park was worth the effort though. Quite crowded, as the world and his wife had had the same idea about enjoying the park in the unseasonably warm sunshine, but good nonetheless. It seemed to provide everything you wanted on a warm day in the city. From large lawns perfect for a bit of sunbathing to winding paths through the trees, should you fancy exploring. From statues and follies to gaze at, to play areas for letting off steam. There was even a secluded bar, perfect for a chilled glass on a fine day. Sure, certain bits, like the Imagine memorial, were very crowded, but still worth visiting to pause and reflect. Besides, if you wanted the tranquility of quieter parts, it was easy to wander into areas like the ramble.

We sat down by the Bethesda Fountain and took a few selfies (or should that be couplies if you take a picture of two of you?) with the water as a backdrop. Delighted with ourselves at how hip and cool we must be if we could pull off such a trick at our age, we were even more amazed when we looked back at the pictures and they didn't look too bad. I thought we'd have ended up taking sky shots. Or floor shots. Or simply broken the camera. We even successfully managed a quick selfie smooch photo. Which of course embarrassed everyone, especially the kids, when we got home and looked at the photos together on the TV, having forgotten about that one.

The light was starting to go, so we walked back to the hotel – yes, more walking – to get there in time for their free cheese and wine session. This is something the Casablanca does (as I'm sure do others) every evening between five and eight o'clock. Given we had tickets for the theatre later, we thought it made sense to use this is as a bit of free prinking. (Pregaming I think they call it in the US). Or in other words, a few drinks and a bite before going out. It did the job well.

This was the show I had pre-bought before Alison's birthday and we had front row seats, right in the middle. The play was *A Gentlemen's Guide to Love and Murder* and, like a lot of New York, was amazing. I'm not really a theatre person, although over the years I have accompanied Alison to shows in cities such as Liverpool, Manchester, Newcastle and

London, as it's something she loves. I say this, because this was the best show I have ever seen. Honestly. I know that's becoming a theme now, what with Eileen's cheesecake, Ample Hills ice cream and now this, but it's true. This was simply different class to anything I have seen before, and I sat there like a small child at a firework show.

The only way I can describe it is that if the Manchester Theatre scene (big regional city in the UK) is like The English Football Championship (second division national football) and London's West End is the Premiership (top level national football), then this was the Champions League (top level international football). Ok, so the tickets weren't cheap, but you got what you paid for. The theatre was in good nick (a lot of the ones at home to be honest are a bit shabby – apparently it's their charm); the acoustic quality (presumably a combination of the acoustic system and the theatre's sound insulation) was top notch; and the quality of the singing & acting was top class.

The play was a musical comedy about the English upper classes, and they had even nailed the accents perfectly. As opposed to a lot of US films where badly done English accents seem to be considered an art form. Think *Ocean's 11* for instance (which was a good film, apart from the bizarre cockney accent that wasn't even needed for the story line), Dick Van Dyke in *Mary Poppins*, and so it goes on. The only bad thing was being told at half time drinks cost $13 for a can (not even a pint!) of (warmish) lager. Well that, and we kept getting involuntarily spat over by the cast as they were singing – a downside to a front row seat I hadn't considered before.

At the end of the show I broke into an impromptu standing ovation (which takes some doing when you're in the front row not knowing whether anyone will follow), but I didn't care it was that good. As the crowd filed out, we stayed put and shouted down to the pit "encore, encore" and hollered how great they had been – the orchestra were top quality musicians as well. To our surprise, the conductor popped his head up and we ended up having a bit of a chat with him. We were again very complimentary and it was nice, because he then shouted down to his musicians, "See, I told you people cared!"

We did, they were great.

Tunes were now being played by our tummies, reminding us we hadn't actually had supper, just some cheese and crackers. So what to do? Well, at the risk of turning into another Shake Shack evangelist (and no, they are not paying me), there was only one option…… Shake Shack!

I'd read in online forums comments from devotees wondering whether Shake Shack were putting addictive substances into their food and I was starting to think they might be right. Perhaps this explained their fantastic growth rate after all. We'd been here Saturday, Sunday, Monday and now Tuesday and had visited a Shake Shack every day, despite still eating at lots of other places. It was a good job we were doing so much walking.

This time we had the regular burger (also very good) as by now, we were working our way through the menu in a scientific manner. This wasn't just straight addiction you know. As part of a belated health drive we skipped the fries, trading them instead for a Shackmeister lager as a nightcap. Then, as Zebedee said, it was time for bed.

Scorchio! (And I Thought New York was Supposed to be Cold in Winter?)

Today was forecast even hotter than yesterday, so another rejig of the plans was called for. With the sun shining we thought outside things would be best, so we hit the High Line – a former railway, converted to a public park – and walked its entire length over the next hour or so.

It's under one and a half miles long so you can see we meandered, stopping to take in the views and sculptures along the way. Some reviews had suggested skipping its top end (just north of the Hudson rail yards, at West 34th Street); that it would be better to join half way along. We thought that missed the point though and decided to do it from the start. Ok, the first half wasn't as spectacular as the latter parts, but the flip side was that it was a lot less crowded. You also got good views of the Hudson River, which was something we hadn't anticipated. The whole walk, or more correctly stroll, was uplifting. Not solely because walking through an oasis of tranquillity and green in the heart of any city is always nice, but also seeing what people can achieve with imagination and determination.

The High Line, for those unfamiliar with it, was originally a raised railway built in the 1930s, to the West of Tenth Avenue. Remarkably, prior to that, trains ran directly along Tenth and Eleventh Avenues. Inevitably, accidents with people and cars, who also used those popular thoroughfares, were common. To warn pedestrians and motorists, riders on horseback accompanied the trains, proceeding in front of them, waving red flags by day and red lanterns at night. However, despite the best efforts of the West Side Cowboys, as they were known, hundreds of people still died. Many of whom were children. To improve the safety of Death Avenue, as Tenth Avenue had become colloquially known, the railway line was elevated to run above street height. It didn't track straight above the streets, but instead carved a path between Tenth and Eleventh Avenues.

A safer and more efficient use of space, this provided other benefits, such as trains being able to operate right into some of the warehouses on the route. Over time, however, businesses relocated to cheaper areas, and the warehouses became apartment blocks. Demand for freight dropped, and the rail line fell into decay and disrepair. An unused eyesore for the city, needing ongoing investment to keep it safe, eventually it was scheduled for demolition.

Local residents believed something better could be done, however. Two men, Joshua David and Robert Hammond, felt it could be preserved and reused as a public space, and formed the not-for-profit organisation, Friends of the High Line, to champion this. A competition was run to elicit ideas for its use, which lead to the blueprint for the park it is today. They then had the guts, determination and perseverance to make this a reality. To persuade the railway company to allow them to transform the site (and later even donate it to the city). To convince countless other companies to sponsor the project and provide the funds to make it happen (some estimates have put this in the region of $150m). Not to mention the tenacity and patience of working with the City Council and goodness knows how many interested parties.

What they achieved is astonishing and today it is an oasis in the heart of the city that's home to: almost one hundred different types of tree and shrub; two hundred varieties of perennial plant; forty forms of grass; twenty breeds of vines; twenty sorts of wetland plant; and seventy varieties of bulbs. It is a remarkable transformation.

Indeed, the High Line has been so successful, it's now a blueprint for urban renewal in many cities around the world. Complete respect to Joshua David, Robert Hammond, and everyone involved in whatever part of the transformation. Because ultimately an awful lot of people had to work together to make this happen. It is humbling.

As we approached the end of the line, we descended to explore the Chelsea Market (between West 15th Street and West 16th). A block long and a block wide, it was where America's best-selling cookie, the Oreo, was invented in 1912, when the building was a factory of the former National Biscuit Company (Nabisco). Nowadays, it is a thriving indoor food hall and craft market with a large variety of vendors and made for a fun diversion. Until we got to this swish looking cooking ingredients shop with a bar in it.

Too early in the day to be drinking, we mooched about until we saw these fancy salts for sale. I know it sounds a bit odd, but they were basically coarse grains of sea salt infused with different flavours, such as pepper, chilli, merlot (what's that all about?) and so on. Anyway, the shop helpfully had signs saying you could try the salt before you buy – suggesting you sprinkle some on the back of your hand and then lick it off. Lovely. I can't think of anything nicer than licking pure salt off the back of my hand. Flavoured or not.

"Ooh look!" said Alison. "This one's supposed to go nicely on your steak, shall we try it?"...... You've already worked out who was going to be the guinea pig here I'm sure.

Probably my biggest mistake (what happened to with age comes wisdom?) was to say "not too bad, could work well," or something silly like that to that first one.

"Oh good, let's try this one then (merlot)," was the response. Or was it a directive? I still can't be sure.

Horrible, that's all I am saying, just horrible. If you do go, don't try the merlot.

"Oh well, probably a bit unlucky," said my darling wife, "try this one"...... this cycle was repeated systematically for the next few minutes until I started to resemble a rabid dog begging for water......

Fortunately, I saw one which could put an end to this madness – ghost chilli flavour. Because after that I knew there would be no point in any more tastings as you probably wouldn't taste anything else again. Sadly, I was right on the not tasting anything else again...... for a long time.

Do NOT try the chilli one.

I think it's supposed to be used as a rub to tenderise/marinate meat as opposed to licking neat. At least it got me out of trying any more. I reflected that I had just been through some sort of torture. And to cap it off, here I was, now raging with thirst, and not ten feet in front of me was a lovely looking craft beer bar. Yet I knew if I started indulging – apart from potentially losing the day – it would only dehydrate me even more. For those who used to watch a pretty naff, but now cult, quiz show in the UK thirty years ago called *Bullseye*, looking at that bar (don't forget it was a hot day as well) was one of those "this is what you could have won" moments.

The market as a whole had about fifty smallish shops. So apart from the torture zone I've just described, there were bakeries, clothes stores, food stalls, craft jewellers selling inexpensive bangles and trinkets, as well as a cooking accessories shop. The latter was an interesting store selling everything from equipment for the catering trade in bulk through to stuff for the home market. Everything from seriously heavy duty pans, perfect for steaks, through to those fancy accessories that you simply must have, like the things that cut cucumbers into swirly shapes that resemble a vegetable slinky toy. Which of course you never use again once you've got home. For the record, I added a lemon zester to our collection of things that will never see the light of day again. (I already had one of the fancy cucumber spiral cutters, thank you).

We were lucky as well because one of the chic clothes shops was having a sample sale at huge reductions. (I think this is where they sell off designer stuff that's end of line or has been used as bait/samples to get the big stores to buy a production run). I was even luckier as there was a big line to enter and the store was only letting people in when others left. It was clearly going to be a while before we got in, so best not waste a nice day in line. That and Alison figured by the time we were in, there would be nothing good left anyway.

We dutifully climbed the stairs back to the High Line, even though it was only three more blocks to the end, just so that we knew we had done it top to toe. We had had a good time, but it was a lovely day and although hot, the sun is low in the sky in November. As a result, the skyscrapers block out a lot of the light, making it shady and cool in town, and so we headed for the seaboard. We walked down through Greenwich Village, which seemed a nice area, and eventually, after crossing down through the Financial District and strolling a few blocks more, we emerged at South Street Seaport.

It was a strange sensation. Only a couple of streets from the river you are in heavy shade, and it feels like an overcast day at home. Then, as you pop out onto South Street, you're suddenly bathed in glorious, warm sunshine. We also had a bit of a bonus. After last night's great show, we had decided to go and see another today and queue up for tickets from the discount ticket booths. They go on sale at 3 p.m. (for a

7 p.m. show) in Times Square and we had been told the lines were often long. Best get there early. It would have been a bit of a pain, breaking up the day having to journey back up there, but at the Seaport there is also an official TKTS booth which also sells the reduced tickets. I had read that the tickets there go on sale a bit earlier and, as we were passing at about noon, I thought I would chance it. Wey hey, they were selling them already! Turns out they had been from eleven – for some reason they sell them earlier down there.

The first show we fancied was *Wicked*, but we were told no chance they never go on discount. Never mind, we were in luck with our next choice, *Jersey Boys*. We got 50% off and got seats twelve rows from the front (great view and no spitting) and right in the middle. Result! Not only great tickets at a good price, but now the day was freed up, as we didn't have to be anywhere fixed until 4.45 p.m. when we had tickets for Top of The Rock (TOTR).

We enjoyed the sun and the shore for a while and then decided to cross Brooklyn Bridge again. I must admit, I've got a bit of a thing about bridges. Although we've lived in Manchester for over thirty years, our spiritual home is Newcastle upon Tyne in the North East of England, a city with many bridges. (Including the famous Tyne Bridge, which was actually built by the same teams and to the same design as the world famous Sydney Harbour Bridge. They even pioneered certain techniques during its construction, that they would then later use in Sydney). Anyway, we figured we had enough time to do the bridge both ways, to Brooklyn and back, whilst also taking in a visit to Juliana's in between for lunch.

Although it was a lot busier than Sunday, the walk across was still excellent. Even second time around. Plus, as it was a lot warmer and sunnier, the views across the river were even more spectacular. Although, it would have been better still, if people spent a bit less time looking at themselves through the camera lens and a bit more looking out at the views. A quick selfie is one thing – primping, pouting and preening as though you are a top model in a photo shoot for *Vanity Fair* is another. Particularly when most of them weren't model quality. In the end, tired of politely waiting every three feet for another Kate Moss wannabe to finish, I think we must have bombed more photo shoots than the Luftwaffe in World War II.

We got to Juliana's about half-past two so didn't need to queue for a table and sat at a counter, right at the back where you could see the guys making your pizza. Whilst I couldn't say whether it was the best pizza in the world or not, it certainly was the best pizza we've ever had. Light and airy, not too cheesy or greasy and full of flavoursome quality ingredients. Not cheap at $30 for one I should add, but we did order one with prosciutto ham on it and there was lots. Plus, the one pizza fed us both comfortably. I also got to finally have that much-wanted beer to wash it down.

Being stuffed, we made the return journey across the bridge somewhat slower than on the way out. That suited us though, because the views when crossing from Brooklyn to Manhattan are so much better than the other direction. Without having to turn and look back, you are constantly presented with Manhattan's majestic skyscrapers in the distance, the beauty of the bridge in the foreground and, melding the scene together, the East River. As you progress across the bridge, there is also the perception that Manhattan is like a giant magnet, pulling as you draw nearer. Although admittedly it doesn't feel like that on the initial uphill section of the bridge. After crossing back and a slight panic attack on my part – I was five foot six when we left for New York, and I started to worry all this walking might be filing my legs down – we decided to take no more risks and caught the subway up to the Rockefeller Center.

The Comcast Building situated at 30 Rockefeller Plaza (or The Rock as it's better known) may only be New York's 26th tallest building at the moment.* But although its observatory decks, at 850 feet above street level, are over 400 feet lower than those at the Empire State Building and One World Trade Center, many people think it offers the best panoramic views of NYC. Its proximity to Central Park certainly helps. Although, you'd best go soon. In the city that never ~~sleeps~~ stops that may well change, particularly with the development of Central Park Tower, Steinway Tower and others.

If I am honest, the views from One World and Rockefeller are incomparable. It's like comparing chalk and cheese. One is higher and

---

* Including all the spires and architectural adornments that builders use to make their structures bigger.

sexier; the other better for Central Park, with a classic beauty. I am glad we saw both of them. Whilst TOTR is excellent in its own right though, the Rockefeller Center is so much more than just a great vantage point.

Covering 22 acres of Midtown New York across its many buildings, it was intended to be a city within a city. Underground passageways, complete with shops, connected its buildings so that in theory you never needed to leave its confines. Or at least pop your head out if the weather was inclement. During the 1930s Great Depression, its construction provided a critical boost to the economy, creating between 40,000 and 75,000 jobs. Indeed, according to Daniel Okrent, whose book *Great Fortune: The Epic of Rockefeller Center* is probably the definitive work in this area, by the time the core of the complex was completed in 1939, the number of people visiting each day was equivalent to the population of the 51st largest city in the United States.

It's also virtually a public art gallery, as those responsible for its development commissioned a stupendous amount of works to adorn the art deco styled buildings. Whilst, it is impossible here to do justice to the number of wonderful items across the Center – there are just too many – for those minded, it is certainly worth a detour to undertake your own tour.

Inevitably, a lot of the art dates from the 1930s, such as *Prometheus* (reputed to be the most photographed sculpture in New York), but the Center has continued to evolve. So you can find pieces such as Michio Ihara's, *Light and Movement*, from 1978 with its almost 1,600 gold-plated metal leaves. Or Michael Hammer's amazing 35 foot high waterfall, *Joie*. Installed in the Grand Atrium Lobby in 2005, it has 14,000 Swarovski crystals hanging on 450 individual strands. Heaven only knows how they go about cleaning that and keeping it all sparkly.

Pieces are strewn everywhere. From grand inspired murals on walls and ceilings, through to artefacts on everyday items, such as low relief castings on elevator doors. The overall effect is spectacular, and you're never quite sure you aren't wandering around a tastefully put together museum or the artfully furnished residence of a seriously wealthy individual. Perhaps both.

As a result, the Center is also renowned for the vast quantity of art across its art deco buildings. In 1987 it was declared a National Historical Landmark. Interestingly, as well as the artworks specifically commissioned for it, the Center has also inadvertently spawned its own. The classic black-and-white photograph, that now adorns many picture frames and posters, Lunch atop a Skyscraper, that captures eleven construction workers enjoying a break, whilst perched precariously on the edge of a steel girder, high above a city below, was itself taken at The Rock during the building of its 69th floor on the 20th September 1932.

Interesting too, was the controversy the Center became embroiled in when it fired Diego Rivera from his commission. Possibly the preeminent mural painter of the time, he filled his work with themes reflecting his staunch Marxist beliefs. In this case, painting in Vladimir Lenin, in a suitably admiring manner. Something a little too much for the world centre of capitalism, certainly given the mores of those times. It lead to his dismissal and the destruction of the entire mural. It was also his downfall.

The TOTR, like most of NYC, was also great, and recommended, with the following provisos:

We had read to get the best of both worlds you should arrive before sunset and experience both day and night. At that time of year, I had calculated that might be about 4.30. But you had to specify your time of visit when buying your tickets and I made the mistake of listening to the lady who worked there. After a while it became obvious that she was new, but I thought she knew more about the venue than she did. Regrettably, as it turned out, I probably knew more about it than her, which says a lot. She suggested a 4.45 p.m. ticket time. She was wrong. Particularly, as once you're at the top you can stay as long as you want.

It takes quite a while to get to the top of the Center, what with security checks and queues for the elevators. I reckon we finally got to the top about 5.10. There was still some light, but in reality it was dusk, and fading fast. The views were still good, and the nighttime one significantly different from that with light, but it would have been a lot better to have been there thirty minutes earlier. Then you could have fixed in your brain the rivers, and Central Park in particular, so that when the night scene arrived your memory could interpolate the missing bits between the lit up buildings.

Fortunately, I was now switched onto the elevator lines and noticed as we went up there were massive ones to go down. Way more than going up. Ostensibly lots of people stay till sunset and then leave. Given our show tickets were for 7.00, I didn't want to miss it through being stuck in a line for an elevator that's only a minute's ride down. (Actually, forty-two seconds to be precise – with elevator speeds that reach 1,200 feet per minute). So we enjoyed as much as possible of the views and experience, whilst making sure we left sufficient time to get down. This proved a good decision as the lines for the elevators took about thirty minutes and we only made it to the theatre with ten to spare.

I didn't know the story about Frankie Valli and the Four Seasons, so I watched *Jersey Boys* both enjoying it and fascinated as the story unfolded, which added a charm all of its own. And what I said before about Broadway being Champions League versus everything else was reinforced.

Great theatre, great acoustics, and the cast and musicians were once again top notch. Honestly, these guys were good enough to be in a top band in their own right. The only downside was the price. Even though the tickets were 50% discounted, it was still expensive compared to UK prices, with two tickets in the stalls twelve rows from the front, albeit in the middle, costing $165. But if I am honest, it was still worth every penny, sorry cent. Ultimately, you pays your money, you takes your choice and with Broadway, from what I've seen, you pay for what you get. I now understand why everyone raves about Broadway shows. Whenever we next return, a show will be in there somewhere. Even for a theatre pleb like me.

The show over, we floated back to the hotel with the tunes still in our heads, pausing to take some pictures of Radio City and its Christmas Tree all sparkling and lit up. As it was our last night, we also stopped in Times Square to try the Revlon Love is On screen, one more time. Luckily, with it being late in the evening, it was now scrum free, and we finally managed to get our photo inside the heart. It had been another wonderful evening in New York City.

Back in the hotel however, I suddenly realised I was shaking. At first I was slightly concerned, then it dawned we hadn't been to Shake Shack today and it was probably just withdrawal symptoms...... only kidding. But the truth is, we hadn't been there today and had eventually proved it could be done. An Englishman in New York, surviving a whole day without a Shake Shack!

Hell, Where Did the Last 5 Days Go?

You could tell we'd been here too long. We slept well and were no longer amongst the first into breakfast. Breakfast was as good as ever.

Whenever you have to travel home on a holiday, it's always a sad feeling. Not going home, but the thought your holiday is over and you're faced with a long day of travelling ahead.

The great thing about New York though is there is still so much to do. So instead of kicking your heels and moping about until it's time to go to the airport, you're off, up and out there.

Unfortunately, the weather had turned and it was now overcast with passing showers. "Sprinkles" as they called it on the news channel, which is a far nicer term than we use in England for that light rain – "spitting" for those of you who are curious – and something I shall now try to adopt and introduce in my country.

The English on holiday, as those who have met them in such circumstances will know, would normally be delighted by this turn of events. Our weather is by and large so poor that we consider it almost compulsory to have good weather on holiday. Were back home to have good weather whilst we are away, however, that would not be good; and frankly if we were away and had bad weather whilst back home had good that would be nothing short of a total disaster. No matter how good the place was. Alright this last sentence may be a slight exaggeration, but not much. Perversely, the thing that pleases the English the most, is when you've had great weather and the day you leave turns rubbish. Honestly. Notwithstanding that you are leaving, that you won't be there, doesn't matter. It means you've extracted the maximum possible value from your holiday. (And of course if back home has been bad as well, well it's like a royal flush, things just couldn't get any better).

So why unfortunately then? Well, it meant we could now squeeze in some last-minute shopping, for those items we simply couldn't live without, ahead of us going to MOMA – the Museum Of Modern Art. On the positive side, at the top of the rock, we'd bought a combo ticket – TOTR and MOMA for $45 instead of $32 just for TOTR so that saved us a little. MOMA is $25 on its own.

Whilst officially representing the Museum of Modern Art, I'm not sure MOMA shouldn't more fairly stand for Must Of Missed the Art, which pretty much summed it up for both of us. Although I'm not an art buff, I wouldn't describe myself as an ignoramus either. Whenever we, or I, go anywhere we try to take in a gallery of some sort and have been to a wide variety. From large to small, from traditional to quirky, we have marvelled at many kinds of paintings and sculptures, encompassing all sorts of different artistic styles. Even when in the National Gallery in Trafalgar Square, London and some of the classical paintings personally left me cold. Either because I didn't like the look of the scene, or whichever pompous monarch, primped in all their regalia and wigs from whatever century. I still appreciated the endeavour involved. I still marvelled that I was looking at something several hundred years old and understood that it was not surprising that it appeared so faded. I still reflected in awe at the effort expended, particularly given that they were painted hundreds of years ago, and the lack of resources then widely available. But I'm sorry, with a few exceptions, MOMA left me cold. In fact, we both started to find the whole thing as surreal as most of the art.

When we got there, it was fairly busy – goodness knows what it's like on a Friday evening when you can go for free. This was a constant theme and I don't think there was a piece of art that you could peaceably appreciate on your own. It wasn't so bad that you couldn't see the art (except for a few star pieces that were mobbed, requiring you to wait for a good view). But it wasn't like many galleries where you can get lost in the art and not really be conscious of others around you.

Although we had tickets, we were still directed to join a queue to exchange our nice TOTR/MOMA tickets (printed on laminated card with a pretty picture) for a flimsy piece of cash register roll paper. Why? I don't know, but it clearly made someone happy somewhere. We were then directed to another line to check in our bags and any drinks/food we were carrying. And then if we wanted it, which we did, we had to join a further line to get the iPods for the free audio guide. We were instructed to leave personal photo IDs as a security deposit, which is fair enough, but they wouldn't accept – indeed weren't allowed to accept – our passports for this purpose. The museum appeared to have been taken over by the bureaucracy police.

Luckily, I had my driving licence on me and left that with the relevant desk. I say luckily as I had read before we went that many places didn't accept driving licences as ID for buying alcoholic drinks, but insisted on passports. These joyful little processes over – which took a good twenty minutes out of our day – we were ready to visit the art.

I should also add here that except for one genuinely nice and friendly guy where we checked our bags (who I also tried to tip, but he couldn't accept it), the staff were the most miserable bunch we met in our whole time in the city. Now whilst I had commented that staff in restaurants were professional, albeit not overly friendly, the staff here at MOMA, pretty much across the piece, including those on the floor, were...... well I can't think of words to describe them that don't come across as terrible. I found them condescending, patronising and aloof. Possibly even arrogant. They certainly didn't seem to enjoy their jobs very much. Given that they have to spend a lot of time working with the public, perhaps it might be time for a career change. It felt like the great unwashed had just walked through their hallowed halls, and they were the ones tasked to deal with it. Oh well, each to their own, or perhaps I am simply an ignoramus after all and clearly not worthy of interacting with these people. Maybe I am part of the great unwashed. I shall try tugging my forelock next time.

When we finally got to the art, with a few exceptions which I will come to, most of it was just bizarre. I won't rattle through the repeated oddities/interesting items depending on your point of view – by all means go online at moma.org where you can browse through them. Although I'm sure they cheat as lots of the items on line had no image attached and I'm convinced they were the really flaky ones. Anyway, as we shuffled from one piece to another, we increasingly kept shaking our heads, thinking, "nope sorry don't get it" or even "*WHY* is this here?"

You'd look around – and it's worth noting here that most people had the audio guides on, so there wasn't much communication going on. It was like being in a library, where everyone is walking around wearing headphones. Anyway, you would look around and everyone seemed transfixed. And you'd start thinking: "Is it me?", "Why don't I get this?", "Oh no, maybe I am part of the great unwashed after all." But then I thought, perhaps they're all in the same boat as us and those transfixed expressions are just glazed over faces trying not to appear uncomfortable.

The nadir was reached when we got to a piece called *Bicycle Wheel* by Marcel Duchamp. By all means look it up, but it's basically an upturned bike wheel attached to a kitchen stool. I actually thought I'm in the wrong job. When I get home, I'm getting into the garage, knock a few pieces up and hey presto I'll be on a fortune. And you haven't seen the state of my garage.

Anyway, this piece was in the audio guide (not all pieces are), so we dutifully listened to the piece being described. It was an interview with the artist followed by a commentary which – in a very sombre and serious tone – described this item as that particular artist's most important contribution to twentieth century modern art. Well I'm sorry, but at that point I couldn't help myself and I started giggling.

By sheer chance Alison had teed up her audio guide at about the same time as me (you have to queue them up separately for each piece you see) and must have got to the same point at the same time as me. You could she was trying to stop herself from laughing as well, and you know what it's like – the more you try and hold back the giggles once you've got them the worse it gets. And when two people are suddenly both doing it, at some point the dam breaks, and before you know it we were both laughing out loud rather uncontrollably. And of course the scene just got worse and worse. Soon we were pissing ourselves (probably not far off actually) whilst the rest of the room serenely wandered around with their heads angled on one side (in that funny way people do when looking at art, or something they don't quite understand), wondering what the freak show was doing in the corner. Shamefully the freak show was us. Sadly, after six days in New York, we had become like the guy on the C train in Brooklyn and it was now us that people were stealthily sliding away from. But you know what, I didn't care (probably much like the guy on the subway). I was just thinking this is all the emperor's new clothes. It was time to leave.

That said, I said I would mention the exceptions. They do have a few pieces which are wow moments. Although Warhol's *Untitled from Marilyn*

Monroe and *Campbell's Soup Cans*, both of which we had wanted to see, weren't on display (they have so many items they have to rotate what they put on view), we did get to admire some of Monet's *Water Lilies* from his garden at Giverny, an artist whose work we like a lot. (Please forgive me going off at a slight tangent here, but "Giverny" is also a great song by Chris Rea from his *On the Beach* album).

We also got to see another one of my favourite paintings, Salvador Dalí's *The Persistence of Memory*. Or "Time Melts Away" as I like to think of it (the painting that has various stopwatches either melting or flying away). To me it's both a nice picture and a clever piece of art and to see it in real life, was one of those moments that will not only live with me forever, but to be fair only happened by going there that day. I was surprised because it's actually quite a small painting when you see it in reality. I had imagined it would be bigger, I suppose because you're normally used to seeing it blown up on posters. Nonetheless, it was excellent.

I was also surprised to learn that I was wrong in what I had always thought about the foreground of that picture. In my mind, symbolising how time flies, I believed that melting watch was on the back of a winged creature in flight. Turns out it was something completely different. According to MOMA itself, "The monstrous fleshy creature draped across the painting's center" is "an approximation of Dalí's own face in profile, its long eyelashes seem disturbingly insect-like or even sexual, as does what may or may not be a tongue oozing from its nose like a fat snail."

Quite.

Well given that art, like beauty, is in the eyes of the beholder, even if I've been wrong all these years, I'll stick with my original interpretation of time flying away on the wings of a bird, thank you very much.

Anyway, our next port of call was Ellen's Stardust Diner, near Times Square. I'd read mixed reviews of this online where some people said it was good fun and you should go, whilst others had said "overpriced tourist hotspot" and so was unsure. My tourist trap concerns had been reinforced when talking to some locals whilst shopping who'd told us not to go – "just touristy". They insisted there were much better eating places for food quality, even though we'd said we were only after burgers.

Nevertheless, Alison had read about it on Mumsnet and really fancied it, so the decision was made. To be fair, I thought we are tourists, it's part of the tourist experience, and it's our last day, why not?

So off we went. And it was like a diner, with diner type food. The difference though is that the waiters sing songs to the customers. It's pretty much like a constant Karaoke going on, as each waiter serenades in turn. Most of them are good singers and aspiring wannabe Broadway performers. Indeed, the manager said sixteen of the staff that year had been recruited to Broadway shows. Periodically during the songs, a bucket is passed around for contributions, which is over and above the standard tip for service. A little unusual, and not to everyone's tastes, but apparently it's used to help the waiters in their careers. So for instance, the funds from this whip round might be used to pay for professional photos, recording tapes and so on. As a whole, the restaurant is quite an interesting concept and something different. In some ways, I suppose it's also a bit like a showcase. You must be decent to sing there and if the people producing shows need extra bodies, going to Ellen's saves them traipsing all over, knowing they'll get a ready-made talent pool to examine.

As for the food? Well, it was slightly more expensive than regular joints, but the burger was large and decent.

Overall, I'm glad we went – it was fun and part of our holiday experience. For us though, once is enough, unless we visit again with a different crowd. For instance, if we returned with the kids (sadly grown up now) or a group of friends, as it would be cool to share it with them.

Our time was nearly up. We'd packed in a lot, but there was still so much left undone. The Metropolitan Museum of Art, and its priceless exhibition collection of three Fabergé eggs (on display until November 30, 2021); the Whitney Museum of American Art; the Tenement Museum, with its insights into the lives of early immigrants to New York; the Bronx Zoo; Roosevelt Island and its quirky cable car; The Statue of Liberty herself and the opportunity to climb her crown and visit Ellis Island; the Intrepid Sea, Air & Space Museum, and countless others. We hadn't left yet, but we already needed to come back.

Fortunately, we still had an hour before we had to collect our bags, so what to do? Now, for all those of you thinking Shake Shack, you'd be wrong. But close, as you know, they do a mighty good pint of

Shackmeister ale. No, instead we thought we have to end this on a total high, so let's hit Hell's Kitchen and the Ample Hills Creamery at Gotham West Market. Taking no chances, we both chose their Salted Crack'd Caramel and you know what...... even second time around it was still the best ice cream I have ever tasted. No pun intended – it put the icing on the cake to a great holiday and visit.

Miami & The Keys

Hace Calor Aquí

Airlines are always tweaking their prices up or down depending on how full their planes are and the time left before a given flight as they try to maximise their income whilst ensuring valuable seats aren't empty. Sometimes though, they run super promotional fares when trying to establish a new route to encourage people to use it, or at least use them when flying that route. Which is how we came to go to Miami.

After our trip to New York with Thomas Cook, inevitably we had been put on one of their mailing lists and not too long after we returned my inbox had pinged with a mail saying something like, "Roll up! Roll up! Flash Sale! From midday tomorrow for 24 hours we will be selling 299 return tickets direct from Manchester to Miami for £299. First come first served. This offer expires 24 hours after our sale starts or the selling out of our 299 special price tickets if earlier." The only other stipulation was that you had to fly out and return in May, but you could select any duration for your trip. In theory, if you wanted, you could go for the whole month, still for £299.

This seemed a great deal. Unfortunately, I hadn't been keeping on top of my emails that week and my heart sank as I noticed that it was already a day old. Luckily though, I realised I had still opened it with about ten minutes to go before the sale was about to start. I did a quick scout about via Google Flights to see what the normal price with other carriers would be at that time of year (just because they tell you it's a good deal doesn't mean it is, sort of thing) and found this was a genuine offer. Particularly as it involved a direct flight and not a horrible transfer via Heathrow.

We were now deep into our Midwinter at home (a season that seems to last for about eight months of the year in the North West of England) and I can tell you that the thought of some sunshine meant it took me about 299 seconds from reading that mail to check those prices and call Alison at work.

That said, to say she is not normally enamoured to receive a call at work, is a bit of an understatement. Believe me, these calls are not to be made lightly and are only reserved for the direst of emergencies. Honestly, you would probably choose to walk across a live minefield ahead of making a frivolous call to my wife whilst she is working. Seriously. The pain would be over quicker in the minefield.

Anyway, looking out of the window at another freezing grey sky, as the wind and rain lashed onto it, I decided that the prospect of a couple of weeks of sun and warmth in Southern Florida classified as a suitable emergency.

I will admit here to a slight heart stopping moment as the ring tone of her office phone started. I even considered putting on a Chinese accent to disguise my voice. Then I remembered where this got me the last time I tried that trick and decided to man up instead. Either that or go for the approach adopted by Jake Blues in the classic film *The Blues Brothers* when he's confronted by Carrie Fisher with a machine gun in a tunnel, as he and Ellwood try to make their escape from the Illinois Police. The part when he begs and whimpers for his life. I went for the Jake Blues.

Amazingly, when I asked her what she thought, Alison simply said, "Yes, why not? The best things are always done on the spur of the moment. Let's go for it!"

Woo-hoo! Result! This is why I love this woman so much. Well that, and the fact that, unlike Carrie Fisher's 'Mystery Woman', she didn't machine gun me.

So a couple of moments later I was in the on-line queue for tickets and now, a couple of months later, here we were flying into Miami International Airport (MIA).

The first thing that strikes you about MIA is what a dump of an airport it is. Or at least was when we went. One minute you are thinking about the gateway to Southern Florida and all the glitz, sparkle and wealth of Miami Beach and the next, you are greeted by threadbare carpets, peeling paint, ESTA machines out of order and a general feeling of decrepitness. It made our home airport of Manchester – which, despite supposedly being a major international airport, is consistently ranked in the top three worst airports in the UK – look amazing.

Now we'd experienced long immigration processing lines at Orlando some years ago (and have also appreciated the difference of fantastic, quick processing at both JFK and Boston), but this set new standards. Unfortunately, at the wrong end. We spent almost three hours in the immigration hall as the long line moved forward interminably slowly, although not without excitement to keep one entertained as we shall see. With the amount of people in the queue, the air-conditioning units couldn't keep up and it was stiflingly hot. Either that or Miami is so hot and sultry, they regarded this as cool. The sweat and the stench was awful. Just awful. Worse than a teenage boy's bedroom after they've had friends to stay on a sleepover.

The second thing you notice is that it appears English is the second language here. That, and Cuban visitors seem to have a different approach to queuing than that considered regular in the UK and US.

The US Border Force had helpfully gone to the trouble of trying to impose some form of order and arranged those snake-like rope systems you see at theme parks. This didn't seem to deter our more intrepid friends, however, who regarded them as mere objects of American curiosity. Slight annoyances even. That hindered their main business of pushing, shoving and general wailing in order that they might form a queue how they knew it should be done. Namely, one big seething mass of people all clambering to get through to the front at the same time. And so what if those Brits and Americans think our way is inefficient and unfair? At least it's way more fun.

The Border staff must have had the patience of saints. Even when they managed to restore some semblance of order – and for a short period we had something resembling the sort of line that you might normally see at an airport – it wasn't long before the more enterprising found a new strategy to deal with this inconvenience. This time, they simply started just walking past people, or perhaps more correctly straight through people, to the front.

I would have said slaloming past people to get to the front, but that would imply something akin to a skier piling down a mountain or a moving car zigzagging through motorway traffic. Either way, it would have implied (a) speed – which was not something to be associated with this queue; and (b) spaces to fit through – which there weren't any, as every available inch was being used up. Instead, it was more a case of just shoving people to one side and then walking past or over them, before repeating the manoeuvre and advancing up the line.

Unsurprisingly, as others realised the efficacy of this new tactic, they also adopted it and before long we had total mayhem once again. We've not yet been to Cuba, but everyone I've spoken to says nothing ever gets done there, which is why everyone still drives around in 1950s American cars. I wouldn't be surprised, as they're probably all too busy fighting each other in what they regard as queues. Bus journeys, shopping trips, you name it, must all take five times as long as they would anywhere else. Or maybe I am just a miserable git, and this is what passes for fun.

Once the latest queue-jumping tactic had broken down, one exceptionally uncouth bunch started shouting in Spanish at the nearest Border Force guard. The border guard, who I knew was bilingual from when she had earlier tried to help someone out, decided to cock a deaf ear and ignore them. Undaunted they then decided that the best approach would now be to repeat the process, but this time in English.

"Hey Baby!" shouted out their ringleader. "Hey Baby!", clicking her fingers as well for good measure. And, in case you were wondering, no she wasn't passing time by trying to sing along to Bruce Channel's early 1960s hit. I couldn't imagine ever trying to use this as a means of trying to initiate a conversation with a border agent in the UK, let alone in the United States. Nor would I like to imagine what might happen to me if I did. Clearly however, this must be how one goes about attracting the attention of those in authority in Havana. Although, I'm still not sure I am going to try it, even if I ever get to Cuba.

Anyway, as mentioned previously, the Border Force must recruit their people from Mother Teresa's missions or something, because at this point I would have snapped. Somehow, the poor guard kept her composure, however. Before telling them – now in no uncertain terms – that any more of this and they would be sent to the back of the line.

As by this stage some people had already been sent back, this seemed to do the trick. For about five minutes.

All I can say is a three-hour immigration process is not what you want after a long transatlantic flight at the best of times. Imagine what it's like when you've got to spend those three hours in stinking, sweltering conditions, earning your place in the line by taking on hundreds of others, seasoned in what seems to be their national sport. It's no wonder that Thomas Cook stopped this route after one season.

Eventually we surfaced at the top of the queue and were processed as courteously as always. The third thing that hits you in Miami is the heat. As soon as we stepped outside the terminal building, it was like a cross between opening a hot oven door and having someone shine one of those old-fashioned spotlights right up close to your face.

We had decided to stay in downtown Miami (as opposed to Miami Beach), as we would be going down to the Florida Keys a few days later. Miami's public transport is quick, easy and cheap, and was a great way to get to our Airbnb. Unlike New York, we had an uneventful journey from the airport, as we transitioned from the Metrorail system (that took us from the airport to the centre of town), to their efficient Metromover. (A free mono rail system that services the downtown area). Although we didn't have any real hassle, something that might have had a lot to do with the armed transit police that sporadically got on and off the Metromover cars, you could still sense that Miami had a real edge to it.

Our accommodation was on the downtown side of Edgewater and a good base for the downtown district. It is regarded as a nice, up-and-coming area. Even so, as we walked the five minutes from our Metromover stop to the flat we were renting, we still passed more than our fair share of panhandlers and winos.

After dropping our bags off at the flat, we decided to catch a bus to Miami Beach. Whilst there was no exciting queueing this time, we were still provided with plenty more free entertainment in the five minutes we had to wait for it. Who'd have thought Miami would be the city that kept on giving?

This time the spectacle was provided by a person loudly having an argument with themselves. This was quite interesting, especially with all the self-generated counter arguments he kept throwing at himself. We couldn't concentrate on the debate too much though, as separately another two people started fighting. Although the fighting only started properly, after we'd first been treated to a suitable period of increasingly loud, aggressive verbal sparring. Whilst slightly alarmed by this latest turn of events – in America, with its wide proliferation of guns, you never knew quite where this might lead – we took some measure of comfort from passing locals, none of whom seemed to bat so much as an eyelid. Presumably this was some sort of everyday occurrence around these parts. Fortunately, our bus arrived on time and we didn't have to endure the show for too long. Even more fortunately, none of our entertainers boarded it.

Crime statistics in Miami are improving, probably helped by the increase in police cameras from 16 to 160 across the city in 2018 alone. Nevertheless, it still has a higher than average crime rate and there is no question that this is a tough city. Where we come from, people think of gritty cities as cold, previously manufacturing dominated places like Manchester, Liverpool, Leeds, Sheffield, Birmingham, Newcastle, Glasgow and so on. With the exception of Birmingham and Scotland's Glasgow, all in the North of England. I guess in the US that might also apply to the Rust Belt across parts of Wisconsin, Ohio, Pennsylvania and Southern Michigan. Again, cold, tough, Northern places.

For some reason in the UK, probably because of our climate and where most people holiday, we don't associate sunshine with rough places, but relaxed, happy people. Just because Miami has sea and heat though, it doesn't stop it being any less gritty. It was a strange sensation for us.

Although we weren't planning to visit the Beach area properly for a couple of days, we had decided to briefly visit it now as part of our strategy of batting through to beat the jet lag. Its bright lights and crowds of people would all provide that vital energy boost. Along with its vast choice of eateries. A key element in staying awake long enough is appropriate sustenance, and eagle eyed Alison had spotted that Miami Beach possessed…… you guessed it…… a Shake Shack!

Now I promise you, this book is not one big advertisement for Shake Shack (and I will try not to mention the place again). But it had been months since our last fix; we needed something for supper; and the stars just seemed to align in that direction is all I am saying.

Do you feel lucky, Punk!

It was still dark when we awoke, thanks to the jet lag and time difference, but we were still greeted by a magical panorama. The condo we had rented was on the 41st floor of a new tower block development near Margaret Pace Park and the views over the city, as well as out across Biscayne Bay, were stunning. With its lights lit, the city sparkled like an immense field of illuminated Christmas trees. A scene enhanced by the reflections thrown on the water. Whilst our vista may have been different to the classic ocean beach views or magnificent mountain scenery that people normally describe when asked their ideal view, it was still stunningly beautiful in its own right. Breathtaking, in fact.

Our view also encompassed the Port of Miami and at this early hour we could see the cruise ships entering and parking up, ahead of the new day dawning. Miami is the largest cruise port in the world, something you got a sense of based on the number and size of boats coming in, and it was fascinating, sitting with a cup of tea, watching as they delicately nudged into their berths. In reality, the process is akin to lots of buses entering a busy bus depot, except that the sheer size and splendour of the liners made it a much subtler, grander operation. Transfixed, we could have sat there for hours. Indeed, we did until, with Miami facing east, the icing on the cake arrived with the sunrise. From 41 floors up, it too was splendid.

Whilst the colours of light generated by a sunrise are similar to a sunset – albeit in reverse – it's interesting how the two feel so different from one another.* With sunset our natural body processes are telling us

---

* Purists will argue here that at dawn, because the air is usually at its clearest (due to less human generated pollution at night), more brilliant reds and oranges can make their way through the atmosphere so we are actually able to see slightly different colours than at sunset. They will also argue that although at dusk the light is more diffused, it is also more scattered by pollution particles and so creates a wider wash of colour. Maybe they just like to argue.

to wind down for the night and there seems more tranquillity, along with the poignancy of another day passed. At sunrise, however, our bodies are telling us to wake up, get up and go, added to the excitement of a new day ahead. It's impossible to say which is better. Perhaps due to something in our primeval DNA, both appear wondrous events of nature. Sunrise or not however, my body didn't need to tell me to move as I had the luxury of an Alison to jolt me out of my trance and let me know that the shower was now free – and best not to waste any hot water.

We took another trip on the Metromover, followed by the Metrorail so we could enjoy breakfast at a fancy bistro in the upscale Coconut Grove district. Dining Alfresco, savouring the warmth – even in the shade, Manchester's leaden skies seemed a million miles away. Eggs Benedict, good coffee, stretching back in our chairs, the long flight soon faded away. Ah, it was all so civilised. As was Coconut Grove. A nice, if quiet, part to wander around, before we made our way back to the centre of town to see the Bayside Marketplace and a mooch round the core downtown area.

The Bayside Marketplace is currently rated the top thing to do in Miami on Tripadvisor – something sports fans of the Dolphins, Marlins and Heat might have something to say about. However, it is also the number one most visited tourist attraction in Miami. Although, that may say a lot about Miami itself. In reality, it's just an open air shopping centre, with an upmarket slant, plus lots of kiosks and places where you can get knick-knacks. With over one hundred shops and eating places, it's certainly not shabby and has a great location right by the waterfront, but we hadn't flown thousands of miles across the Atlantic to do a bit of shopping. So, after a quick refreshment stop, whilst taking in what to be fair is a good view, we tottered off towards the other parts of downtown.

Maybe it's because Miami has Miami Beach only a few miles away, with its hundreds of restaurants and shops hoovering up a lot of demand, but the downtown part of Miami doesn't have that much to it at all. Not for a city of its size. Yes, there are shops, restaurants and bars, as you would expect. There is also the basketball arena for the NBA Miami Heat team, as well as The Adrienne Arsht Center for the

Performing Arts – to be fair America's second largest such centre. It's just that, for the most part, downtown Miami doesn't feel like a big city.

Perhaps that's because Miami itself isn't as large a city as you might expect. Although it's part of the seventh largest metropolitan area in the United States, that conurbation also includes the separate cities of Fort Lauderdale, West Palm Beach and Miami Beach. Miami, as a city on its own though, doesn't even make the top forty most populous US Cities, ranking behind places such as Oklahoma City; Louisville, Kentucky; Albuquerque and Tucson to name a few. Let alone the more obvious candidates such as New York, Chicago, Los Angeles and so on. Whether it's because Miami itself is smaller than you might imagine or whether it's because the beach is where it's all at, sadly its downtown didn't feel anything special.

Ordinarily we would have walked to our next stop, Wynwood Walls, as it was only a couple of miles away, but by this stage it was already 35°C (95°F), with a scorching sun, so we decided to grab a cab. It didn't look great as it pulled up, but when we got in, it was even worse. All I could think was "Blinkin Blimey, what a wreck." It was so down at heel, it made the airport look like the Ritz. With more rattles and bangs than one of those old-timer wooden roller coasters, I wasn't even convinced it would get us to the end of the street, never mind Wynwood.

At the risk of harking back to *The Blues Brothers*, this would have given their car, the Bluesmobile, a run for its money. And after the police had finished chasing them at that. In fact, you would have been forgiven for thinking you had just stepped into the original Bluesmobile, except this might once have been painted yellow. Honestly, I kept looking at the floor plate half expecting a hole to appear at any second, and our taxi to become a Fred Flintstone mobile instead. If we'd had to finish the journey propelling it using our feet, I wouldn't have been in the least bit surprised.

Our driver was an amenable old hand who'd been around a bit, and he pointed out various bits of the area to us. He told us that Wynwood used to be as rough as a bear's nether regions, but for some reason that he was still trying to fathom, it was now a major tourist site. Creative types had moved in, he said, lured by low rents and/or abandoned buildings, and then persuaded outsiders that the graffiti sprayed everywhere should be considered art. Somehow it was now regarded as a hipster hangout. He asked us if tourists to the UK were as dumb as in Miami. Actually odd was the word he used.

For us, Wynwood was a dichotomy. There is a wider district called Wynwood, that used to be a manufacturing and warehousing centre that has clearly seen hard times, but now seems to be rejuvenating. Then at its centre are the Wynwood Walls themselves. The Walls are an area where graffiti artists are invited to express themselves and showcase their work. Conceived by a guy called Tony Goldman, who had been key in transforming New York's decaying SoHo area into an arts hub in the 1970s; he wanted to create an area for the greatest street art ever seen in one place.

Although most of the artwork is spray painted or wheat pasted, a lot of the murals are superb and put to shame a lot, if not most, of the stuff found in New York's MOMA. That said, sadly, it all felt a little contrived; a little forced. Maybe because of its success.

The Walls themselves are in a fenced area, best described by the renowned urban artist Gaia as "like a gated community of murals" and you shuffle round in a busy line of people. In that sense it is no different to any major art gallery, but somehow it seemed odd. Maybe it was just our lack of experience in seeing art in this sort of setting, but somehow the original spirit now seemed diluted; a little artificial; a bit ersatz. You wondered how many people were there to enjoy the art and how many because they'd been told it was the place to go by Tripadvisor. Regardless, we spent an enjoyable hour and then ventured out into the surrounding area.

Outside the Walls, the area is still festooned with graffiti. Perhaps drawing inspiration from the Walls themselves, much of this is also in the format of large murals and pictures. Albeit painted on the sides of real warehouses and street walls, as opposed to a dedicated area. Some of these were also truly excellent, but hardly any of the visitors that had mobbed the official walls, seemed inclined to venture less than a hundred yards outside, and into some of these side streets. So many were so good, it seems unfair to pick out a few, but some of our favourites included a Boy with oversized glasses called *Tongue* by Brazilian artist Sipros, of the Bushwick Collective group of artists; a, quite literally giant, *Panda* by Ernesto Maranje; a Woman's Face in three stages from surprise to horror called *Happy Shock* by Jeff Henriquez (also from the Bushwick Collective); and *Size is no measure of greatness* by Italian artist ZED1, a modern art inspired piece in which a little bird defends itself and its companion against a large unidentified, clawed beast. All of which were to be found between the Concrete Beach and Wynwood craft breweries.

As you might expect, with two working craft breweries within four hundred yards of each other, and each with a tasting room, we visited them both. Of the two we preferred the Concrete Beach Brewing Company as it had an outside bar, with shade if needed, and it seemed a crime to sit inside on a day as gorgeous as this. It had also entered into the spirit of art in the neighbourhood with some quirky pieces of its own, like the front end of a car, converted into a seat for two. Plus, it had a nice circular bar that ran inside and out so even if you sat in, you still felt the nice day outside. Most importantly, it had a good range of beer and so we enjoyed a couple, whilst drinking in the sunshine, before we wandered back to our apartment.

Although Wynwood is still a challenged area, we decided to walk as it was still broad daylight, only a mile to our apartment and we would go past Miami's number one rated donut shop. The donut shop took some finding – being hidden inside a larger building with little visible signage. A building also cloaked from top to toe in murals. Apparently at times it's dead easy (no pun intended) to spot with queues up to forty-five minutes long snaking outside. These must be good donuts. When we went, however, there was no such line of people helpfully waiting to provide clues, and walking through the area was an unsettling experience. Believe me, repeatedly having to cross streets to avoid people frenetically spray-painting walls in front of you, whilst you frantically scour for any sign of what might pass for a donut shop is as fretful as it sounds. Particularly, when accompanied by the sound of sirens and police cars hurtling around every few minutes.

In addition to its vast selection of different varieties, the donut shop was expensive. But Alison is to sweet things what I am to beer and having risked life and limb getting here – potentially truer than figurative – she was going to make sure she enjoyed every last moment and cent. This started with the choosing process.

"Ooh this looks nice. Shall we go for the Brown Butter & Salt one?"

What's interesting is this time the 'we' meant her, as distinct from the salt shop in New York's Chelsea Market, where that time we meant me. And women wonder why men find it hard to understand the language they speak at times.

"And what about if we get a Maple & Bacon one too?" I don't know why I am putting question marks here.

"And how about the Mini Key Lime Pie one?" she continued.

"Can I say No?

"No."

"Then we should get one of those as well."

"What about the Coconut & Lychee? They sound lurvely."

"Honey, you know these are costing about four bucks each with tax?"

"Cheap at half the price."

"Certainly cheaper than a divorce," I muttered.

"What was that?"

"Oh, nothing. I was just saying certainly cheaper than the White Chocolate Tres Leches. Don't they also look great?"

I am learning you see. I also figured that if we bought our body weight in donuts, we might be able to wear them as body armour, should we actually get attacked on the next stage of our walk back to our apartment. Plus, we'd have no money left, leaving not much to rob.

To be fair, the donuts were all delicious and whilst not cheap, were large enough to keep us going for days. Helped by us buying so many. After making it safely back and a quick recharge – nothing like a cup of tea to refresh the soul – we were off again, this time to Little Havana, on our way to the baseball game to watch the Miami Marlins.

We'd heard that the best fish restaurant in Miami was a place called La Camaronera Seafood Joint and Fish Market. As from there it was only a ten-minute walk to the ballpark, it seemed perfect for a pre-match meal. When time is short, it's always good to grab two birds with one stone. The Metromover didn't run there though, so we caught a bus from the centre of town. Little Havana, as its name implies, is a neighbourhood composed of predominantly Cuban migrants. Like many cities, people from similar origins cluster together, so Miami also has districts comprising those originating from Haiti, Puerto Rico, South America and so on. When we landed at the airport, I had thought from the luggage carousel boards that it was sheer chance that we had arrived at the same time as a host of flights from Argentina, Bolivia, Cuba, Colombia, Mexico, Peru and Puerto Rico, but in fact over 70% of Miami's population speak Spanish and are of Hispanic background. The effect is such that, apart from indicators like American flags flying on public buildings or the style of police uniforms, most things that you encounter are in some way Hispanic. From the writing on signs, to the shops, to hearing people talking. You don't feel you are in an American city.

The food was very good, but please don't let the description of restaurant mislead you. A better clue is the use of 'joint' in its official name of Seafood Joint & Fish Market. Put it this way, it was more like a decent British chippy where you can eat in as well as having counter service. Rugged it may have been, and perhaps it helped that I spoke passable Spanish, but it was good, honest, fresh seafood. There was also the bonus, that if you didn't fancy anything from their regular selections, you could buy a piece of fish from their market counter and then ask them to cook it how you wanted.

As well as eating its food, I've always been a great believer that to fully appreciate the culture of a nation, you need to attend its sporting events. Major League Baseball is right up there alongside American football and basketball in the US psyche, and so it was with some excitement that we entered Marlins Park. Especially with it being a nice, shiny, fairly new stadium.

The heat of the day had ebbed and it was now a lovely warm Saturday evening. Groups of guys, couples and families wandered in munching their hot dogs and popcorn. Kids were eagerly bouncing up and down at the thought of a night at the ball game. It was a relaxed, happy, anticipatory atmosphere. Whether we had picked a bad game to go to though, or whether the Marlins were crap that season I don't know, but it wasn't the best introduction to one of America's most loved sports.

The first innings ended 0-0. This was not a good start.

The second also ended 0-0. This really was not a good start at all.

Miraculously, someone hit something in the third innings and Atlanta scored two runs.

Miami didn't, however.

The fourth and fifth innings then reverted to type with no runs either.

Atlanta lucked out again in their sixth innings, so that by the bottom of the sixth, with Miami going into bat, the score was still 0-2. I thought I was watching a football (soccer) match, other than that the players run in football. Oh, and the crowd sings. It was dire.

Somehow both teams seemed to rally themselves sufficiently to actually hit the ball and lumber – even jog would be too quick a word for these guys – the 120 or so yards required to complete a run, and the game ended with the Braves beating Miami 3-1.

In the whole game, only twelve people had hit a ball. Just think about that for a second. Miami sent twenty-seven men into bat, of which only five managed to hit a ball all night without being run out, caught out or it being out of bounds. And they say Americans don't get cricket; they find it too boring.

Now, despite being English, let me point out that I am not an ardent cricket lover (save for when we beat the Australians in the incredible test series of 1981 and 2005 and when we won the World Cup final against New Zealand in 2019). I can think of better ways of spending five days than watching a match that might not even yield a winner. Which, given the amount of rain we get, often happens. In fact, despite popular preconceptions, most English people also prefer action sports. But if cricket is boring, what the hell do you call it when you sit there for three hours to watch a ball being hit twelve times, or only once every fifteen minutes? Cricket might often result in a draw, but at least they're hitting the ball every minute or so whilst they are playing.

Pitch … strike, pitch … strike, pitch … strike-out! Pitch … strike, pitch … ball, and so it continued. It was like watching paint … dry.

Every year, over three million packets of peanuts are sold at American baseball games. Apparently it's so that people can expend their nervous energy shelling them and then be able to eat them without having to take their eyes off the game. Well, we could have had a sit down, silver service, gourmet tasting menu and not missed anything.

It was then that I realised that much as I love America, if this nation really does adore baseball, I could never truly be an American. Not even if I lived here for thirty years. Oh, and I'm not even going to get involved with how a competition can be called the World Series when it's only open to teams from the United States plus Toronto.

So a bit of a shame, as it was a flat way to end what had otherwise been a good day. Little did we know, however, that things were soon to get dramatically worse.

We came out of the ground and I had been planning to flag down a cab, the way you can at any major European sports stadium I can think of. The police however had cordoned off two blocks around the ground, so there was no way a cab could get in. Not a problem, I thought, we'll get one as soon as we're outside the police's restricted zone. Easier said than done.

There were no taxi ranks, or none that I could see, and any taxi pickups were only for people who had pre-booked. Although we hadn't yet been Uberised, I had taken the precaution of getting a card from the taxi driver who had given us a lift to Wynwood earlier. I tried to call him, but for a whole host of reasons, all of which conspired against me, my mobile phone wasn't working for calls to US numbers. For the first block or so outside the police cordon there were still lots of people about, and I figured that it would only be twelve or thirteen blocks before we were in the centre of town. I thought we could walk it – it should only take about twenty-five minutes.

I was wrong. I was thinking like a European, but we weren't in Europe. We were in America, in one of its rougher cities, and if that wasn't enough, we didn't know the area. After walking two blocks (on the bright side only ten or eleven to go) we realised we were all alone. Clearly the locals knew something we didn't – never a good sign.

After another block, a guy on a bike started circling about. And he didn't look the cycling type. I knew we could be in a lot of trouble here if we were unlucky enough, and I started thinking as fast as my little mind could process. I was looking everywhere, with my eyes darting as discreetly as possible – so as not to convey the impression of being lost or scared.

Then, a couple of blocks to our right, up a hill, shining like the star of Bethlehem, I spied a sign for a drugstore and petrol station. It was our saviour. It must have been 250 yards away, but it was light and would have people; where we were was dark and had no one, save for our midnight rider. It was the longest 250 yard walk of my life. We got to the store to be greeted by its security guard – who was armed. He was a genial, older guy and we explained our problem.

"You don't want to be walking around here," he said.

"We realised that, pretty quickly."

"No, really, you don't want to be walking around here." He was ramming his point home. "You're not from round here, you're going to get in trouble. You'll probably get robbed."

"But we've not got much to rob, and we're not dressed flashily or anything."

"Then that's worse." He continued his lesson to us, "It's obvious by the look of you, you're not from round here. This is a poor neighbourhood and whether you have money or watches or cameras, or not, people will assume that if you're not from round here, then you will have those things. And if they rob you and you haven't any, they'll either not believe you or get angry. Or both."

He didn't need to say anymore. I had learnt a vital lesson, just in time. Miami is not Manhattan. It doesn't have its public transport system, it's a lot poorer, and whilst there are parts of New York that you wouldn't want to walk around late at night on your own, you've got to work a lot harder to get to them. Miami is a lot smaller than New York, which means you can be in the wrong neighbourhood a lot quicker than you realise. Of course, it's not only Miami. At home, there are parts of our big cities that I wouldn't wander around alone in the middle of the day, let alone at night. The difference is at home, you know which parts lead where. At home, you understand the clues.

In my defence, most large European sporting events would provide plentiful public transport options out and a place where you can easily grab taxis and naively I had assumed it would be similar here; I had thought ahead and got a taxi card and number; I'd also made sure I had the international roaming options set up on my phone and account before we left. I had simply been extremely unlucky to have a series of things go against me. At the same time, I was also lucky. Lucky to have learnt a massive lesson without any real harm being done.

Anyway, the old guard was great and, with his phone, sorted us a taxi, from a firm he trusted, to get us back safely. I shall always be grateful.

Life's A Beach!

Most people, apart from those living there, think Miami and Miami Beach are effectively the same place. That Miami Beach is the beach district of Miami, rather like Bondi Beach is a suburb of Sydney. However, although it's not five miles away, Miami Beach, incorporated almost twenty years after Miami itself, is a completely different city. Legally, physically and culturally. Separated from Miami by Biscayne Bay, it is a set of islands, connected to the mainland by a series of umbilical cords in the guise of various bridges and causeways.

Despite it being another hot sunny day, we thought we would walk the three miles via the road connecting the mainland to the Venetian Islands and then onto Miami Beach itself. It was a fine walk with, as you might imagine, spectacular waterside views. Although man made when dredging Biscayne Bay, the Venetian Islands themselves are still picturesque, with some stunning real estate on them. Heaven only knows how much these things cost,* but it was certainly a far cry from grittier Miami just over a couple of miles away. The other side of the water, it could have been on the other side of the moon.

We walked down Lincoln Road, which describes itself as a Mall, but Europeans would think of it as a pedestrianised outdoor shopping street. (Although cross traffic was still allowed at the intersection of each block). It runs for about half a mile, across six or seven blocks, each of which is crammed with fancy stores, fancy restaurants, fancy ice cream parlours and so on. Overwhelmed by fanciness, after a couple of days on the other side of the water, we made our way to Ocean Drive where we were then assailed by Lamborghinis, Ferraris, Bentleys and all manner of luxurious cars cruising up and down. Their occupants posing, preening and flaunting. You felt like you'd walked into an

---

*Actually I looked in an estate agents – they ranged from $1.5m to $22.5m and upwards.

exclusive club where membership requirements were wheels costing at least $100k.

Sadly, when we saw a young couple in a Chevrolet Spark (think something one up from a Smart car), they were the ones who looked incongruous. Stopped at a red light, they just looked embarrassed. Something I could relate to having years ago driven our family people carrier, a Renault Espace, up the Ferrari lined gravel drive of a posh hotel I'd booked as a special treat for our tenth anniversary. That day I cringed as I handed the concierge my keys. Much in the same way as the poor young driver was now, as he tried sliding under his steering wheel. You could see him thinking, "as well as options to avoid Tolls and Motorways, why the hell didn't my Sat-Nav give me an option to avoid areas not meant for cheap cars."

And of course there is Casa Casuarina, Gianni Versace's former mansion, something everyone stops to look at, certainly judging by the number of people taking photos outside. Apparently it's America's third most photographed home, behind The White House and Graceland. Bought for just under $3m in 1992, after he fell in love with the building whilst visiting Miami Beach, Versace reputedly spent in excess of $30m remodelling it and filling it with marble, frescoes, sculptures and opulence that one can only imagine – not to mention buying the hotel next door and tearing it down in order to install a swimming pool with over a million mosaic tiles. Famous house guests are said to have included Madonna, Princess Diana and Elton John. Except these days you can do more than just imagine the opulence, with Casa Casuarina now converted into a hotel anyone can stay at. Well, if you can run to the cost of a room – which as you can imagine doesn't come cheap on the road for high rollers.

Opposite, the beach was as gorgeous as the mansion and most of the motors. Fine, golden sand, nice warm water and herons that provided entertainment diving into the sea, plucking out fish. All set against a brilliant blue sky. It was almost too beautiful for words. As were many of the people bronzing themselves. As I disrobed, I began to worry that tragically, here on this beach, I might be the equivalent of that Chevrolet up against the Ferraris. Fortunately, I spotted a few trucks nearby and suggested we park our towels near them. We lay there for a good while, soaking up the sun, the sea air, the sounds of the waves on the shore. Aaaah, it was bliss.

Not everything was perfect in paradise though. Something we discovered after an hour or two, when our mouths told us it was time for an ice cold beverage. The obvious thing was to hit an establishment on Ocean Drive opposite the beach, but the prices were just insane. Sod our mouths watering, this was eye watering. We should have guessed it from the cars out front, but if this was the place to flash your stash, it was also the zone to lash your cash.

It was more than that though. For us, the feel was all wrong. Please don't write us off as old fogeys here – we can party hard with our friends and even (for a short while) with the best of them. But there is a big difference between partying when you want to and partying because you're expected to. The closer you looked, the more you realised it was people coming here and paying through the nose because they'd been told it's America's party resort; or it was groups of guys, either on business trips or a weekend away with the boys. It just felt false and without substance. Or as they say in Manchester, "All fur coat and no knickers."

It felt like one big money making washing machine. Put yourself in the middle, get spun round a few times, and pretty soon you find you've been rinsed of all your cash. God help us when we get to be dried out by the mangle, I thought to myself.

Now, please don't misunderstand me, I'm happy to spend hard earned coin when it's worth it. I also know those providing the service have to make a profit. It's just that it's normally better when done a little more subtly. It's hard to relax and enjoy things when you feel you're getting right royally screwed over. Rather detracts from the ambience somewhat. Unless you're completely pissed up – which, on closer examination, it seemed most of the other customers were. That, or they owned key fobs with horses on them.

To restore some sanity, we decided to move a couple of blocks back on the Venice principle – i.e., whilst you need a mortgage to get a cup of coffee in St. Mark's Square, there is also a full-time population and a lot of service workers in Venice who don't get paid much. So for those prepared to walk a couple of hundred yards off the beaten track, things become almost normal again.

Even a couple of blocks away from the front though, we were still paying three times what we had the day before, for the same beer in the craft brewery. Nor, I might add, did we have any spray paint artwork to admire either. Although admittedly, the journey home would probably be less stressful. Usually I let the barman keep the change, but I just couldn't bring myself to do it. Mainly because there wasn't any.

Aside from the Versace mansion, you might be wondering why I hadn't mentioned the grandeur of the Art Deco Historical District on our walk to the beach. Well, that's because we had opted for a guided tour of the area and having finished our drinks, that was where we were now heading.

It was the first time in our lives that we had booked a tour, having previously been put off by preconceptions that you would be in a group with hundreds of other people. Not only that, but most would be toting cameras with lenses big enough to make NASA proud. All whilst sporting gaudy Hawaiian shirts, which if they didn't endanger your eyesight, the flash of ample white flesh from beneath almost certainly would. You would have to walk at the pace of the slowest, which would invariably be somewhere between slug and tortoise, due to some special snowflake moaning about their sciatica or lumbago. Or just generally moaning. Still, at least they would have had a good day out, as it would give them a new audience and at least another fifty poor beings to share their aches and afflictions with.

Due to the size of the group, no one beyond the first two rows would hear anything anyway. A situation often not helped by some wittering inveterate telling their companion about the trials and tribulations of their trip to the Post Office last Tuesday. Before launching into a long story, about how things hadn't been the same at the bridge club since old Fothersdyke had been expelled for passing the port to the right. All without taking breath. And at full voice, given their hearing isn't what it was.

On top of that, the teenage tour guide would be bored to the back teeth from doing this six times a day, seven days a week, every week from here until eternity. In an attempt to get home quicker, they would then rattle through things so fast that the poor sods at the back would only be arriving at the latest point of interest, as they were wrapping up.

People would start pushing, some would start shushing, whilst others would be organising an escape committee.

Unless it's a German organised tour of course. I once got caught in the midst of one of these whilst walking around the coast of Menorca in Spain. Where the Germans are concerned it's the complete opposite of a shuffling, ambling tour. They might also be octogenarians, but they move at a speed closer to a forced march. Woe betide anyone who doesn't keep up the pace. You don't get through the Maginot Line in twenty-four hours by worrying about those at the back you know.

I'm not sure how it happened – I must have been daydreaming or something – but before I knew it I was in the middle of their group. Whether they had spotted me glinting in the sun and had zeroed in before I got away I don't know, but what was certain was for about fifteen minutes I marched with a German walking holiday tour. It was a nightmare. Not just because I don't speak a word of German apart from "Ja", but because I have never been so exhausted in my life. Seriously, these guys march quicker than I can jog.

As I kept smiling inanely at whatever they were saying, you could see them looking at each other quizzically.

"Who's the new guy?"

"I don't know, I thought he was with you."

"With me? I thought he was with you?"

"Seems a nice guy though, always smiling."

"Seems a bit simple if you ask me."

I kept expecting one of them to rumble me, and their leader to exclaim, "Ha ha, for you Englander, zis valk is over!"

Knowing I had to escape, I considered stopping to tie a shoelace, but thought this might prove fatal, with me being crushed by the back half of the phalanx. In the end, my moment came when we turned a corner and not wasting a second, in case there were no other opportunities, I threw myself to the side. Lying there, I was exhausted.

Still, it had the benefit in that for fifteen minutes I covered a lot of the island – I was virtually carried along in their slipstream. It was like being in a peloton. Although, I'm not sure pelotons go as quick as a German tour group when it gets up a head of steam.

Either way, organised tour groups weren't for us, we thought. We had seen plenty examples on visits to London, Chester and even our fair city of Manchester, now that it too has been discovered.

Miami Beach's art deco architecture is iconic though. In fact, it is the largest collection of such buildings in the world and we wanted to do it justice. Particularly given limited time available. Either that or we have now also reached the age required to join most organised tour groups. That said, we did a bit of research and selected a company that had nothing but rave reviews, even if they had written most of them themselves.

Actually, my line about writing their own reviews was unfair as our tour guide was brilliant. We might also have dropped lucky, because as well as us and our guide, there were only two other people on the tour. The others being an American father and his son, who was about to head off to college. Sadly, that meant we would now be the slowest in the group.

Miami Beach was a mangrove jungle until 1870, when purchased from the Federal Government by two Quakers, Henry and Charles Lum. A touch ironic, considering what it became famous for. The Lums paid the princely sum of 25 cents an acre. How times change. Their initial plan to farm coconuts was unsuccessful, however, and it wasn't until forty years later another crop grower and Quaker, John S. Collins, hit upon the idea of developing the area for holidays instead of crops. The intention was to serve the growing city of Miami and wealthy people from the northern States. This plan was much more successful, and it meant that Miami Beach took off as the art deco movement was taking a hold around the world.

We learned about key art deco concepts such as symmetry, streamlined patterns, geometrical shapes and a desire to be modern for the age. The latter often reflected in themes around transportation, communication and mankind's technological progress. As a result, some buildings are styled to signify an ocean liner or a rocket. Others have artistic details added, such as train tracks running up them. Art deco buildings also often included ledges, representing eyebrows, above square or long rectangular windows. To convey the impression the building had eyes and was watching you. Whilst inside, decorations made heavy use of inlaid materials, highlighting angular geometrical forms.

In the case of Miami Beach, the inlaid symbols served to point guests to secret drinking and gambling dens. As well as expanding through the art deco period, Miami Beach also grew heavily during the time of prohibition. Recognising the demand for these vices, hotels created distinct rooms to provide those services. Whilst attached to the hotel, they would be separate enough from the main buildings, so the hotel could claim any drinking or gambling den discovered in a police raid was nothing to do with them. Why they didn't even know it was there, and were as appalled as the police to discover this going on, sort of thing. Art deco styled shapes such as triangles, or card themed ones such as diamonds, were inlaid into hotel floors, disguised as decorated borders. If you looked carefully though, they would guide you from reception to the nefarious room.

Perhaps unsurprisingly, many Miami Beach hotels ended up controlled by organised crime syndicates. Apparently, one way you could tell if a hotel was mob owned – and therefore whether it was more likely to have a gaming room before you checked in – was its height. After the Great Hurricane of 1926 decimated large swathes of Miami Beach and Southeast Florida (a hurricane so powerful that if it hit today, it is estimated would cause circa $235 billion of damage) stricter building codes were introduced to limit building heights. Somehow though, mob controlled hotels always seemed to be a little higher.

Although the Government got its revenge when it decided to use Miami Beach as one of its major training centres for the US Army and Air Force in the Second World War. It requisitioned 85% of Miami Beach's hotel rooms as troop quarters. Four years of occupation by troops in boots left the hotels, shall we say, no longer in pristine condition. By then, with gambling legal in Nevada, the crime bosses thought it easier to relocate and redevelop their businesses in a more conducive environment.

The rise in Las Vegas lead to a corresponding decline in Miami Beach. Over time, from being America's playground, it became God's waiting room for retired snowbirds. Its demise continued for several decades as ever easier jet travel made other holiday destinations more attractive. Until, in misguided efforts to relaunch Miami Beach, developers started tearing down the old hotels and buildings to replace them with newer, shinier models. Ironic, as today Miami Beach's Art Deco buildings are one of its biggest draws.

They might have completely succeeded, were it not for the heroic efforts of a lady called Barbara Baer Capitman and the Miami Design Preservation League, something she was instrumental in founding. Their combination of candlelit vigils, standing in front of approaching bulldozers, and lobbying media and politicians, succeeded in highlighting the area's plight. As a result, in 1979 the National Register of Historic Places officially recognised the Miami Beach Architectural District.

As our guide took us into some of the older hotels, he pointed out how stairs would often lead up and away as you left reception for your room. Not only is the city of Miami Beach practically at sea level, but the Florida limestone, on which it sits, is porous. This means water can rise through it, something the sea does at particularly high tides, or King Tides as they are known. Even back in the 1920s and 30s this biannual phenomenon was a problem with water flooding ground floor receptions, irrespective of whether there had been a storm. (Hence why even ground floor bedrooms were built on higher levels than the main reception). But these days, with global warming and consequential rises in sea levels, it's much worse and getting progressively so. It may yet prove a greater threat to Miami Beach and its historical Art Deco District than even the wildest developers. Unless long-term solutions can be found.

The city authorities are trying their best. As well as changes to building codes, a huge public works programme is underway to raise the level of essential amenities and infrastructure. Power stations, sewage and water treatment plants are all being addressed. Even the roads and pavements are being raised. Like King Canute trying to hold back the tide, it may not be enough though. The National Oceanic and Atmospheric Administration predicts that by 2070 Miami will flood daily, compared to the half a dozen times a year at present. Ultimately, Miami Beach was claimed from swamp and, if nature gets its way, it may one day return to that.

Having finished our tour, we still had time to grab supper at the 11th Street Diner before making our way back across to Miami. A Miami Beach institution, the Diner is a restored original art deco Dining Car, much like those that graced a lot of the US from the 1920s to the 1960s. Beautiful from the outside, its sleek, shiny aluminium form wraps around the corner of 11th Street and Washington Avenue. It looked like a cross between a silver train carriage and the skirt of an inflated hovercraft, made from platinum.

Inside it was also wonderful, with everything just as you imagined. Red leather stools sat alongside a white formica serving counter; leather banquettes huddled either side of tables, in a series of low level booths; vintage American memorabilia adorned the walls. Perhaps best of all was the menu which featured that other All American classic, the milkshake. In a staggering, salivating twenty-six different flavours.

As well as the other American staples you would expect from any self-respecting diner such as burgers (twenty-two different types in addition to building your own); omelettes (twelve versions); pancakes and waffles; they had a veritable miscellany of wholesome, filling, if less than heart friendly, food. And all at prices which, if not true diner, were more regular America than Miami Beach. The diner, along with our art deco interlude, nearly went as far as restoring our faith in Miami Beach.

We were glad we went to Miami and Miami Beach, otherwise we would always have been wondering what it was really like. Besides, its art deco district is truly great and its wider popularity means that it must suit lots of people, even if not us. Plus, I can see how Miami Beach makes a great base for a stop before a Caribbean cruise. But, we were also glad we had gone, as with our changing climate who knows what the future holds. At least we saw it whilst it was still there.

Now, however, it was time to hit Key West.

Water, water everywhere, not any of it a drop to drink

The drive from Miami to Key West encompasses one of the world's great drives. Specifically, the stretch of Overseas Highway that starts just north of Key Largo and continues for 113 miles until it ends in Key West.

I know some people might take issue here and say hold on, what about The Icefields Parkway in Canada between Lake Louise and Jasper? Or California's Route 1* from Monterey to San Luis Obispo, taking in the Big Sur? Or the Mount Cook Road in New Zealand? Or The Blue Ridge Parkway? Or any of numerous crossings through the Alps from the Brenner Pass to La Route des Grandes Alpes.

I could go on and on here, because there are many great drives in this world. The point is not which is *the* best, or which should comprise the top ten. It's impossible to be definitive on these things anyway, particularly as different people prefer different things. Instead, it is to recognise that this is a special journey and to enjoy that moment you're in and the company you're with.

I guess all I am saying is that on a warm sunny day, with a light breeze in your face; the Gulf of Mexico to your right, a gleaming bright turquoise blue; the Atlantic Ocean on your left, sparkling as it reflects the rays from the rising sun as though topped with hundreds of glittering diamonds. For me, the Overseas Highway is right up there.

In your 113 miles, you cross a staggering forty-two bridges and forty-three islands (or keys as they are called down there) and pass numerous others. Most of the time you have amazing sea views. Often in front of you, to the left of you and to your right, at the same time. Even when you're on an island instead of a bridge crossing water, many of the keys are so narrow that you can still see both the Atlantic and the Gulf.

---

* Maybe the Americans save Route One for all their best drives as for some reason the Overseas Highway from Key Largo to Key West is also called Highway 1.

Viewed from a map or a plane, in the bright southern sunshine, the Keys are like a string of pearls joined by a necklace made of road. Strung out in an arc that heads Southwest. The highest point of the route, on Seven Mile bridge, is only 65 feet above sea level, and even then that's only to allow clearance for ships under the bridge. For a lot of the journey you are as good as at sea level, which combined with the slenderness of some of the keys, makes you feel that you are virtually driving through the ocean. At times, particularly if it's a high tide or there's a bit of wind, you can see the water lapping at the shoreline, only a few yards from the side of the road.

Actually, Seven Mile bridge is only 6.8 miles long, although that is splitting hairs, particularly as it provides one of the highlights of the voyage. One of the reasons for this is that it's a rather odd sensation being on a bridge for so long. Driving for over ten minutes across nothing but ocean.

Heaven only knows what it's like to cross the 23.9 mile Lake Pontchartrain Causeway in Louisiana. Not only is that America's longest road bridge, it is also the World's longest continuous road bridge over water. It is even longer than the width of the English Channel at the Straits of Dover – and it's hard to conceive driving from England to France across the sea. Indeed, Lake Pontchartrain Causeway is so long, there is an eight mile stretch in the middle during which you can't see land from either side. It can be so disorientating, and spook out some drivers so badly, that the Highway Patrol have to station cars at various points across the Causeway. They are there not only for help and reassurance but also to drive affected motorists and their cars to the other side when necessary. One for the future, when visiting New Orleans no doubt, but I digress.

One of the other reasons Seven Mile bridge is a highlight of the voyage is because once you've crossed it, you've only got forty miles left to Key West. I know this sounds inconsistent with me earlier exclaiming this as one of the world's great drives. It's just that long stretches of the journey are restricted to 45 mph or less, albeit for good reasons. Allied to limited passing places, this results in a long journey. Now blame it on evolution if you like, but we human beings are quick at adapting to our environment. As a result, we get desensitised when we experience the same vista, smell or tastes around us after a while. So although the ocean views are magical, unless you're some kind of professional stoic, after forty, fifty, sixty miles of similar panoramas, tragically, you start to take them for granted.

Instead, you start focussing on new stimuli, like the incredible number of tat shops and advertisements that start lining the route as you appear in one settlement or another. The towns on the way to Key West also have to make a living, and so you see any number of billboards telling you why you must stop off at that point. There and then. The biggest collection of seashells, the cheapest T-shirts for miles, best Key Lime pie in the Keys, and so it continues. After a while, it seems this is repeated virtually every time you make landfall, which given forty-two different bridges, you tend to do with regularity.

Signs implore you to stop off and experience "The Real Keys" as they try and lure you from your main aim of getting to Key West. But with exceptions, like Key Largo's John Pennekamp Coral Reef State Park, or Bahia Honda State Park's excellent beach, it all feels a bit like after the Lord Mayor's show. Even if these anticlimactic diversions are beforehand, but you know what I mean. Local traffic aside, pretty much everyone is gunning for Key West. Besides, with Key West's population being half as much as the rest of the Florida Keys put together, who is to say Key West isn't the real Keys anyway?

After a while of driving so close to the waterline, you also start to realise how vulnerable this area is to hurricanes. Lying a mere seventy miles north of the Tropic of Cancer, although not officially in the tropics, Key West still has a tropical climate. Consequently, the Keys pick up their share of hurricanes during that season. With Key West having only been permanently inhabited from 1822, it is hard to know precisely how many hurricanes have made landfall over the years, but a review of records to then suggest they visit the region more frequently than one might think.

Between 1835 and 1870 seven hurricanes hit Key West, or the Florida Keys, with that of October 1846 destroying or damaging all but eight of Key West's then six hundred buildings. Whether due to better recording, as more people settled in the area, or whether because of global warming, or perhaps a bit of both, the twentieth century was worse with at least thirteen. Some of these are within living memory, such as Hurricane Irene in 1999, which inflicted $600m worth of damage on Key West. Or 1992's Hurricane Andrew, a category five storm which had sustained wind speeds of 145 miles per hour and gusts of up to 175 mph. Arguably the worst, though, was the Labor Day Hurricane of 2 September 1935.

Wind speeds were believed to be 185 mph until the instruments stopped working. Unofficial measures suggested gusts exceeded 200 miles per hour. People, literally, had their clothes ripped from their body.

The atmospheric pressure was officially recorded at 892 millibars. Normal sea level atmospheric pressure is 1,013. Although *officially* beaten by Hurricanes Gilbert in 1988 and Wilma in 2005, it may well have been the most intense ever to hit the United States. Unofficial accounts have suggested it may have been 880, potentially less. To put that in context, at that level of barometric pressure, those houses that weren't being washed away, were exploding.

Let me say that again, because it is almost unfathomable. Houses weren't being blown over by the wind; although undoubtedly some were. They were exploding because the air pressure was so low outside – in much the same way a plastic bottle in an aeroplane expands as you climb from ground level to cruising altitude.*

Survivor accounts talk of the windows in their houses blowing out, not in. Exploding outwards, not inwards. Almost as if the air outside sucked them in.

The Storm of the Century, as the Labor Day Hurricane is also called, made landfall at Islamorada, about 80 miles north of Key West, with a storm surge in excess of seventeen feet. With Islamorada having a high point at only five feet, it doesn't take a genius to work out what happened next. Almost all buildings between Tavernier, ten miles to the north and Marathon, thirty miles to the south were destroyed. Islamorada was virtually obliterated.

Sadly, almost five hundred people lost their lives – nearly half of the population of the Keys, excluding Key West, at that time. Many of those who perished were World War One veterans constructing the Overseas Highway that we take for granted today. The exact number who died will never be known. They were literally swept away.

---

* Aeroplane cabins are pressurised to reduce the effect.

As you drive it, and see first-hand how the land is only at sea level, or at best marginally above; how little there is in the way of tall structures, or natural barriers, for protection; you begin to appreciate how helpless those people, and the surrounding keys, were in the face of that storm. To have been there must have been horrific – trying to ride out the storm, whilst waiting for the train that had been sent to evacuate everybody. The wind, the noise, the fear. Not to mention the final moments as the water from the storm surge washed over the island.

People talked about the noise being so bad, it was like everyone, *and everything* was crying. Survivors said even the buildings themselves sounded like they were screaming. Those that lived to tell the tale – and it's amazing that any did – were predominantly those washed into fallen debris which acted as makeshift rafts, or those that managed to cling to things that remained tethered to the ground, like palm trees. Although quite remarkably, twenty people somehow survived when the cottage they were sheltering in was lifted whole from its foundations, carried (and not swamped) by the water surge and then redeposited on dry land as the water receded.

Tragically the order to evacuate was given too late, and the relief train to remove the residents and veterans never made it. It arrived at Upper Matecumbe Key, Islamorada at the exact time the storm surge hit and was itself washed from the tracks. All that remained standing was its engine and coal tender. Miraculously, no one aboard the train died.

A memorial in Islamorada commemorates those who perished in this sad affair. It can be found just south of mile marker 82, on the left-hand side as you travel towards Key West.

The bigger tragedy, if that is possible or even an appropriate use of words here, is that the order to evacuate seems to have been delayed by bureaucratic wrangling. President Roosevelt ordered a full investigation into the incident, but shameful officials down the line appear to have conducted a cover up, asserting that no blame lay with the Federal Emergency Relief Administration. Instead, they concluded that this was an act of God beyond the capabilities of man to foresee that level of devastation. And therefore, the necessary level of planning required for an appropriate evacuation and preparations.

They must have worked fast because they filed their 'comprehensive' report within four days of the presidential order. Only after critical reports from the esteemed writer Ernest Hemingway (who travelled by boat from Key West, in order to personally visit the area in the immediate aftermath); from senior people in the Veteran's Association; and disparaging press coverage, were other, more thorough, more damning reports conducted. Even then, a full explanation still didn't appear to come out in the Congressional Hearings conducted. Seemingly the right questions were never asked and the appropriate facts never volunteered, and the hearings concluded that it was an act of God rather than failings in administration that were to blame.

Either way, the survivors on the ground still needed help. Real, tangible help and not just inquests, reports and paper. Aid, that also seemed to be slow in arriving. It all added to the sense of isolation felt by locals and the belief that those on the Keys were separate from the rest of America. An America that didn't really give a damn.

As well as being emotionally isolated, the damage to the railway now also meant that the Middle and Lower Keys were, once again, physically isolated. Except for passage by sea or air. After a while it becomes easy to understand why those from the Keys feel different to the rest of the US.

With the storm destroying over forty miles of train track, it also meant the end for the Overseas Railroad. If anything positive came from this, it was things like the Overseas Highway salvaging what bits of the Overseas Railroad it could. Like the bridge thirty miles to the south that had survived and was modified to become the Overseas Highway's original Seven Mile bridge. As a result, on the 29th March 1938, the road that the veterans had helped build finally became a reality, and Key West was joined to the mainland by road.

In the new millennium Key West has suffered badly again, from Hurricanes Wilma in 2005 and Irma in 2017. Irma's path had predicted a direct hit on Key West, but a last-minute swerve saw it make landfall twenty miles up the road at Cudjoe Key. It hit with wind speeds of 130 mph and a storm surge of ten feet. Whilst Key West was spared, almost 1,200 homes were still destroyed in the Keys alone. Highway 1 was once again washed away. This time, at mile markers 37 and 75.

Lessons have been learned from history though, and a well-planned evacuation saw a staggering six and a half million people leave their homes in good time. That said, the storm's size as well as its ferocity meant it still wreaked devastation. Hurricane-force winds swirled in an eighty mile diameter vortex, as it crept north and west across Florida, meaning tragically 84 people still died in Florida alone. The United States suffered damage in excess of $50 billion.

You might wonder why I am detailing these hurricanes in so much length. Well, aside from giving due respect to the people and the suffering they have endured, to create what for most of the time is a paradise on earth – a paradise that we can now relatively easily enjoy – it gives an insight into the character of the Conch people; those for whom the Keys is home. It gives a flavour of the resilience that comes with routinely having to live with the destructive threat of these immense forces of nature. A sense of the spirit that arises from the constant realisation that everything can disappear, so make the most of it. It is part of what makes the Keys and Key West special.

You might also reasonably be wondering why these people continue to live in a zone that can be so downright dangerous, not to mention destructive of what they own. It's not an easy answer, but is probably an amalgam of things: (a) most of the time the weather is not like that and they can go years without a major hit; (b) when the sun shines, as mentioned above, it is a veritable paradise; (c) these people are incredibly resilient; and perhaps most importantly (d) at the end of their day it is their home. It's where they have been born and raised, and it's where they have their families and friends. As one survivor of the Labor Day Hurricane said, when his son asked him what they would do now and where they would go, "Son. The only thing that you and I own today is a little bit of property in the Keys. That's the only thing we've got and everything else is gone. We go back and we make the best and we start over."

Driving from Miami to Key West will take you at least three and a half hours. And that's on a good run with no stops. However, the length of the journey, coupled with the stunning scenery, means that it provides a great decompression between the madness of Miami and the calm that is Key West. It's almost like a mini detox programme.

When you finally arrive in the Old Town part of Key West, the feeling is truly wonderful. You actually sense that you may have stumbled into a magical world, lost in time. So magical was it that my heart didn't just skip a beat, it skipped several. Which at my age is not something you want happening too often.

Key West is the complete polar opposite of Miami in almost every way I can think of, except maybe that they're both in Florida. It's calm. It's hassle free. There's little crime. Traffic is no longer a nightmare (indeed cars now seem to be outnumbered by pedestrians). And then there are the buildings. The others you discover later, but the first thing that strikes you are the buildings.

With the odd exception, the vast majority are all either one or two stories high. Even Key West's tallest building, the Crowne Plaza Hotel on Duval Street, only reaches five stories. Gone are the brash high rise sky scrapers that line Miami's waterfront. Instead of wave upon wave of glass buildings glaring garishly in the bright southern sun, most buildings are finished in wooden clapboard and painted in beautiful pastel colours that absorb the light and blend into the surroundings.

Then there are the trees. All manner of charming specimens line the roads, from palms to figs to orchids to mahogany. Along with a few, even more exotic types like banyans and kapoks. It's like a super-sized botanical garden.

Key West is nearer to Cuba than Miami, yet the overall ambience is no longer Hispanic, even though, as you might expect, there is a reasonable proportion of the community that is. Instead, like the climate, it feels like an outpost of the Caribbean. There is a strong harbour vibe – perhaps because you are never more than half a mile from the sea, but surrounded by buildings not beaches; boats not bikinis. Whilst the look and feel of the wharf buildings and neighbouring streets make you imagine you've stumbled onto a set from *Pirates of the Caribbean.*

The next thing you notice is how stress free this place is. Most people seem to walk or cycle around rather than drive. Even walk is stretching it a bit, saunter would probably be a better descriptor. There are plenty of bars, but you never sense things are going to kick off or get out of hand. They say it's a place full of hippies, but there are certainly no weirdos. Nor are there any panhandlers, vagrants or threatening individuals. Even chickens (and by that I mean the fowl kind rather than the cowardly kind) freely roam the streets. I have seldom felt so relaxed in my whole life.

Checking into our hotel, the Eden House, the chilled out vibe continued. The duty manager, whom I'm sure was wearing flip-flops, handed us an ice cold beer, so we could have a welcome drink whilst he took us on a tour of the property. As we took that gorgeous first sip, he explained they know most people will have had a long drive to get there, so they just want to ease them into the Key West Spirit and start their holidays on the right foot. Wow.

We walked past a pretty little pool, also surrounded by exotic foliage and even, tucked away in a quiet corner, a hammock. Behind and above the pool was a little bandstand type structure, again tucked away, only this time inside it was one of those swinging porch seats for two people. It was like walking into a private tropical oasis and yet someone's back garden at the same time. It was so lovely I thought Alison was going to spontaneously combust.

Prior to approaching our room, the manager pointed out a cute little bar made from coconut trees, complete with a thatched roof made from the palm fronds. He pointed it out, not because it was also so sweet, but because that was where happy hour was held every day between 4 and 5 p.m. And – here was the rub – simple gin, rum and vodka cocktails, such as a Gin and Tonic, a Bacardi and Coke and so on, were all completely free! I swear as he said that I saw little wisps of smoke starting to come out of Alison's ears. Time was pushing on and it was now early evening however, so we just dropped our bags and made our way to Mallory Square. Besides, I didn't want to risk any further outbreaks of smouldering.

Mallory Square is a plaza which butts up to the Gulf of Mexico and is one of *the* places in Key West where people routinely go to watch the sunset. Like the rest of Key West, it's captivating, tranquil and charming all at the same time. Crowds line its quayside, watching as the sun slowly glides across the sky before slipping under the horizon and into its bed for the night. For a couple of hours until the final few minutes of the sunset proper – when everyone's eyes are focussed on the main attraction – buskers and performers entertain the crowds, alongside vendors selling all sorts of street food and knick-knacks from crepes to crap.

Some artists are regulars and even become small celebrities in their own right, although given the level of tips they hustle from the appreciative throngs I'm not surprised. It seems to be a lucrative business that pays more than most full-time professional careers. Still good luck to them, I'm not sure you could ever pay me enough to swallow a sword or breathe fire. Although when in a bad mood, the latter seems to be something my good lady does quite easily for free.

We were both just so captivated by everything going on around us. Like Key West, it was just enchanting. Although this was obviously for us tourists, somehow it was different to other holiday resorts we'd been to before, albeit in Europe and the Canary Islands.

Yes, people were on holiday and having a great time, but it didn't feel forced. Nor were people too hyper – all pent up and waiting to explode on their annual break that they'd worked so hard and waited so long for. Instead, everything just seemed so calm, so relaxed, so nice. If we hadn't already guessed it from our earlier drive in, and tour of our hotel, we knew there and then Key West would be a special place.

Life's A Blur

Key West is the sort of place where days just slide by. You wake up later than usual, which is needed from the carousing the night before. You mooch about a bit before having to make the big decision of the day – shall we have a pool day or a beach day? Or perhaps both. Invariably you go for both.

You wander out into the scorching heat and the humidity that wraps around you like a blanket. It's not so oppressive as to be debilitating, but it's enough to mean that exertions are restricted to ambles and saunters. There's no brisk walking here, let alone anything as insane as jogging. But that's ok, because everyone else is doing the same and it just adds to the laid back vibe of the place. You're hot, but you're chilled.

You stop off somewhere for a treat, like Eaton Street's Glazed Donuts or for a piece of Key Lime pie and a coffee, before visiting one of the local sights. You then wander to a beach for a bit of sea time, before strolling back to the pool to catch up on your reading or sleeping.

You wonder why you're spending so much time on loungers as by now you're so laid back you're practically horizontal anyway.

On the way back to the pool, you make sure to soak up some more of the ambient vibe. By now you are addicted to this place and its way of life, and you need another infusion of its charm. At the same time you also realise you need to top up your sugar levels and so have either a piece of Key Lime pie or a donut and coffee. Whichever it was you didn't have in the morning. As a real indulgence, sometimes you will also have a frozen Key Lime pie that's been dipped in chocolate and put on a stick. That way, you can eat it like a lolly whilst walking from the coffee/donut shop to your hotel.

After some time by the pool you freshen up with a shower before going out somewhere nice to eat, then onto a bar to catch some live music. After that, things become a bit hazy. Tomorrow the process repeats itself.

It's wonderful!

To a certain extent this scenario plays out on a lot of beach holidays, well at least for us anyway. But here's the thing, Key West isn't really a beach resort.

It only has four beaches (Higgs, Smathers, Simonton Street and Zachary Taylor State Park). Some people claim a fifth, C.B. Harvey Rest Beach, but to me it seems an extension of Higgs Beach. Higgs isn't that large anyway, whilst Simonton Street is tiny. I've had duvet covers that are larger. Although it has a cracking location right in the heart of town.

To be honest, the beaches themselves aren't that wonderful either. Nothing like those you'll find in the Caribbean; or parts of the Mediterranean, such as the island of Menorca; or elsewhere in Florida like those at Naples, Siesta Key, Anna Maria Island or any number of its other award-winning beaches. You certainly wouldn't go there solely for a beach holiday. But maybe that's what has saved Key West.

It is so beautiful, so charming and so captivating you wonder why it hasn't been destroyed by tourism. Perhaps if it had great beaches in addition to its other charms, it would have been. Although of course had it been overrun, it would no longer have its other charms. Don't misunderstand me, Key West relies on and has a lot of tourists. It's just that it receives and welcomes them without losing a lot of the innate charm that attracts them in the first place.

Perhaps it's a combination of factors that have kept Key West the way it is. Firstly, a location that is not simply out of the way, but literally the end of the road. This place is not merely at the end of a cul-de-sac, but at the end of a one hundred mile long cul-de-sac, with not a lot between. (Apart from a beautiful drive). In many ways, it's like journeying to the end of the world. To make the journey, you've really got to want to go there. Which helps protect it from unwanted outside influences and those who might encroach on it and chip it away.

Secondly, there is a lack of top notch beaches, which means again those who go to Key West do so for its charms, tranquillity and character. Rather than just its sun, sea and sand.

Thirdly, the local council goes out of its way to help maintain the integrity and character of the island. For instance, a few years back when the cruise ship terminal was developed there was an uproar from locals who didn't want the sunset views from Mallory Square being spoiled by big cruise liners passing back and forth from the docks. So the council passed a law (at the risk to a loss of cruise income), requiring all cruise ships to leave at least two hours before sunset. As a result, Key West's legendary sunsets have been protected.

Fourthly, the people themselves. The combination of feeling apart from the rest of the United States and not needing to conform; of being more sensitive to how precious life is and how fleeting it can be. (Borne from annually having to live with the threat a big storm could wash away everything you have worked for, not to mention your loved ones); of possessing the grit and resolve required to come back again, once a major storm does visit. It all means that these people are tolerant, friendly, welcoming and relaxed.

Accordingly, they live with a great sense of perspective. It may be why the official philosophy of Key West and the Florida Keys is "One Human Family – celebrating the unity, equality and diversity of all people worldwide." For certain, they really embrace life. Particularly during the non-hurricane season, when it seems that almost every other week they have a festival celebrating something or other.

All manner of celebrations seem to take place, from sports festivals to food festivals; music festivals to fishing festivals; boating festivals (that include Offshore Racing World Championships); arts festivals, literary festivals, on and on it goes. From Pole Vault in Paradise, an event for top national pole vaulters, to its legendary Fantasy Fest. Although the latter is quite a departure from its usual tranquillity.

Fantasy Fest is a week-long, clothing optional, alternative celebration of Halloween where most of the participants use artistically styled body paint in place of clothes to try and create exotically themed costumes whilst preserving some modesty. Even so, I'm not sure that's one for us – sadly my body is not in sufficient shape to disrobe publicly, with or without body paint. I'd probably need an offensive weapons licence before they let me in. Even then, I'm not sure I could afford the amount of body paint necessary to prevent bystanders still being horrified.

Although, I might be being hard on myself here. One thing I've noticed, when we've accidentally strayed into nudist beaches when holidaying in the Mediterranean, is that by and large the older and saggier you are, the more likely you are to have fewer clothes. It may even be the first rule of sod's law.

Even if Fantasy Fest isn't for everybody, it gives an insight into the tolerant nature of Key West, and that feeling of we are different round here. As are their New Year's Eve celebrations, where they have not one, but four venues celebrating – all whilst cocking a snook at Times Square's extravagant dropping of the ball ceremony. Instead, in Key West, they'll drop a big conch shell from Sloppy Joe's Bar; a Key Lime wedge at Sunset Pier; a pirate wench, from the mast of a schooner in the seaport; or, for good measure, a drag queen, from a balcony on a house in Duval Street.

As well as some bawdy whilst crazy festivals, they also specialise in the just plain crazy. From March's Smallest Parade in the Universe, where all parade floats must be under 18 inches long; to July's Papa Look-Alike Contest, where more than one hundred contestants compete to see who most resembles celebrated writer Ernest Hemingway.

In April the Conch Republic Independence Celebration (CRIC) lasts over a week with everything from ship races to Cuba, to the self-billed World's Longest Parade. (So described because the parade snakes all the way down Duval Street and therefore stretches all the way from the Gulf of Mexico to the Atlantic Ocean). There is a Dog Fest – for the canine variety and not some of the rougher specimens that might attend Fantasy Fest – as well as a re-enactment of the Great Sea Battle that preserved the Republic's independence.

"What's this?" I hear you cry. Isn't this isolationism thing going a bit too far now? The Independent Conch Republic? These people sound worse than those Cornish secessionists who constantly want to break from England. Except that in Key West, they actually did it.

Back in 1982, concerned with the flow of illegal drugs and immigrants into the United States from its difficult to police southern coastline, the Border Patrol set up a checkpoint south of Florida City. Just north of where the Keys join the mainland. They searched vehicles, asked people to show their papers, and did all the things you might expect at a border patrol. Except that this was a checkpoint in the middle of a road in the contiguous United States.

The local council were concerned at the impact on the tourist trade. (You can imagine the tailbacks that were arising, adding to an already long journey). They were also indignant that Conch people, as Floridians and US citizens, should have to provide documentation in order to travel to another part of their state, let alone within their country. Understandably, they protested to the US Federal Government.

When their protests failed, along with attempts at getting a court injunction to stop the roadblocks, they thought if you will treat us as citizens of another country, we might as well be. So at noon on the 23rd April 1982 the City of Key West, now calling itself the Conch Republic, declared secession from the United States of America.

As a symbolic gesture to declare war, a stale loaf of Cuban bread was broken over the head of a man dressed in a US Navy uniform. Then, one minute later, Mayor Dennis Wardlow, who by now was named Prime Minister Wardlow, officially surrendered to the US Admiral and Union forces at Key West's US Navy base, bringing an end to the conflict. He then claimed a billion dollars for foreign aid, citing war relief needed to rebuild his nation after its long siege! The event attracted a lot of publicity and whilst the short lived sovereign state didn't get the billion it requested, the point had been made. The roadblocks were removed soon after. An unexpected bonus was also the boost in tourism from all the coverage.

Amazingly, another incident erupted a few years later. In September 1995, forces from the United States 478th Civil Affairs Battalion of the US Army Reserve decided to practise their invading foreign country skills by landing at Key West. Quite why a civil affairs reserve battalion should need to practise invading a foreign country anyway, is also a mystery. But they had decided they needed to, and that they would execute a training drill, where they would treat the island as if it were a foreign nation. Unfortunately, no one had thought it might be a good idea to speak to the council of Key West about it first.

Understandably, the Council was rather put out again, particularly as they only found out about the exercise through local media. Miffed, and sensing another welcome opportunity for some free marketing, they responded by publicly announcing their intention to defend their 'nation' and issued a call to their citizens to mobilise forces. The next day, the 478th Battalion were met on land by locals forming blockades on the Overseas Highway, and at sea by locals in a schooner. The invaders were then repelled, jokingly – these guys in the reserve still carry guns after all – with water balloons, conch fritters and once again more stale Cuban bread.

As you might imagine, there was another storm of publicity and the US Army issued a letter of apology. According to the Florida Weekly newspaper, the Army issued a tongue-in-cheek letter commenting, "That the exercises in no way meant to challenge or impugn the sovereignty of the Conch Republic." The following day, the US Army took part in an official surrender ceremony. Only in Key West.

Festivals aside, there is also a fair bit to see and over the days we visited The Little Whitehouse, where President Harry S. Truman used to spend his Winters whilst working on state business; the Botanical Garden; Fort Zachary Taylor; the Customs House; the Lighthouse; the ship wreck treasure museum, which tells the story of Key West's original economy and its ship wrecking heritage; as well as its aquarium. We also saw Ernest Hemingway's house, along with its cats, which due to a genetic mutation have six or seven toes. Something rather in keeping with the quirky nature of Key West.

Whilst none of these are in the realm of must see sights, which to be fair are more normally associated with visits to major cities, they all add to the overall whole that comprise this place. Key West isn't just a beach holiday, nor is it a sight-seeing holiday. It's not a honky-tonk bar band break, nor a detox chill out recuperation. Instead, it has a bit of all these, and somehow the whole is more than the sum of its parts. Perhaps that's part of her magic.

We ate in all types of restaurants of which the best, although you would never have guessed it from the outside, was a place called Bien, about a ten-minute walk north of the historical centre up Eaton Street. Outside it didn't look much more than a shack with shade, but the food was first rate and the prices reasonable. Probably because it was that bit further out. It was so good we returned a couple of times to work our way down the menu. Not one dish disappointed.

But that's another one of the added bonuses of Key West. Yes, they have full scale dining – at full scale prices – if that's what you want, but littered around are food trucks and shacks, many of which are excellent.

Sometimes they work Key West style in a sharing arrangement where both sides win, like Garbo's Grill, which serves excellent Tacos and Burritos out of a small scale silver food truck in the garden of Grunt's Bar. You get great grub in a serene setting, washed down with a beautiful beer from the bar. Everyone's happy. As an aside, it's opposite where Pan Am first started in business.

We went to all sorts of different locations for the legendary sunsets from Mallory Square to Sunset Pier. We even tried the deck of the US Coast Guard Cutter Ingham in the Truman Annex Waterfront Park. They were all good, but the best of all was when we set sail on a sunset champagne cruise with a company called Sebago.

We chose their cheapest option, the Catamaran Champagne Sunset Sail, which cost about $40 each. Although it still included unlimited champagne within that package. There were more expensive options which offered things like inclusive food, or more exclusive, more prestigious boats, but we figured we'd grab a bite to eat back on shore. Anyway, with it being our first time for this sort of thing (dipping our toes in the water, you might say), we thought the budget version was the best for our needs. Especially as it still provided unlimited champagne.

We set sail ahead of the appointed time for boats to leave the harbour and enjoyed a pleasant trip around the island before heading out past Sunset Key and Wisteria Island. That way, we would have an unobstructed view of the sunset when it came.

Mallory Square is good, but at certain times of year the sun sets over Sunset Key, about four hundred yards offshore. Whilst still good, it's never quite the same as when it dips below the sea.

I had been sceptical about claims about the unlimited champagne, thinking it would either be a cheap substitute or that pouring might be rather, shall we say, slow. I am delighted to say I was wrong on both counts. Either that or they had gone to a lot of trouble to relabel bottles of inferior product with champagne labels. Even I doubt that was the case. The only trouble was, the glasses kept on slipping down too quickly. For once it wasn't because I was trying to squeeze every last cent out of our tickets either, but because everything, rather like Key West, just felt so right.

We toasted our first glass with a "Cheers!" to each other as you might imagine, and our second with a big intake of breath and an, "Aaaah, this is the life!"

Believe it or not our third was to a, "Bloody Hell, look at that!" as we saw, and I swear that I am not making this up here, something that looked like a round motorised raft, not much bigger than most large kitchen tables. On top were perched six chairs, surrounding a tiki bar with coconut palm fronds for its roof. Like us, it was also sailing around in search of the perfect sunset, whilst its occupants enjoyed a sundowner. It was like having friends around for a dinner party and then taking your table and chairs out into the ocean. At first I thought I must have lost count, and we had drunk more than I realised. Then I remembered we were in Key West, where it seems pretty much anything goes.

As I got refills for our fourth, our lovely bartender asked, "Are you guys English?"

"We are," I said. "How can you tell? Is it our accents?"

"No," She replied. "It's the rate at which you're getting through the champagne."

Now before you think (a) blimey these guys must have been putting it away – maybe he did lose count after all and he imagined the whole floating tiki bar thing, and (b) clearly it's true everything I hear about Brits abroad being booze buckets, I should like to add that she then clarified her last statement. Much to my relief.

"Yeh," she continued, "I think we have quite a few of you on board tonight," which was true. "You guys *really* seem to like your champagne." Also true, the UK is France's biggest export market for the stuff. She then explained how American customers tended to prefer the lager beer that was also available as part of the range of drinks offered with this package.

I was dumbfounded. Honestly, I again thought I must have miscounted my drinks based on what she had said.

"So you're telling me, that our ticket prices are all the same and that we can choose anything we like from champagne, margaritas, normal wine, beer and soft drinks and the Americans by and large go for the beer?"

"Uh huh," she said in that nonchalant way, that implied she saw nothing at all odd about it. Other than the English seemed to be a rather strange people who had a curious obsession to imbibe their body weight in champagne before the allotted time for the cruise was up.

At that moment, if the baseball in Miami hadn't already told me I could never be an American, here was conclusive proof. And they think we're strange.

When Alison sent me back for our fifth, I wondered if the sea was getting a bit of a swell, as walking to the bar seemed a trifle wobblier than before. However, conversations with other passengers revealed this not to be the case, and I thought "better slow down here, or it'll be man overboard" and me swimming for that tiki bar. It also dawned on me why Alison had me doing the dirty work of the bar runs, whilst sensibly she remained seated.

When the sunset finally arrived though, like Key West, it was tremendous. Indeed, it was the best sunset we have ever experienced in our lives.

We are lucky to have had some magical ones together over the years, with highlights including those whilst picnicking on a beach, a glass of cava in hand in Menorca, Spain. Sometimes the simplest things are the best. For some reason though, everywhere we have been from the Mediterranean to India's west coast, at the last moment the sun has always been obscured by a bit of cloud. Even on a cloudless day, there has been a haze on the horizon for the sun to sneak behind. Even with sunsets over sea instead of land. People say it's a common occurrence in the Mediterranean. But here, in Key West, despite clouds dotted around the sky, there was nothing – absolutely nothing – that masked the sun's descent into the ocean.

When we stepped ashore (local boats are allowed back into harbour after dark) we made our way to mile marker zero in Whitehead Street. With it being our last night, we wanted to have a look at the beginning of the journey that awaited us in the morning. Mile marker zero is the sign that officially signals the start (or end depending on your direction of travel) of US Highway 1. Although it's just another road sign, there still feels something pretty cool about standing at the start of a road that stretches 2,369 miles. In this case from Key West, Florida all the way to

Fort Kent, Maine in America's Northeast. Particularly when that road is also called Route 1.

You get much the same sensation at the bottom end of Whitehead Street, which is where we headed next. There you get to stand beside a large concrete buoy signifying the Southernmost point in the whole of the contiguous United States.* That said, if you want to take a photo you had best get there early in the day or, as we were doing, late in the evening. In between it is besieged by cruise ship passengers standing in long lines waiting for their moment in the sun, with the southern buoy. It's one of the most photographed spots in America.

When the cruise ships depart before sunset however, it becomes all yours. As does Key West, which is when it becomes even more special, if that were possible. From the moment the day trippers depart until sometime the next morning; with no more cruise liners docking and next to nothing in terms of traffic from the Overseas Highway, it feels as if you're part of a special, private party. Much as in the days when English pubs used to have secret after hours lock-ins, before our drinking hours were relaxed in 2005. At this point the bars, many of which have quality live bands playing, come into their element. There are so many bars, and so many good groups, that you start to choose your establishment based on the band rather than the beer.

Anyway, having done both major markers, or perhaps I should say Key markers, it was now time for supper and we thought prior to grabbing a group, we'd end with a typical southern style barbeque joint. We found one conveniently located between our last two stops, called Charlie Mac's. Although we only chose it for the exquisite barbecue aromas emanating from within, it turns out they have a state-of-the-art low and slow hickory smoker on the premises. Along with their signature rub and barbecue sauce, it made for succulent, smoky, tasty ribs and brisket. Put it this way, if you like barbecue food, big sports TVs over the bar and decent rock music playing as a backdrop, you won't go wrong here. Except that you will be stuffed.

To be fair, the waitress tried to warn us. "Before you all order, I should tell you that our portions are large."

---

* There is a slightly more southern point, but it stands on US Navy property and is not accessible to civilians or tourists.

"Blimey," I thought, "and we're Europeans best go easy here".

"Thank you," I said. "We'll skip starters. I'll just have the brisket"

"And you ma'am?"

"Just the ribs for me," said Alison.

"And you sir?" she asked turning to our son Josh, who believe it or not, by now was at university in Michigan and thought it would be nice to come down and see us for a few days with his American girlfriend, Karina.

"The Crusher Burger please," he said, choosing from the burger menu.

"Are you sure, sir? It is a very big dish." This was an interesting line I hadn't been expecting. It was reminiscent of the New York knishery sales patter, whereby the waiting staff go out of their way to make you reduce your order. Particularly as, unlike me, Josh is a big guy. Six foot one and built like a centre half, this is a student athlete that doesn't just consume several thousand calories a day, but devours them. Maybe this is a new sales technique they are pioneering in the States, I thought to myself. Perhaps they're working on the reverse psychology principle.

"Oh," he said. This approach also took him aback. "In that case, me and my girlfriend will share the Crusher Burger. Is that ok with you?" he asked, turning to Karina. He really wanted that Crusher Burger, but it was nice to see that he did the gentlemanly thing and checked with her first. That and the fact that he had twenty years first-hand experience from me as to what's likely to happen if you neglect to consult your better half.

When our meal came, we couldn't believe our eyes. The plates were so loaded that it was a wonder the waitress carrying them didn't suffer an industrial injury. Perhaps that was why she was trying to dissuade us. Appropriately named, The Crusher comprised four quarter pounder patties, loaded with brisket, pulled pork, bacon, four slices of cheese, onion ring, lettuce and tomato. All in a bun topped off with their signature sweet barbecue sauce and accompanied by fries, coleslaw and some corn. There was no way this was fitting in either of their mouths. So, given they were sharing, we asked for a set of step ladders and chainsaw in order that we might have a chance of cutting it into manageable pieces. Before Josh took the lettuce leaf out explaining, in all seriousness, that he was on a diet.

Tragically the waitress was right, and despite only ordering three mains between the four of us and neither starters nor desserts, we still couldn't get through everything. Delicious as it was. As she'd been on the money with the food, we thought we'd pick her brains on the area.

"Tell us," I asked, "what's the best thing about Key West?"

"Oh, that's easy," she replied. "We're so far from everybody else, we don't think of ourselves as American down here!"

The quantity of food aside, Key West had been wonderful and we would be back. Back to the Eden House, back to Bien and back to Charlie Mac's. Back for the sunsets, back for the bands and, for sure, the Sebago champagne cruise. Indeed, if the truth be told, we would relive it all over again.

The only thing we'd change is to hire a mustang for that next drive down, drop its roof and really feel the wind rushing through our hair.

Boston

Smile you might even enjoy it!

We had decided to visit Josh in Michigan and stopping for a few days in Boston en route seemed too good an opportunity to miss. Although, that wasn't what I was thinking as we started our descent.

You see, flying into Logan airport can be an invigorating experience. The runway is on a small promontory, a couple of miles outside downtown Boston itself. A finger of land jutting out into the sea, that alone might make for its own interesting microclimate. But, coupled with Boston's notoriously changeable and rainy weather (its annual rainfall is a third higher than that of even Manchester, itself famed for its precipitation), it can often make things, shall we say, rather lively.

Aircraft normally take off or land into the wind – it aids their lift on take-off and eases their descent on landing. As a result, airports around the world try and align their runways into the direction of their prevailing wind. That way, most of their flights experience optimum conditions. It says a lot then, when you find out that Logan has six runways, aligned in different directions.

Even the airport itself notes, "Due to Logan being located on the coast, ideal wind conditions are far from common and [so] are just one of the factors that are considered when the FAA [Federal Aviation Administration] selects a runway to use. Other factors that are considered include: ground visibility, cloud coverage and ceiling." I think you're beginning to get the picture.

It also turns out, not only is Boston rainier than Manchester, it is also much windier than even the renowned Windy City of Chicago. In fact, it is the windiest major city in the United States. And that's just based on wind speeds, not direction – which as we've already seen appears to be a law unto itself.

When we left Manchester the weather had been unusually decent, but by the time we landed in the early afternoon it had changed into the Boston ecosystem. Suddenly, what had been a smooth flight turned into a rollercoaster ride for the last fifteen minutes. On the bright side, you might say all this added excitement was a free bonus.

It certainly appeared the pilot wanted everyone to get the most value and fun from the trip, as he opted to land the plane in three stages rather than the usual two. First our left wing touched down, prior to us skating for a few seconds on one wheel, until he also managed to get the right wing down, before finally completing his hat trick with the nose another few seconds later.

"Good afternoon ladies and gentlemen and welcome to Boston Logan International Airport!" All we were missing was him shouting "Yeehaw!" and appearing from the cockpit wearing a Stetson.

We were processed through immigration quickly and courteously, which made our first experience of meeting a native Bostonian all the more surprising. Looking for the quickest way to downtown (you can get a free shuttle bus from the airport to the town centre proper) we approached an airport employee sitting beside a load of left luggage. I could see they were busy doing nothing in particular. Other than some form of transcendental meditating with their eyes open. Or in their case, staring into space.

Before I could even open my mouth though, we were met with "If you're not with British Airways I can't help you." Nor in an overly friendly manner at that. The words might have been polite, but the tone wasn't. Honestly, I hadn't even squeaked a word at that point.

"I was only going to ask where I could get the shuttle bus to downtown," I responded.

"Are you with British Airways?"

"Uhm no, but can't anyone catch the shuttle bus?"

"I can't help you" was her final reply. After which she just looked away and got back to minding the luggage. Or staring at the wall.

Well, "thank you Ma'am," and welcome to Boston.

Eventually we found the shuttle bus stop, which it turned out wasn't that difficult, and made our way towards the centre. The shuttle bus is great. It's free – always a bonus – and within twenty minutes you're at South Station, a key hub for Boston city centre.

Although here is an interesting thing. Your trip from the airport to the city centre on the bus is free, but when you want to return, you have to pay. Even for the same route, and via the same bus. Now why is it free to go into the city of Boston, but you have to pay to leave it? Hmmm……

The city has a good, efficient metro system that covers many of the places you would want to go. Like most major subway systems, they offer a card which you can top up with credit and then reuse as you want. Again, like most metro systems, it's cheaper per ride if you use it than if you pay separately for each ride. They call it a Charlie Card. It's free to get and, you are told by the Transport Authority's own website, they're available from MBTA (Boston's Transport Authority) Customer Service Agents at most major bus and subway stations.

So why then, when we approach a Service Agent at South Station and ask (politely) for a Charlie Card, do we get the reply,

"Why do you want one?". In another less than helpful way. Sadly, something becoming a theme.

"Well, we want to ride the subway a few times and we understand that using a Charlie Card would be better." Unbelievably, these were not the right words to unlock the key to the magic door that would get us one of these, clearly hallowed, items.

After a somewhat protracted process which took several exchanges as I tried to find new ways to explain why we might want one, we finally got our hands on Charlie's golden ticket. Alison was just silent in disbelief at this point. Fortunately, I remained calm throughout and thanked the assistant in question. Instead of smiling sardonically and thanking him sarcastically, which I had been pretty close to. (After I had my paws on the card, of course).

I say fortunately, because not moments later, as I tried to load some cash onto the card, the sodding machine wouldn't respond. Forcing me to ask once again for assistance from the same, super unhelpful, representative to show me how it was done. Somewhat unbelievably, we then had to go through another similarly excruciatingly protracted process.

Then I started thinking. Apart from the Border Security people who were professional and helpful, the first two Bostonians we spoke to were up there with the most unhelpful, miserable people I have come across. The team at MOMA were comedians in comparison. Welcome to Boston indeed.

Sadly, this was a theme repeated during our three days in the city. Some people (such as at the Sam Adams brewery or the bartender in the Ginger Pig or in the bars around Fenway) were great. As always, you can find good and bad wherever you go. But a lot of Bostonians we met came across as dour and miserable.

Maybe it's a weather thing? Travelling around I've come to realise that the sunnier and warmer a place is, the more chilled out and welcoming people seem to be. And vice versa. Miami may have been a tough city, but on a one-on-one basis, the people were still friendly. Street entertainment, aside.

Or maybe Boston just thinks a lot of itself because it's home to two of the world's greatest Universities in Harvard and MIT; home of the late President J F Kennedy; and home to the Red Sox baseball and Celtics basketball teams, both leading teams in their respective sports?

Now you could be forgiven for wondering why I am going on so much about this. To start with, I've never held much store about preconceptions and believe you tend to find good and bad everywhere. Good people, bad people; kind people, mean people; friendly people, miserable people and so on. For the same reason, I tend not to prejudge people until you've had a chance to properly interact with them. But by and large many people we met from Boston were at best curt and reserved. Many times they were downright rude.

Almost to confirm the point, when I undertook some research in Google, and typed "Why are Bostonians …", before I could finish my sentence Google auto filled my search. (As it often does). Without any prompting, Google automatically added the words "so rude". The search now read, "Why are Bostonians so rude." It was nothing to do with me. Mr. Google could have added "so fab", "so cool", "so clever" or any number of descriptors, but he chose to add "so rude". As an alternative, his second and third options were "so cold" and "so mean" respectively. And that's all he offered me.

By way of comparison, I tried typing in some other places to see if they were all the same. They weren't. For Californians, Google offered "Why are Californians moving …", to which there was then a variety of states, such as Texas, Idaho, and so on. After that, the next offering was, "so weird". The options for Floridians were, "Why are Floridians called crackers" and something to do with unemployment. Even Texas, which a lot of Americans seem to have a strong view about, after "so rude", in first place, came, "so proud", "so nice", "so rich" and interestingly, "so tall".

I tried another search engine, Duck Duck Go, which whilst recording all the searches across the internet, doesn't record yours personally, in case I was biasing results based on what I typed. This was becoming a great game! The results were a similar story, though. Indeed, Duck Duck Go only offered me one option for Boston – "so tough", in case you were wondering.

Now remember, these search engines only interpolate your searches based on what the billions of netizens type into their browsers. Either that or maybe Messrs. Google and Duck Duck had also been to Boston.

That said, I am told that whilst Bostonians can be initially reserved, at least when they are friendly or kind, you *know* it is genuine. And once you win them over, apparently they are both fiercely loyal and friends for life.

Anyway, we decided we were not going to be bothered about being too cool for school and decided to go exploring. People say that in Massachusetts if you don't like the weather, just wait five minutes. Well, amazingly, by the time we surfaced in downtown Boston the sun was beaming down and it had turned into a lovely day. We had to squint, and squint hard. Until our eyes had adjusted from the gloom of the subterranean Bus Terminus to the blinding sunshine outside. But when we opened them, what a view.

Behind us was South Station, which once you get away from the terminus is a beautiful building. Standing imposingly on its corner, it makes a diagonal as it looks downtown towards the Old State House. Built in 1898, to act as a transportation hub for the centre of Boston, it demanded grandeur. And it has it. Five stories of granite, built in Neoclassical Revival style, featuring grand arches, imposing stately windows and a magnificent clock. All topped by a majestic stone eagle with an eight foot long wingspan.

By 1913 it was the busiest train station in the world, handling some 38 million passengers. Yet, unimaginably, it was almost demolished in the 1970s to make way for an engineering company's corporate headquarters. Thankfully, it was saved by a group of concerned citizens who got it listed on the National Register of Historic Places, and it has now been restored to its former glory. It is a great way to enter a city.

Looking straight ahead, contrasting with South Station's Neoclassical architecture, was the view of the high-rise buildings of the financial district. Modern and gleaming, stretching up as if trying to touch the sun, they also made quite a sight. In particular, the John Hancock Tower (now known rather less charmingly as 200 Clarendon) was stunning – its mirrored windows reflecting the bright sun and odd passing cloud across its sixty story blue glass facade. A blue tint was especially incorporated into the reflective glass to blend the 790 feet high building with the sky on a clear day. It does a great job. I know I was critical of Miami's incessant glass palaces, but whether it was the blue tint that did it, or that the sun wasn't as blinding as in Miami's southern latitudes, the John Hancock Tower looked amazing.

Unfortunately, problems with the initial design of the Hancock building also meant those same glass panels, each weighing 500lb, had a nasty habit of detaching themselves from the building during its construction; plummeting towards the ground, whenever it got especially windy. Aside from injecting a little frisson of extra excitement into the lives of everyday folks walking around downtown in the early 1970s, the problem became so bad that the police had to close off local streets whenever wind speeds reached 45mph.

The building became known locally as the Plywood Palace, as each departed pane of glass was replaced with boarding panels until an answer could be found. Locals joked Boston had the tallest plywood building in the world. The solution wasn't straightforward, but thank goodness they persevered, because seeing that Tower on a sunny day, with a few small white clouds for contrast, is quite a sight.

Having taken in the view for a bit, we decided to head up to the Common, a fifty acre green space in the heart of Boston and site of the oldest public park in the United States of America. We asked for directions from a UPS guy delivering a package who, despite being in the middle of a job, was really helpful. Not overly friendly, but certainly not rude, and to be fair he was busy. It was progress.

The Common with its wide, open lawns, trees, monuments, fountains, pond and even band stand was reminiscent of a park in central London. Albeit on a smaller scale. It was a delight to amble around, helped by it now being a warm, sunny day. We just mooched; enjoying the warmth and the sunshine, taking in the scenery, stopping here and there, as we looked at various bits of interest. Before treating ourselves to an ice cream and resting on a bench by the frog pond. Boston Common is great for mooching.

It's also great for catching sight of the Massachusetts State House. Particularly that day, with its golden roof beaming majestically in the afternoon sun. Designed and built by architect Charles Bulfinch, who was also responsible for the Capitol Building in Washington, it is considered one of the best pieces of Federal-period civic architecture.

Completed in 1798, with large Palladian windows in perfect symmetry studding its red brick walls, it has a noble appearance. What strikes you though, are its tall white columns and that gleaming dome on its roof – a dome gilded in 23 carat gold leaf. On a sunny day, it is an arresting sight.

Designed to show the strength of the newly independent country, whilst engendering confidence and respect for the legislature, it demands your attention now. Let alone then. It genuinely fills you with a bit of awe, and you end up having one of those wow moments. One can only imagine how much more amplified that feeling would have been over two hundred years ago, in a much smaller, skyscraper free city.

We wandered to our hotel, checked in and recharged ourselves with the obligatory cup of tea before diving back out.

Our hotel wasn't far from Quincy Market, which Tripadvisor will tell you has loads of boutique stalls and eating places. As well as being home to a replica set of the bar from *Cheers*, the famous comedy series starring Ted Danson, Woody Harrelson and Kelsey Grammer amongst others that ran for over ten years on prime time television.

Most reviews of Quincy Market were fairly positive, and the photos looked good, so off we went. Sadly, it was a disappointment. Seriously crowded and seriously overpriced. In short, we'd walked into a tourist trap. As if to confirm the fact, many of the boutique stalls were selling tourist staples typical the world over, albeit with the crucial local twist. So you could gleefully expect to buy I ♡ Boston sweatshirts, key rings, paper weights, underwear and so on. Actually, I may have made the last one up. Although, just because I didn't see any, doesn't mean you couldn't get them.

Disenchanted and hungry, we decided to get something to eat from one of the thirty or so food stalls within the Quincy Market food colonnade. Sadly it was a similar story, with the food offerings no better than you would get from the food court in a large shopping mall. Except the prices were a lot higher. This was nothing like Manhattan's Gotham West Market, even if it was in a nicer building. We couldn't bring ourselves to pay twenty-one dollars for a lobster roll, Boston speciality or not, so settled on a Chinese noodle dish. It offered more vegetables than its competitors and looked relatively freshly prepared.

Once served, you then had to find somewhere to sit in a central communal seating area where people shared benches and tables. Or if you are clever, you send your other half on ahead to stake out some seats whilst you queue up for the food. With Alison being the smarter partner, I drew the 'find some seats' straw. Apart from requiring laser-like, fighter pilot target spotting skills to even locate a seat in the first place, this then required the athleticism of Usain Bolt to secure it, and the physical presence of an American Football Linebacker to keep it. Or in my case, sheer luck followed by a skin thick enough to be impervious to the death stares from other customers circling for places. Whilst I sat at one without anything to eat.

One of the best tactics I've found in these situations is to engage in conversation with the people around, particularly if they already have food. It makes you look both part of a bigger party and that you have a rightful place to these seats as your group is eating. The lady opposite me actually had a lobster roll, so I asked her what it was like. When she told me the bread was ok, but she was still looking for her lobster, I briefly thought I might have pulled. Only joking, that hasn't happened to me in over thirty years. Even then, my close friends still regard that occurrence as something from Roald Dahl's *Tales of the Unexpected.*

However, I soon realised that she meant she needed that fighter pilot eyesight to find any pieces of lobster in her roll.

It was a shame as I wanted to like Quincy Market. Completed in 1826, it is also in another very elegant building. Built from grey granite with twenty-two foot tall Doric columns, it looks like a mini Parthenon. It's also another National Historical Landmark.

In many ways it reminded me of Covent Garden in London, both architecturally and also because it would once have been a thriving, bustling real produce market. Now, with the passage of time, it has morphed into a tourist trap. Again, much like Covent Garden. Yes, like Covent Garden, it had atmosphere, theatre and a bustling street scene around it, but it just felt too manufactured and expensive. One of those places people go to tick off the list and say they have been there, without necessarily enjoying it.

Covent Garden, albeit much larger, is also great to visit, soak up the atmosphere and take a few photos, but you don't find many Londoners eating or shopping there. Ironically, not only are the two similar in many ways today, they share the same evolution. From once booming market to latter decay, through to today's tourist attraction. Rather poignantly perhaps, when Quincy Market was created in the 1820s, it was modelled on London's Covent Garden.

We decided to move on, and as fans of the series, set off to find Cheers and see if we too could sup a beer in Norm's seat. I know you can probably predict the next sentence, but whilst the bar did justice to the original set, is a proper working bar and has some real items from the series (such as Sam's Red Sox jacket), it was so crowded that it lacked the ambience or magic you might have hoped. To us, it felt more like a themed bar and restaurant.

As an aside, those who want to see the bar that was used for the outside shots of *Cheers*, should head up to 84 Beacon Street. It used to be called the Bull & Finch pub and in 1982 won the award for Boston's best bar. These days it is run by the same company that owns the Cheers bar at Quincy, and although downstairs it wasn't the same inside as the *Cheers* set, the outside is the real deal. Plus, inside it is a smaller, cozier bar than that at Quincy providing for a better feel, whilst upstairs they have recreated a replica of the bar used on set. Cutting our losses, we headed out and wandered around the Faneuil Hall Market Place area, which is the name given to Quincy Market, Faneuil Hall, and the shops in the surrounding vicinity.

Faneuil Hall is also a wonderful building with a rich history. Completed in 1742, it was given to the city by rich merchant Peter Faneuil who believed the city needed a central marketplace as it grew. Amazingly, despite him offering to pay for the building, there was considerable opposition as people were concerned that in a centralised market traders would collude and raise prices. Built of redbrick with seven white arched Palladian windows across each of the three main stories of its front facade, it is a worthy sight. With Quincy Market, twenty-five yards in front of it, the two fit well together.

Outside, we spotted a Christmas shop in the area around Quincy. Now, we have always been a bit of a sucker for Christmas shops so in we went, if nothing else to get a bauble for the tree to remind us of our trip to Boston. Sadly though, it was another disappointment.

We were just about to leave when we overhead the conversation between a group of people. The women were visiting Boston from Sweden and expressing similar levels of disappointment with the shop to that we felt, when the man they were with said, "Yeh, it's not very good. This is nothing compared to what we've got in Michigan."

"Really?" enquired one of the ladies.

"Sure. In Michigan we've got the largest Christmas shop in the world," he replied.

WHAT!!! I don't know who looked more surprised, his companions or us. Michigan is pretty much a mid-state in everything. Midwest in location, middle of all the states in terms of population, middle in terms of geographic size, etc. Not unreasonably, you might have thought the largest shop in the world would have been elsewhere instead. Such as one of the more populous states. Or one of America's largest cities. Indeed, anywhere other than Michigan. Given that Josh had never mentioned this, to us rather important fact, I just had to find out more.

"I'm sorry," I said, interrupting. "Did I just hear you say that Michigan had the largest Christmas shop in the world?"

"Oh yes," he said in a completely matter of fact, not at all boasting, polite sort of way. Before explaining how big it was, how amazing it was, and so on. All in that understated manner I have since come to realise is part of the charm of many people from the Midwest. He told us it was in a place called Frankenmuth, a small town that we had never heard of, which made us even more incredulous. Nevertheless, I filed this information away and was delighted that our trip into the Christmas shop hadn't been such a waste of time after all.

Deciding our luck was on the up, and that it wasn't long before we could respectfully call it a night, we decided to chance our arm at any decent looking local bar and grab a night cap. Purely for medicinal reasons, of course. We stopped at a place called The Ginger Man, not too far away on State Street, which looked alright from the outside. As soon as we stepped inside though, boy did we realise that we were on a roll now.

If you are a beer lover, or a whisky lover, it was fantastic. With seventy-four beers on tap and a further seventy-nine in bottles or cans (not to mention over one hundred whiskies and other spirits) it was a beer/whisky lover's paradise. They even reprinted a drinks menu daily to reflect their latest offerings. As you might imagine from a choice this extensive, pretty much everything was catered for. Styles ranged from super light through to treacle, and from alcoholic strengths that were driver friendly, to are you sure this isn't wine?

Whilst they had regular brews, like draught Guinness, they also had more exotic sounding concoctions such as Hermit Thrush Brattlebeer. No, really. Or perhaps the cheerful sounding Jolly Pumpkin Bam Biere; the intriguing, Zero Gravity Conehead; the rather racy, Lawson's Finest Maple Nipple; through to the rather bizarre (if you hadn't thought the previous ones were strange enough), Hoof Hearted Thanks For Letting Us Play Tonight. Words fail me on the last one, but in case you were wondering that's a 5.5% American Pale Ale from Ohio. And these were just a small selection of the ones on tap.

Whether it was the names of the beers failing to give clues to their taste; whether the jet lag was kicking in; or whether we were just overwhelmed by the sheer amount of choice, we just stared blankly at the menu. We were like rabbits in headlights, hoping vainly that something would leap out from the page and grab us. Without being so potent that it flattened us.

In the end we prevailed upon the bartender for his assistance and he didn't let us or the city of Boston down. In fact, like the Ginger Man, he was brilliant – helpful, friendly and spot on with his advice.

Alison settled for a sensible, characterful wheat beer. (The 4.1% Notch Dog & Pony Show in case you were wondering). I, however, in a vain attempt to put some hairs on my chest, even at this late stage in my life, opted for one of the versions of rocket fuel. Who says you can't make beer with a 13% ABV? As usual, her choice was the better one.

But whilst mine might have been hard going, at least it had the desired effect of helping fight the jet lag by knocking me straight to sleep when we got back to our room. The difficulty would be getting back there. Something I discovered when standing from my chair as we went to leave.

Thank God! Not everywhere around here costs an arm and a leg

After a decent sleep, which I put down to last night's Sledgehammer That Knocks You Out Cold IPA (not its name, but really should have been), the benefits of the 5 hour time difference meant we were still up early. Really early in fact. Something we were about to find out as the café we'd decided to go to for breakfast was still shut when we arrived.

Our tummies wanted food though, so rather than go wandering off we stayed put for the few minutes until it opened, which turned out a good decision on various fronts. (I knew we were on a roll now). Firstly, within half an hour of opening the café was rammed, and we would never have got a seat. Always a good sign. Secondly, we had the most amazing French Toast we have ever had. End of. The best we'd ever had until that moment and still the best we have ever had.

It was called Honey Crunch French Toast and I can only describe it as French Toast, but after dipping the bread in eggs they must have rolled it in honey and then some sort of cornflakes prior to frying it. Or perhaps it was the cornflakes first, then the honey. I'm not entirely sure, as we've never managed to recreate it exactly at home. Despite trying repeatedly. Anyway, it was amazing and to finish they served it with some maple syrup on the side. Umm umm. Honestly, I can still taste it now.

We were in Boston's North End, an area famed for its Italian eateries, as well as Paul Revere's House. Paul Revere was a leading figure in the libertarian movement and, as every American schoolchild knows, his ride through the night to alert senior Patriots Sam Adams, John Hancock and the people of Lexington and Concord of advancing British troops proved a key moment in the American Revolution.

The North End is an interesting mix of buildings. Predominantly composed of redbrick, square structures, each only a few stories high, with narrow streets and tiny alleyways, it reminds you of many a neighbourhood in New York. Yet, interspersed amongst all this are several historical buildings that differ markedly. Not only because of their historical significance, but also because of their dramatic difference in style to the rest of the neighbourhood.

No better example exists than that of the house owned by Paul Revere, where visitors will find a grey timber-framed house dating back to 1680 only two stories high. The contrast with its surroundings is so vivid that as you start to walk down North Street, you can immediately see it standing out, almost defiantly. So too, with the Old North Church on Salem Street. Famous since the evening of April 18, 1775, when Robert Newman held high two lanterns from its steeple as a sign from Paul Revere to Patriots across the water that the British Redcoats were advancing to Lexington and Concord by sea, and not by land via the Boston Neck. Although also constructed from red brick like most of the surrounding area, its tall white steeple is so distinctive, that it's almost as though it's there to say "look here, this is where we gave the signal that started it all."

Both sites lie on the impressive Freedom Trail, a two-and-a-half-mile walk that takes you past buildings and places in central Boston that were a key part of the events which lead to the American Revolution. Or are of other significant importance in the early history of the United States. The route is very well done. Information panels explain the significance of each stopping point, whilst the city has cut an actual marked line into the pavement. They have even cut it into roads when the trail crosses them. It means even complete idiots like me, with the navigational skills of a lemming, can't get lost. It is wonderful.

So, now standing outside the Paul Revere house, we decided that as the city had gone to so much trouble to make it easier to visit and learn about these sites, the least we could do was to follow it and see where it took us. Which, as it turns out, is around much of downtown Boston. From Boston Common to the Bunker Hill Monument, across the Charles River, via a lot of history in between.

As much has already been written about the Freedom Trail and all the locations it crosses, it would be inappropriate to take you through a detailed tour of it here. Suffice to say that it's a great way of seeing and learning about some of the key places in the early history of Boston and the United States. It is also great for getting a sense of the central Boston neighbourhoods and their distinct characters and vibes.

And that is something of the charm of Boston. It's small enough to walk round and cover a lot of it quite quickly, but at the same time the various neighbourhoods each have a very different feel and distinct identity. Whether that's characterised in that area's ethnic community, its buildings or its general surroundings. Within a three-mile walk starting in the North End, you can feel like you're crossing several countries and continents before you end up in Newbury Street, west of Boston Public Park.

The North End, with its large Italian community and tight streets; its alleyways of low rise redbrick buildings, feeling like of a suburb of New York, transitions into the Waterfront. An area that is similar to Liverpool, England with its vast expanses of river leading to a heavily developed peninsula on the other shore.

Cutting back up into the financial district, you could have been transported to Wall Street or any number of the world's financial centres. Although, amongst all the high rise steel and glass, you are still able to stop and admire the diminutive three story Old State House. As well as the nearby, similarly modest, Old South Meeting House. Both remain distinctive and beautiful, whilst dwarfed by the surrounding skyscrapers.

Detouring into Chinatown reminds me of the Chinatown area and surrounding streets of our home city of Manchester, England; its low rise redbrick buildings differing notably from those in the North End. Each is longer – more oblong – and looks more Victorian warehouse than the North End's squarer structures, that resemble individual houses or shops within a terrace of properties. Again, narrow roads and little alleyways shoot off here and there, but now are full of the sights, smells and sounds of a bustling Chinatown. The similarities don't end there though. Like Manchester, Boston also has a Chinese Gate and a sizeable Chinese community. And where Manchester is second to London for the UK's largest Chinatown, Boston is the US's third – behind New York and San Francisco.

Within a few minutes (like Manchester, it's a pretty compact area), you can be on the Common with its similarities to one of London's many parks and green spaces. In the space of a couple hundred yards, it's like being transported a couple of hundred miles.

From there, a walk through the Boston Public Garden brings you to Commonwealth Avenue. With its pedestrian walkway flanked by lawns, enclosed under a canopy of trees, it is reminiscent of many boulevards from great European Capitals, such as Paris or Madrid.

After Commonwealth Avenue, you can choose to head left for a brief walk to the upscale shopping district of Newbury Street, often referred to as the "Rodeo Drive of the East." When built, it was again designed to imitate Europe's leading cities of the day. Or you might turn right and head up Massachusetts Avenue to cross the Charles River via the impressive Harvard Bridge. Heading right would also allow you to stroll along the waterfront via the Charles River Esplanade. It is a different experience again to the waterfront walk from the North End to the Aquarium.

The Charles River walk was still to come for us though and after we had finished the trail, our stomachs told us it was time for sustenance. This time we headed for Boston Public Market and its neighbouring Haymarket. Although less than five minutes' walk from Quincy, what a contrast. Here was a real foodies market specialising in seasonal, locally sourced food, with everything produced or originating from New England. Including lobster rolls that you could recognise as such, without the need of an eyeglass. (And five dollars cheaper than those at Quincy).

With a huge variety, you were spoilt for choice of quality food to eat. Then we remembered that this was *the place* that we had seen a UK celebrity TV chef use as the backdrop for his USA cooking/travel program when he visited Boston. Oh well, better late than never. Anyway, we probably still would have gone to Quincy's just because everyone says you have to. Even though they say with age comes wisdom. Sadly, something I seem to be taking forever to learn.

Unfortunately for us, the Haymarket next door was shut as it only opens on Fridays and Saturdays. It was a shame as this is a market that specialises in fresh food and produce at ridiculously low prices. Bostonians say it's where local traders sell the excess fresh produce they haven't managed to shift wholesale. It would explain why the prices are a third to a quarter of what you would pay in a regular store...... and that's before you haggle. (Something you can try at the end of the market early on a Saturday evening with traders prepared to accept discounts for what is left rather than throw stuff away).

Nevertheless, now comforted after a pleasant lunch, we thought what better than a couple of beers to wash down our food and aid the digestion. And so off we set for our next destination, the Sam Adams Brewery.

Set in the Jamaica Plain district, a little over four miles Southwest of downtown, you can easily get there by taking the Orange Line subway to Stony Brook station followed by a walk of about five minutes. Brewery tours are offered, as long as you go around in an organised party, and afterwards there is a tasting session of some of their brews. Best of all, it's free! Yes, FREE! In a city that seems more expensive than Manhattan, the Sam Adams Brewery tour, tastings and even a small souvenir glass are all free! Incredible is all I can say.*

Our tour started by us signing up for a slot and showing ID to confirm we were over twenty-one. I know many visitors to the US who clearly look older get irritated when they have to go through the process of proving their age to purchase or consume alcohol because things are a lot more relaxed where they come from. But even though I am greyer than a koala bear, I don't mind. Aside from respecting the laws of the country I am choosing to visit, it only takes a couple of seconds. Plus, it allows me the indulgence of thinking maybe, just maybe, they do think I look that young.

Anyway, age verified, we joined the rest of our group and had an interesting tour around with guides who took time to explain the brewing process, what made Sam Adams different and so on. It was particularly nice to learn how everything began when founder, Jim Koch, brewed the first batch of Boston Lager in his kitchen in the early 1980s. He found an old family recipe in his dad's attic, entered his brew into a competition and did rather well. The rest is history, and nowadays the Boston Beer Company produces a staggering four million barrels of beer every year. Clearly, it has been a popular recipe. But it's also inspiring to see how one person working hard and producing a great

---

* At the time of writing. The brewery asks for (not demands) a modest donation which goes to local charities.

product can grow their business from kitchen table to a billion dollar turnover enterprise in thirty or so years.

After the thirty-minute tour we retired to an indoor sampling area where we got to try three different Sam Adams beers – their regular Boston Lager along with a couple of their other brews, one of which was a seasonal ale. They actively seek your feedback on the drinks to help with their market research, which as well as a splendid idea is a nice touch. Our tasting worked by having people sit communally on picnic style wooden benches. Then, following a few words from the Master Brewer describing the drink we were about to try, a pitcher was placed on each bench for all to share.

Well, talk about the luck of the Irish. Our roll since the Christmas shop was now reaching unprecedented proportions, as we were paired on our bench with just one other couple. Meaning only four people on our bench, still with a whole pitcher to share. Then, the lady then told us she was driving, and wouldn't be able to sample! So just her husband, Alison & me...... per pitcher. And with one pitcher for each of the three brews we were to taste, even my maths told me that was three pitchers between the three of us. And all for free. Geronimo!!!

Although it hadn't taken me long to work out the sums involved here, at this point I fear I lived up to the worldwide reputation of tourists being dumb, by struggling to find what to say. I was certainly struck dumb.

For a while all I could do was hang my mouth open, whilst my brow remained furrowed with that look of confusion. Sadly at this point, with my mouth open, and finger raised, I had the floor. It was clear to all I was about to communicate something. But try as I might, nothing seemed to be coming out.

By now my growing audience had assumed, given how long I was taking to deliver whatever precious words might eventually emanate from my mouth, that these must clearly be pearls of wisdom. Everyone sat on the edge of their seat. Breath was suitably bated.

Tragically, brow still furrowed, all I could utter was, "I'm sorry. I know the Boston accent is hard to understand for out of towners, but did you just say you were driving?"

Very patiently, as though responding to someone in their dotage or an imbecile, or both, she repeated that she was.

"So you've come to a free beer tasting, in what has to be said is a brewery that makes great beers, and you're driving?" I responded. Now also talking slowly, as if to ram home how thick I must be, but in reality because I was struggling to comprehend what she was telling me. I was also wondering who was the real imbecile.

"Yes, that's right," she said. Once again, pleasantly and patiently.

"Wow! This would never happen back home," was all I could mutter. Still shaking my head in disbelief.

That said, if it took my brain an age to process what it had heard, it certainly took no time for the apple of my eye to snap me out of things. Taking control of the situation, she didn't waste a second pouring the three of us our drinks.

"If you don't get a shift on, they'll be bringing the next pitcher out before we've done supping this."

Where would I be without her?

The beers we had were all excellent. For the record, the Boston Lager, a Kellerbier and their Oktoberfest.

Half way down our second pitcher we realised we were in danger of biting off more than we could chew. As well as realising that we were the subject of seriously envious glances from the tables surrounding us. So we did the decent thing and started offering pours to those nearby. Soon we were making new friends and with all the ensuing revelry were in danger of creating a mini Oktoberfest of our own. All we needed was the Lederhosen and an oompah band, and we might have been there. All good things must come to an end though. So, after doing proper justice to our drinks, we bade farewell to the friendly and exceptionally patient staff – unsurprisingly we were the last to leave – and staggered out into what was still a really warm and sunny day outside.

Just beyond the tasting room was a pay bar with open air seating. Perhaps we hadn't wanted our visit to end. Perhaps it was me who cracked first with my comment, "Well, we've had a wonderful time, it seems churlish not to give something back."

But if so, it was Alison that finished us off with her, "It would be a crime to waste this glorious sunshine on the subway. How about just one more outside?"

Whichever, it meant that we must have made it all of ten yards before another beer beckoned.

Alison secured us some seats which, surprisingly given the weather, were all empty. Momentarily I wondered whether there had been more drivers than we thought or, whether after all the free beer, people were now baulking at paying what was still only a regular price for another. But then I shrugged my shoulders, reflected how lucky we were to have the place to ourselves on such a fine day, and wandered to the bar.

At first I was a bit disorientated when I got to the counter as I could hear voices, but there was no one apart from me at the bar. Or even anywhere about. Hmmm, just how much have we had, I started thinking. When suddenly, sensing my presence, a barman – leaping like a Jack in the Box – appeared from below the counter.

"How can I help you, sir?" he asked.

"Two pints of Sam Adams," I replied. Predictably, this brought a quizzical look on his face. "Sorry, I meant Boston Lager."

In my defence I explained to him that where we were from, you could only get the Sam Adams Boston Lager and not any of the other Sam Adams varieties. So everyone at home just asks for a Sam Adams when in a pub. Now understanding, he asked us whether we were from England.

"Yeah, Manchester, up in North West England."

"Cool. Do you guys like soccer?"

"Is the pope a Catholic? Although we call it football."

"Gotcha!" and he then explained how he loved soccer (football in America is played with the oval-shaped ball) and that his favourite team was Arsenal. He said he watched it whenever possible and in fact was in the middle of watching a champions league match.

Which, thankfully, explained the voices. Nestled below his bar, to keep it in the shade and the sun off the screen, was a TV beaming out Atletico Madrid and Chelsea. And with Europe being five to six hours ahead of us, this was a game in full flow. It also reinforced to us that it might just be true what everyone had said about Bostonians being sports crazy, and that everyone you met would either love The Sox (baseball), The Pats (football), The Celts (pronounced Seltz – Basketball) or the Bruins (pronounced Broons – Ice Hockey). Clearly, we had another team to add to that list now.

Testing the Beer & Ball Games Theory

As well as being Sports fanatics and rude (or dour, depending upon your point of view), other preconceptions about Bostonians include their love of beer. Which might explain the vast array of choice at The Ginger Man. With us having tickets to see the Red Sox at home to the Toronto Blue Jays that evening, it gave us another chance for some more research. First though, we were off to see an institution that specialised in research of a different nature. Namely, Harvard University. Or Hahvahd, as they like to say it in Boston, in their famously unique accent.

We headed up across the Common and then west through the Public Garden. Similar to the Common being the first public park in the United States, this was the first Public Botanical Garden in the United States. In my mind's eye, I have always associated botanical gardens with glass houses and tropical plants. Rather like at Kew Gardens in London. But although Boston's didn't have those, it still made for a pleasant walk through the city. Particularly over the suspension bridge across the middle of the pond. From there, we walked down the tree-canopied boulevard of Commonwealth Avenue before turning onto Massachusetts Ave and crossing the Charles River via the Harvard Bridge.

The Harvard Bridge provides a great vantage point over the magnificent Charles River with the latter's tree lined esplanades along its banks, contrasting with the onward views to the grand skyscrapers of the financial district. At about two-fifths of a mile wide at that point, the Charles River is double the width of the Thames at Waterloo Bridge and much wider than the Seine in Paris's city centre. This is a bridge and a river that can compare with any of the world's great cities. In fact, at this point it is on a par with New York's East River, and the Brooklyn and Manhattan bridges. In short, this is a big bridge over a wide river. And, whilst the Harvard Bridge may not be as imposing as

Brooklyn's or Manhattan's, nor have the same scale of cityscape screaming for your attention, nevertheless it has a great view and is still pretty special.

With the continued unseasonally warm weather on our backs we could have stayed there for some time, even allowing for the busy traffic at our backs. Until we noticed all these numbers painted on the bridge in all manner of colours. And every now and again the word "SMOOTS" beside them.

This dates back to 1958, when some freshmen were aspiring to join the Lambda Chi Alpha fraternity at Massachusetts Institute of Technology. It transpires that the pledge master (an older student charged with setting tasks for hopeful entrants), was sick and tired of crossing the long bridge home in the notorious Boston weather, without knowing how far he had left to go. He decided a suitable task for the pledges would be to measure the bridge and mark it at appropriate intervals. To make the task harder, because pledge tests aren't supposed to be easy, he chose the smallest of the group, Oliver Reed Smoot, to be the official unit of measure for this exercise. The five frat hopefuls then dutifully measured the bridge from beginning to end, with Oliver lying down whilst his friends painted a line to mark each length of measure (i.e., the end of his body). Poor Oliver would then repeatedly get up before lying down again at the start of each line. Sometime later, made longer by having to hide from passing police at one point, the deed was done. They officially recorded the length of the bridge as 364.4 smoots +/- 1 ear, the latter adjustment being added to reflect potential errors in their measurements.*

MIT students were delighted with these staging posts to help break the drudge of long walks across the bridge. So much so, that as the markings faded over time, successive generations repainted them to

---

* They actually recorded the distance as 364.4 smoots +/- 1 εar, a clever play on words because ε, or epsilon, is the Greek symbol in mathematics for an error or a small increment. As they say, you have to be special to get into MIT. Spare also a small thought (or should that be smoot thought) for poor Oliver. As he himself later said "even at that age, I could not do the equivalent of several hundred push ups or sit ups." Meaning that an unintended consequence for him in this task with all the standing up before carefully lying down again for each measurement, was that the poor soul ended up having to be dragged by his colleagues for much of the way.

ensure their continued use. Indeed, they became so useful that instead of viewing the continual repainting as an offence and chasing away offending students, the police even started using them when reporting incidents, such as traffic accidents and so on.

Fast forward to the 1980s and the Harvard Bridge needed its superstructure replacing. This is not something undertaken lightly. In essence, the bridge needed rebuilding. Amazingly though, the contractors, instead of using standard measures of six feet for the concrete blocks and expansion joints, actually used smoots. So each concrete block and expansion joint on the bridge is now exactly one smoot long. Incredible, but true. (Incidentally, a smoot is five foot seven inches for those wondering).

Nor is it just in Boston where the smoot has taken over. In fact, it is now recognised as an international unit of measure. Indeed, if you go onto Google Earth and use the measuring functions such as ruler, path, etc. it offers you the results for whatever you want to measure in millimetres, centimetres, metres, kilometres, inches, feet, yards, miles, nautical miles or even smoots. So too Google's calculator function, which also recognises the smoot.

If all that wasn't amazing enough, then in a truth is stranger than fiction way, Oliver Smoot himself ended up having a very successful career in measurement and standardisation. He was a Chair of the American National Standards Institute and also became President of The International Standards Organisation. (The world body governing all those ISO standards we see).

And that makes Boston's Harvard Bridge not only unique, but something that even New York would find hard to rival.

We paused to read the plaque commemorating this feat and realised we were now in Cambridge, which people will pointedly tell you is a different city to Boston with its own City Government and City Hall. In reality though, it feels just a suburb within the Greater Boston metropolitan area. Whether it is technically a separate city or practically a suburb of Boston these days, what is remarkable is that it is the only city in the world that's home to two of the world's top ten Universities.

Harvard is arguably the more famous University, founded some 225 years before its younger rival, Massachusetts Institute of Technology (MIT). However, it is the latter that is now actually rated higher by the influential Times World University Rankings. It is also where we were headed next. We took a right and walked fifty metres down Memorial Drive before turning left to walk up Killian Court and then stopped to marvel at MIT's Great Dome.

Sitting atop the somewhat unromantically titled Building 10 (you can tell these folks are scientists and engineers rather than artists), The Dome is probably the most iconic image associated with MIT. Modelled on Rome's Pantheon, it is like a huge limestone turret atop a rectangular building (also of limestone) fronted with ten imposing Ionic columns. One hundred and fifty feet tall, it makes for an impressive sight. Particularly, when you're aware of the many pranks that MIT students have undertaken on it over the years.

Many of these have been funny and clever, but relatively simple, such as beaming a bat symbol onto it. Or making it look like a giant pumpkin through the use of banners draped over and an orange filter applied to the spotlights that illuminate it. Others, however, defy any explanation, let alone logic.

For instance, on September 11, 2006, to honour the men and women serving in the fire service, hackers (the name MIT pranksters call themselves) secured a 25 foot long fire truck to the top of The Dome. Remember, this is a dome on a roof, 150 feet off the ground.

Or in May 2009, to commemorate the upcoming 40th anniversary of the first moon walk, they placed a half-scale replica of the Apollo landing craft on top. Or in December 2017 to celebrate the 100th anniversary of the first powered flight, they landed (tethered) a replica of the aircraft flown by the Wright brothers (complete with a dummy pilot) to its top. In May 1999, they converted The Dome to look like R2D2 from *Star Wars* by using carefully designed cloths and panels placed on its roof.

The list goes on and on. Indeed, it's well worth googling "MIT Dome hacks" to see the huge variety of these over the years. Having seen the pictures online though, to stand there and appreciate the size and height of the building just leaves you speechless. Or gives you brain ache. Or in my case, both.

Honestly, you stand there thinking "never mind the huge personal risks involved," (believe me you would not want to fall off this building), "how the hell would you even get these things up there? Let alone get them up without being seen?"

You look at the sheer height of the building, what little time you would have to evade security patrols, the equipment you would need, and you realise the ingenuity and planning behind these operations is incredible. Then you realise why you never got to go to MIT and why this is one of the World's best Universities.

There was also another question that went through my mind which was "Why the heck would you even put these things up there in the first place?" Although sadly the fact that I could contemplate that, probably also reinforced why I was never good enough to go to MIT.

Unlike many Universities which can be rather stuffy, MIT is friendly and welcoming. They even provide maps so visitors can do self-guided walking tours of the campus and allow you to enter many of the key buildings. Perhaps it goes back to its founding vision of being a different type of educational establishment relevant to the modern world. Who knows? But it's pretty cool nonetheless – a refreshing alternative to the "keep off the hallowed lawns" brigade.

And you know what might have even been the best part? Aside from giving my brain a run out, marvelling at all the hacks I had read about and could now vividly imagine, you felt that just being there, surrounded by all these really clever people, somehow made you a bit smarter too. Maybe it was Osmosis? Maybe it was ESP? Or maybe I was just kidding myself. Either way, it was nice while it lasted.

Deciding my brain could do with a super boost, to which disappointingly Mrs. Stanson didn't disagree, we wandered up Harvard Street to Boston's other well-known college. Established in 1636, Harvard is the oldest University in the United States and certainly feels more blue blood. In contrast to MIT's, more modern architecture, Harvard is square, red brick Georgian style buildings standing around a square of trees and lawns. It is in keeping with a classical University, though not on the same scale as those at Cambridge and Oxford in England. Although, to be fair, they predate the founding of Harvard by well over four hundred years.

We took a tour run by Harvard students, which gave an interesting insight into the history of the college and some of its buildings. Unlike MIT though, there would be no going behind the facades here.

Nevertheless it was worth visiting, if only to get a sense for how the other half live. Or more correctly, how the top 0.1% of students live.

You walked around and listened to the tales of how many ex-presidents of the United States (including John Adams, John Quincy Adams, Theodore Roosevelt, Franklin D Roosevelt, J F Kennedy, George W Bush, Barack Obama), were Harvard Alumni; not to mention Vice Presidents, Attorney Generals or other incredibly rich and influential people. Somehow it would be wrong here to ignore Bill Gates and Mark Zuckerberg. As you drank in the grandeur of the place, you could literally feel the wealth and power oozing out of the walls.

However, even with all that wealth and power, life can still be a lottery. Sadly, three Harvard Alumni perished on board the *Titanic.* (Harry Elkins Widener, scion to one of the richest families in America; John Jacob Astor IV, part of the Astor dynasty and the richest man on board the doomed ship; and Francis Davis Millet, a renowned artist and writer).

In fact, Harry, an avid book collector, was only on the *Titanic* because he was returning from Europe where he had been purchasing rare books. As a result, as a permanent memorial to her son, his mother built Harvard their library at an estimated cost of $4m (circa $65m in present-day terms). That may seem a lot, but there are more than three and a half million books across fifty-seven miles of shelving inside.

The other hand of fate in that terrible tragedy though, was seen in the survival of Harvard student Richard Norris Williams. An accomplished tennis player, he was travelling on board with his father on the way to play in some tournaments.

After the last able lifeboat had been despatched, Richard and his father remained on the sinking ship. With the boat in its last moments, they were almost up to their waists in water, when the forward funnel broke loose and came crashing to the deck. Richard tried to grab his father and jump out of its way, but couldn't save him. His father was crushed to death as it fell. However, as the funnel landed, it created a huge wave which propelled Richard some distance from the doomed vessel.

When he surfaced from below the icy waters, he saw a lifeboat in the distance. It had also still been on the *Titanic* and also washed overboard. He swam vigorously, discarding his overcoat and shoes on the way until he reached it. Because the lifeboat hadn't been readied for dispatch, its canvas sides weren't erected and it was taking in a lot of water. Although Richard eventually managed to clamber on board, he spent several hours waist deep in the freezing water. Not helped by the boat periodically capsizing in the waves and upending everyone into the icy sea. Something requiring the stricken passengers to make their way back to it and clamber inside. Time and time again. So arduous were the conditions that, by the time that boat was rescued, only eleven people from the original thirty to forty estimated to have made it to that lifeboat remained alive.

Although one of the fortunate eleven, Richard had suffered extreme frostbite; leading the doctor on the rescue ship *Carpathia* to recommend amputating both his legs. He refused. Then, after an intensive exercise and recuperation program, he recovered to such an extent that as well as graduating from Harvard, he also managed to win the United States Mixed Doubles. Amazingly in 1912, the year of the disaster itself.

He then went onto become United States Singles Champion in 1914 and 1916, Wimbledon Doubles Champion in 1920 and an Olympic Gold Medal Winner in 1924. He also represented the United States Davis Cup Team from 1913 to 1926. Fate, like the sea, can be a capricious mistress.*

Time waits for no man (or couple in our case) however, and, having broadened our minds, we now needed to push on as we had another demonstration of power and wealth to get too. Namely the baseball, and the Sox against the Blue Jays.

As you know, our trip to see the Miami Marlins had been a bit of a disaster. Every baseball fan you ever talk to though says you must visit the Red Sox's iconic home, Fenway Park, at least once in your life. So, albeit reluctantly, I decided to give it another try. Well, that and the fact that Alison, for some reason I am still trying to fathom, enjoys going to baseball games. Even though I find them monotonous – literally ball,

* As an aside, an interesting insight into the attitudes of the time also concerned Richard Williams. *After* the collision with the iceberg, he and his father left their room and encountered a steward struggling to open the door of a cabin in which a passenger was trapped and panicking. Using his strength Richard broke the door down freeing the passenger. Only for the steward to threaten to report him for damaging company property!

ball, ball with, as we saw in Miami, 12 hits in 3 hours if you're lucky; she says that after putting up with me droning on drip, drip, drip for the last 30 years, she finds them positively scintillating.

Anyway, as well as being told that Fenway, which opened in 1912, is the oldest Major League Baseball stadium still in use, you will also be told that getting a ticket for the Sox is neither easy nor cheap. (With an 820 consecutive game sell out streak from May 2003 – April 2013, they hold the longest run in US baseball history for sold out matches).

However, we managed to secure decent tickets at a reasonable price using one of the reselling sites (StubHub, if you must ask) without too much trouble. That said, as our subway train got within a few stops of Fenway, it was clear that the ground was still going to be pretty full. At that point, it seemed like the world and his wife were on our train, resplendent in all their replica kits and scarves.

By the next stop the subway was crammed so tight, even sardines would have refused to get on. In an effort to avoid the awkwardness that comes from being closer to a stranger than I would like to be with my wife, I struck up a conversation with those around.

From this I learned that whilst our main stand tickets near first base might provide a better view, on a fine evening like this, the bleachers was the best place to be for the atmosphere. "No doubt about it," I was told. And stacks cheaper. I also learned judging by those around us, not only would we experience a raucous atmosphere and save money on our tickets, we would probably also save a fair bit on alcohol. Getting merry wouldn't mean buying any drinks, just inhaling the fumes around.

Our train eventually arrived at Kenmore, which was our chosen stop, and as anyone who has been to a major sporting event in London knows, the whole train then got off. Whether it wanted to or not. Like someone stamping on a full tube of toothpaste, the entire contents of every carriage were emptied onto the platform in a big splurge. Even if you wanted to stay on the train you were out, before attempting to remount after the human wave had passed.

Carried along with the crowd, we soon found ourselves in a bar. Not our choice you understand, we were just propelled along by the swoosh. Well, that's the defence I am sticking to. Anyway, we did our best to mingle in with our new surroundings and promptly joined in with the general commotion. People were singing, being loud, being boisterous.

All whilst having a good time. They were also drinking a whole load more than I have become accustomed to seeing when visiting bars in the United States.

This was nothing like the build-up to a game in Miami and in many ways reminded me of the atmosphere around some of the big inner city football grounds in England like Newcastle, Everton or Liverpool. Or the pubs around Twickenham or Cardiff prior to a big rugby game. Lifelong new friends were made, and everybody was having a great time. Well, until the next morning, when you woke up with one of those almighty "Just let me die – I'm never drinking again" hangovers. Honestly, I'd never seen so many happy people in Boston. Either this was where they let it all out, or everybody around was from out-of-town like us. (Actually quite a few were).

I can also share that it was in this bar that I was cured of one of my little foibles. Although it's a little embarrassing to admit, I had previously been a bit picky about using public conveniences for certain kinds of ablution. Fine for a number one, as we say in England, but not a number two.

Some might think this a little strange I know, but some will also relate to where I'm coming from. Anyway, each of us has our own little idiosyncrasies – this was one of mine. Until that night. Because suddenly in the midst of all the merriment I knew I had a calling to go that could not be ignored. Not unless I wanted to ruin the evening and really embarrass myself in the process.

Whether I'd eaten something dodgy at lunchtime or caught a bug from someone I don't know, but what I did know was I desperately needed to go, and I needed to make it quick. Rudely interrupting one of our companions in the middle of one of their stories with a rather direct, "Will you please excuse me for a moment," I walked – virtually skipped – as quickly as I dignifiedly could to the facilities. Whilst clenching my posterior as tightly as I imagine a drug mule does on entering a customs checkpoint.

I positively burst through the door to the gents to be confronted by several urinals, but – can you believe this – only one cubicle. Thank heavens it was empty and touchdown was achieved by the lunar landing module not a moment too soon. I use a space rocket analogy here, because literally one second later we had liftoff, and it was lucky I wasn't propelled into orbit, such were the forces at the other end. Fortunately, the facilities were those which provided handlebars at the side of the toilet to hold on to. Otherwise, I might have made a head shaped dent in the ceiling.

They say that a lot of visitors to India experience the dreaded phenomenon known as Delhi Belly. All I can say is if this is also a regular occurrence for visitors to Boston, as well as the helpful handrails, I suggest they consider fitting seat belts to their toilets as well.

And I'm not even going to talk about the smell that enveloped the surrounding area. Other than to say it was worse – way worse – than even the most vivid imaginations could envisage. Perhaps most embarrassingly (as if this hadn't been enough) was the chorus of comments I could hear coming from the other side of my cubicle's wall, at most three or four feet away.

The worst were usually when someone new came in through the door, when you would routinely here "Oh Gohhhd!" or perhaps, "What the hellllll!" In all cases, the last word always being horrifically elongated. Until it flowed into a gut wrenching choke as the stench and horror of what they would have to endure for the next couple of minutes hit them.

Other encouraging phrases included the "Just what the helllll is in there?", "Pity the poor guy who's got to go in there next," through to downright fits of uncontrolled laughter.

This was bad enough whilst I was in full flow, so to speak, but apart from having bigger things to worry about, at least I was behind a cubicle. You can only imagine how embarrassing the walk of shame was when I had to leave. After I had cleaned up, I tried to wait around for a gap in the traffic, as it were, but the bar was packed. It was clear that no opportunity to make a break for it would be forthcoming, so I had no alternative, but to make the best of it.

I considered opening my cubicle door, sticking my chest out and leaving with my held head high. But I decided this was nothing to be proud about, and instead went for the head down, shoulders bowed, dog that has been naughty stoop and tried to slink out. It might have worked too, were it not for the reception committee that had stationed itself outside the toilets, curiously awaiting to see the beast that had wrought so much havoc. At a sufficiently safe distance, I might add.

As I snuck my head out of the restroom door, I was greeted with an All-American round of applause and whooping ovation. To be honest, I don't know why they didn't just be done with it and give me a full guard of honour. Mercifully at least with it being just a regular bar, I wasn't the subject of the crowd cam they use inside ball parks to beam onto the stadium's giant video screens anyone who they think might brighten up someone's day.

Anyway, my little affliction now cured – once you've been through that you can pretty much go through anything in a public place – I decided that discretion was the better part of valour; and that whatever dignity I still had might be better preserved were we to leave for the game. Now.

Not sure entirely how, after all those beers, but we made it to the ballpark and even found our way to the right seats. First time as well, thank you. Rather than those annoying people new to a stadium, not to mention slightly tipsy, who proceed to walk up and down each aisle resembling some sort of Pacman on Mogadon. Creating wave after wave of poor souls who have to stand in turn to let them pass.

The boisterous atmosphere must also have transmitted itself to the players. Because both teams were knocking balls everywhere, with the Sox winning 10-7. Either that or it's due to Fenway Park having the smallest field in Major League Baseball.

The next day we were off to Detroit and it was a nice way to end our stay in Boston. Until that point, Boston had been good, but not amazing, in a blow your socks off way. Which is a shame, because underlying that initially unwelcoming exterior is a city that has lots of variety, and its different areas feel distinctive and charming. Not to mention its history. It's easy to get the feeling that you are somewhere truly unique. Whilst there are bits of other cities in Boston, no other city has got all the bits that Boston has.

Once you get beneath its skin, there is a lot to like, see and do. It has a real charm and a uniqueness that genuinely marks it out as different in a good way, rather than just another identikit large city anywhere else in the States or further afield for that matter.

We had done and seen a lot, but there was still so much more to do and experience. The John F. Kennedy Presidential Library; the top of the Prudential Center and its bar with the highest views of the city; the

Museum of Fine Arts, with its nearly five hundred thousand works. Oh, and of course the bleachers!

Michigan

Detroit - This Kid Rocks!

I must admit I felt a little apprehensive before we first went to Detroit. It's story as a boom and bust town and associated problems are almost legendary.

Home to Henry Ford and the famous Model T, which first rolled off the production lines in 1908, by 1910 Detroit had grown rapidly to become the ninth largest city in the United States with a population of 466,000. That was four times what it had been not thirty years previously, and a staggering two hundred fold increase from the 2,200 people who lived there in 1830. By any scale, this was a massive expansion, but it didn't stop there.

After the creation of Chrysler in 1925 and the relocation from Flint in the mid-1920s of General Motors (the world's largest motor vehicle manufacturer for much of the twentieth century), the city kept on growing at a rapid rate of knots. Combined with the continued expansion of the motor industry, Detroit's population peaked in 1950 at 1,850,000. It was America's fourth largest city at that time.

The population had increased by about 35,000 people a year. Every year for those preceding forty years. One can barely imagine the pressures placed on the local schools, health services, policing and road networks.

By the mid-1950s Ford, General Motors (GM) and Chrysler were producing almost 95% of all American cars. Indeed, almost 75% of the World's cars! Detroit, or Motown as it was affectionately known, was home to the American car industry. In fact, you could argue, Detroit was the American car industry.

However, increasing competition from foreign rivals started to put the pressure on and so began a long decline. By the late 1950s the Packard Motor company, an upmarket manufacturer that had been the first to put air conditioning in cars – a manufacturer that at the start of the decade had outsold GM's luxury marque, Cadillac – closed its flagship 3.5 million square foot factory. It had once employed over 40,000 workers and been a beacon of the American dream. It remains vacant today – the largest derelict factory in the world. Vandalised, looted and decaying, for some it epitomises Detroit's decay.*

A decade later and horrific inner-city riots in July 1967 saw over 2,000 buildings destroyed, 43 people killed and 1,189 injured over 5 days. Order was only restored once the National Guard and Army had been deployed – with tanks on the streets. Businesses and individuals flew to more desirable areas. Even that Detroit icon, Motown records, moved to Los Angeles, California.

Detroit's dependence on the Automotive industry saw things worsen still further – if you thought that possible – with the 1970s oil crisis; a period that saw the price of West Texas Crude oil rise from $20 a barrel in June 1973 to $123 a barrel by April 1980. As consumers turned away from big American gas guzzlers to smaller, more fuel-efficient models produced by European and Japanese manufacturers, Detroit's car makers continued to contract. With knock-on consequences for the myriad of sub-contractors supplying the industry. Hundreds of thousands of jobs were lost over time.

With no work, people either turned to crime or left the area. Once thriving communities were abandoned and left vacant. Scores of empty homes competed for the tumbleweed. As Bill Bryson observed as he travelled around America in his 1989 seminal work, *The Lost Continent*, by 1987 Detroit was the city with the highest murder rate in America. Somewhat presciently he also opined, "What it will become like as the

---

* The building was purchased by an overseas investor in 2013 who specialises in renovating and bringing new life to rundown areas with a historical background. They plan an ambitious mixed use development encompassing residential, retail and commercial uses in a project that could span 15 years and I sincerely hope they succeed. At the time of writing however, no tenant had yet started operating, although some site clearance has taken place.

American car industry collapses in on itself doesn't bear thinking about."

Bryson was clearly visionary, but even he might have struggled to foresee the scale of the city's demise. By 2013, the city estimated that one fifth of its housing stock, 78,000 homes, lay empty; and that approximately 60% of its 12,000 fires per year came from abandoned or blighted buildings. That's a statistic that's sadly worth reflecting on, rather than dismissing in one sentence. Twelve thousand fires per year, of which over seven thousand are coming from abandoned buildings. Little wonder that Detroit also carried the moniker of "Arson Capital of America."

The vacant buildings problem doesn't only apply to factories and houses though, but to schools, churches, theatres, train stations and all other aspects of everyday life that were once built for a much larger city. Buildings that now lie unused as the people that once frequented them are no longer there. Many of these empty and abandoned buildings have now either been reclaimed by nature or bulldozed by city authorities to deter arson and other crimes. As a result, certain bits of Detroit appear almost post-apocalyptical, as odd buildings stand, isolated amongst desolate surroundings. Especially in the areas outside its inner core.

Less jobs and less residents meant less taxes for the city authorities; taxes needed to pay for the upkeep of a city's infrastructure – roads, hospitals, public buildings and so on. As well as to pay the salaries of vital public servants such as teachers, nurses, police officers and firefighters amongst many others. And as the city made cut backs, the quality of life deteriorated still further. Meaning more people left, making the situation even worse. And so the vicious cycle continued.

If all this wasn't bad enough, the city mayor from 2002 to 2008, Kwame Kilpatrick, abused his position and weakened the city still further. In 2013, after an extensive investigation by the FBI, he was convicted (and sentenced to twenty-eight years in prison) for racketeering, extortion, mail fraud, tax violations, taking bribes and misuse of non-profit funds whilst in office. The public corruption scandal was so widespread, it saw over thirty other people also convicted. Effectively a city already on its knees had been overpaying for municipal contracts awarded in exchange for kickbacks.

With its population now below seven hundred thousand – a far cry from the glory days of almost two million, and significantly below the level needed for a break-even level of taxation revenue – the city couldn't cope. On the 18th July 2013, Detroit filed for bankruptcy.

So a city that had pioneered the world's most advanced factories and production techniques; a city that had been the first in the world to reduce work shifts to eight hours a day*, whilst doubling the usual daily pay for factory work, was on its knees. Over one in three of those that remained were below the poverty line. The city that had been the first in the world to use traffic signals, lane markings and many innovative features in traffic management, today taken for granted the world over, now had the ignominy of crumbling roads and traffic lights not operating in certain areas due to insufficient funds to maintain them.

This latter piece of information was something I learned to my surprise whilst planning our trip. Along with routine advice from locals that also suggested not stopping at traffic lights in certain areas – either because they wouldn't be working or for reasons of safety. Given we were due to be hiring a car, this was not comforting news.

I also learnt to my horror that when it came to car insurance, Detroit wasn't just the most expensive place in the United States, but virtually off the scale altogether. According to the *2020 The State of Auto Insurance* report by The Zebra, an expert firm on American insurance pricing, the average cost of motor insurance in the US was $1,548 per year...... in Detroit it was $6,208. By comparison, that is more than double the figures for New York and even that hotbed of the South, Miami. At the other end of the scale, the good people of Winston-Salem, North Carolina only had to pay $847. Less than a seventh of those poor souls in Detroit. To cap it all, those eyewateringly high premiums coupled with the challenged local economy meant almost half of all people then drove with no insurance at all. Albeit illegally.

You can now see why I was facing this visit with some measure of anxiety. Detroit was going to be interesting.

---

* As well as being great for employee relations, this was also astute. An example of Ford's relentless drive for efficiency, it meant they could now run three, eight hour shifts a day in their factory instead of the previous two, nine hour ones.

Things did not start well. Having cleared security at Logan Airport, we were greeted by a sign saying our plane was delayed. At first it didn't seem too bad with indications that it would be about a couple of hours. Not great, but not a disaster, and we went for a wander around the airport. When we returned to our gate at the appointed time, however, we were informed that it would be another couple of hours.

I asked if anyone knew what was happening, for another passenger to growl, "That's Detroit for you! Nothing ever works!" This seemed rather harsh, particularly as the airline taking us was a New York based carrier, but in reality reflected the American stereotype of the Motor City. Most Americans have a dim view of Detroit, whether or not they have been there. Usually not.

It also helps explains why whereas most places you go to you can usually buy a T-shirt with I ♡ Whatever town, such as I ♡ MCR, I ♡ NYC, I ♡ Boston, in Detroit the popular local T-shirt reads "Detroit Vs. Everybody." Others may now be copying the style, but it originated in Detroit, created by local designer Tommey Walker.

After another mooch about, we dutifully returned at the appropriate time (now four hours late) only to be told, yet again, that it would be another two hours. Apparently the plane was still en route and hadn't even arrived yet. Wearily, we set off for yet another potter. God job, Boston has a great airport inside – big, clean, bright, with lots of seating areas (most of which helpfully have free electric sockets and USB charging points), and many shops and eating facilities. Rather typifying the way the day was heading though, the first restaurant we chose – Wahlburgers, a rather smart looking burger joint, with a decent-looking menu and a fair amount of TV's to watch some sport and pass the time – was out of Sam Adams's Boston lager. Can you believe that? Apart from me moaning about how the day was sliding, how can a flagship restaurant in Boston's airport run out of the local beer? Sod, "That's Detroit for you," what about, "That's Boston for you."? But it probably doesn't have the same cachet. Anyway, we made do as they say, before returning yet again to our gate.

The good news was the plane had arrived. The less than good news was there didn't seem much activity. By this stage, with all the comings and goings during the day – allied to the fact that we were that day's most delayed plane – you started recognising people and before long we were chatting to those around us. Whether it's because we were all in the same boat, or whether it's because most people were from Detroit and the Midwest I don't know, but what I do know was that all around were pretty regular folk and pretty friendly.

It even turned out that the guy next to us had actually studied at one of Manchester's Universities, just up the road from where we were from. They do say it is a small world. It also transpired he'd been to Boston for a job interview which, in keeping with everyone else's day on that flight, he thought could have gone better. He was speculating whether it would have been quicker to drive the eight hundred miles home rather than fly when the captain appeared, to give us an update on proceedings. He explained the plane had been delayed arriving into Logan because of engine difficulties which had meant they needed to fly a little slower, but they were now working on the engine and hoped to have it fixed soon.

This was something that we hadn't expected. Not the nature of the fault per se, which would mean a further delay, but more the detailed nature of his speech. In England, for a start, we would never have seen the real pilot. (They don't mix with the hoi polloi you know, instead some poor assistant would have been sent out to do their bidding). Secondly, we would only have been told it was due to, technical difficulties. Best not to worry our pretty little heads sort of thing. But of course in America, the Customer is King, allied to which people seem to want to know everything in an inordinate amount of graphic detail. Something you would attest to if you watched any of the myriad of adverts on TV for healthcare products.

I'm not sure which is the better option. On the one hand, you always think honesty is the best policy; on the other when people aren't subject matter experts and aren't in a position to know what the best course of action is, why complicate matters? It can sometimes have unintended consequences. Which it did here.

Because no sooner than the poor pilot (who after all wasn't responsible for the engine problems, just for flying the plane and getting us there safely) had uttered his last word, all manner of people started jumping up and down. And as you can imagine, they weren't best pleased. Comments ranged from the predictable, "That's a disgrace," or, "So, when are *you* going to get us home?" to the rather more forceful,

"That plane is not safe, I'm not getting on it and you can't make me." And believe me, when a Detroiter gets mad, you want to listen. This is also probably why English pilots, who tend to be somewhat more reserved, choose not to engage with us mere mortals.

Whether it was the force of the last suggestion, or whether it was because our plane was well and truly shot I don't know, but what I do know is after what seemed like another interminable wait, we were told that they had decided we would be travelling on another plane after all. Hooray! Just as soon as it got here. Noooo! We were then treated to regular updates on its progress from Buffalo, or wherever the blessed thing was coming from.

As the expectant crowd started to lose the will to live, there were innumerable wise cracks, mostly concerning the state of the replacement plane, which helped pass the time. In England some people call this Gallows Humour (which Mr. Google defines as grim or ironic humour in a desperate or hopeless situation). But, given what Detroiters have had to endure over the last 60 years or so, and still have to put up with, to me it seemed more like Blitz Spirit. (Or according to Mr. Google stoicism and determination in a difficult situation, especially as displayed by a group of people). I was warming to these guys.

Eventually our plane arrived and we finally landed at Detroit's Metropolitan Wayne County Airport. At three in the morning. Our hotel provided a free bus transfer from the airport, but given it was the middle of the night and, apart from our flight there was hardly a soul around, it was obvious we would have to call the hotel and further wait about. Hardly an enticing prospect. When suddenly, our guardian angel appeared, in the form of the guy we had been talking to all those hours previously, the guy who had studied at Manchester.

"Do you guys want a lift to your hotel?" he asked us.

"Are you sure it's not too much trouble?" we replied, trying not to appear too forward or enthusiastic. In reality, we would have bitten his hand off.

"Sure, it's no problem," he said. "You guys will be waiting ages, it's just a few moments for me." Honestly, I could have hugged him.

As we walked to his car he said, "Look I realise you hardly know me, but you don't have to worry, I'm just a regular family guy. There is one small thing though, my car is slightly messy. Please don't think badly of me, it is just a regular family guy's car, but I might just need to spend a couple of moments moving some stuff around."

His car was one of those people carrier type things, like an old Ford Galaxy sort of thing. But being honest here, I am not sure I can adequately describe the scene that then greeted us when he opened the boot and slid back the middle side door.

Having had four children ourselves, not to mention a Great Dane dog, I am used to driving a heap of a car. Mine was forever stuffed with all kinds of rubbish such as boiled sweets, always helpfully melted into arm rests or cup holders; mouldy food, which may or may not have once been banana skins, hamburgers or God knows what else – (usually hard to tell and often found wedged between the back seat and boot after a thorough rummaging about to locate the source of the increasingly pungent smell); residues of sticky drinks, again all helpfully spilled over the seats and absorbed in; along with a myriad of other crap.

This was something else though. It was like he'd asked his wife, or more likely his kids, to take the rubbish out, and instead of going to the dumpster, they'd gone to his car and up-ended the contents of the garbage inside that instead. Repeatedly.

It was piled high with all sorts of trash, tools and other bits and pieces from everyday life. Honestly, you couldn't even see a bit of seat cloth, or boot, or even pretty much floor. Whether, and I can relate to this, he was the kind of guy who never threw anything out, because when you haven't had much, you never want to waste anything. (You never know when it might come in handy sort of thing). Or whether the kids had done this as some kind of joke and he hadn't had time to clean it up before he left for his interview, I don't know. What I do know is, he was still one hell of a guy taking time out at three o'clock in the morning to make sure that two people he didn't know – two foreigners in his land – could get back to their hotel safely and as quickly as possible. For which I am grateful.

I helped clear a bit of seat and rummage around until we found his car park exit ticket and then we were off, only to get the icing on the cake of a very long day. We got to the exit barrier and he presented his ticket, which was in order, to the attendant. Unfortunately, what was not in order was the car park's computer system.

Believe it or not, it was down for maintenance or a system update or something. (I suppose 3 a.m. is as good a time as any to do these things, particularly with no flights scheduled for that time). What it meant though, was they couldn't let us out. Talk about defeat from the jaws of victory. As they say, "That's Detroit!"

"Could you not just let us out anyway?" he asked.

"I'm sorry sir, I can't do that," said the lady in reply. Well, at least she was polite.

"Well, I parked here about twenty-two hours ago," he said. "That's about ten dollars. Can I not just pay you that and go, and then you can process the ticket when the system comes back up?" he tried again.

"I'm really sorry sir, but I just can't do that."

Grrr. Computer says no. Still she was from the Midwest, which meant she remained polite, and to be fair genuinely sympathetic. Although at 3 a.m. that didn't seem to be much of a consolation.

Later that morning, after eventually getting some sleep in, we caught the hotel bus back to the airport so we could pick up the hire car. We piled into the Alamo and I was struck, by not only how friendly the people were, but at the lack of any upsell.

In Europe the big rental companies quote low rates online and then when you're at the pick-up desk, point out to you that although you are insured, you have an excess of €1,000 which they will have to reserve on your card. Or you could of course purchase their excess waiver insurance at a very reasonable price. Well, reasonable in their eyes.

You also know that unless you check the car with the voracity of a police forensic scientist (and take copious amounts of pictures as evidence), they will claim that any slight scratch when you return the vehicle was your fault. Even if it was already there. Then stiff you for hundreds of euros worth of damage. Whether or not they actually get the work undertaken. Who would ever know after all? Unless of course you opt for their generously priced insurance excess waiver policy. Such are the economics of pricing too low in the first place and that business environment I suppose.

To a certain extent, the same also happens in Florida where, as in Europe, not content with selling you expensive reasonably priced excess insurance products, they will also do everything they can to sell you anything. Whether that's extra fuel options, SatNav upgrades (even though most of the cars have them anyway and you will probably still get one if you politely decline the option); child seats – "I have no children with me, thank you"; toll passes, personalised coffee cups, a turndown service, you name it. Actually, I made the last two up, but you get the idea. Although that said, there is probably a sales department working on those as we speak.

But here, in the Detroit Alamo, there was none of that. In fact, they were so friendly, with such a lack of upsell, that I started to worry.

"So I don't need any more insurance?"

"No, you're fine sir."

"So I don't have to worry about an excess if, God forbid, something happens?"

"No sir, everything's fine."

"So, there's nothing else I could possibly need, or should possibly have?"

"No sir, everything's good."

Whilst great, this was also disconcerting.

The lady serving us then asked for my driving licence and on giving it back to me wished me a happy birthday. Bloody hell, she was right. It was my birthday. With the excitement of last night we were both so tired and, preoccupied with getting the car, we had temporarily forgotten. She'd seen it when looking at my driver's licence. It was a thoughtful, nice touch.

We strolled outside to the lot to pick up our car and asked the guy out there which one was ours, when with a big sweep of his hand he said,

"It's your birthday. Take whichever one you want."

"What, any one?"

"Sure. It's your birthday."

"So, we can have any car? Our reservation says we can only have a standard class, like a Buick Verano, Toyota Prius or similar."

"No problem. Today is your birthday. You can take whichever car you want. Go on. Why don't you go and have that big Chevy over there? Whatever you want."

I was dumbfounded. Whether it was because he clearly had a lot of cars and not many customers and so could be flexible, or whether it was because the lady on the desk had radioed ahead to him, what was becoming plain was how different Detroit was from Boston.

You then have to be careful in these situations, or I do anyway. Because suddenly faced with a whole car park of choice, it's easy to lose hours as you wander around trying to pick the very best one. Fortunately, I had Mrs. Stanson with me to ensure no such silliness would occur. We still spent a bit of time wandering around though, because with my suspicious European head on I tried to find a car without any nicks or bumps on. This was more of a challenge than you might think. In fact, in Detroit, it was impossible. In the end I settled for a compromise and went for the nicest car possible with the fewest scuffs and scratches. We then drove to the exit gate, where a lady completed our paperwork in quick sticks time and lifted the exit barrier.

"Excuse me ma'am," I said, as I was now concerned the paperwork had been processed far too quickly and something was still going to bite me on the bum when I gave the car back. "Did you make a note of all the scratches on the car?"

"Which scratches?" she asked, "Can you show me?"

I then pointed out a few small scrapes and scuffs, that although relatively minor, would have been sure to cause a major incident back in Europe. Bless her, she then let out a deep, warm chuckle, and holding her hands apart, like the fisherman who claimed the one that got away was "like this" exclaimed,

"Honey, those ain't scratches!...... In Detroit it don't count unless it's THIS BIG!" *

* Oh and when we gave the car back, nothing bit us on the bum either.

The Clothes don't fit

When you get into the centre of Detroit, it's unlike any other city you have ever been to. The closest approximation might be one of Europe's great cities circa 1950. Long enough after the Second World War to have cleared the bomb damage and raze most of the blighted buildings, but not so long after as to have rebuilt on the vacant lots. Even that isn't truly representative because Detroit's heyday was in the first half of the twentieth century, whilst Europe's cities are much older and their buildings reflect different architectural styles and earlier eras. But the similarity in the gaps between surviving buildings is very apparent.

Everywhere you look around there are spectres from Detroit's grand past, with buildings that would put many modern day cities to shame. It's just that there are huge amounts of space between them. Not as in grand plazas and avenues, but emptiness in the form of vacant plots of land.

Invariably, the lots are rectangular or square shaped parcels of land and it's obvious they were once something. Some have been turned over for surface car parking; for some, nature has crept back covering them in grasses, weeds and the odd tree. Others, sadly, seem to have become convenient places to fly tip, although those tend to be further away from the city centre. The effect is rather like standing in an urban prairie – it's just that skyscrapers and magnificent art deco buildings dot the landscape, instead of grain silos and barns. Of course, buildings on a real prairie would be even further apart, but this isn't like most cities where the scarcity of land means every plot has to work hard and is put to valuable use. No, not in Detroit.

The other thing you realise, but only after a while, is that there is nowhere near the same number of people you expect to see when you are in a major city. And then you remember that its population is almost two-thirds lower than it once was. Detroit's physical size of 139 square miles means you can fit the whole of San Francisco, Boston and

Manhattan in with room to spare. Its population, though, is less than seven hundred thousand, compared to their combined total of more than three million. And when there is a third of the people there once was, there is less demand for shops, offices, factories, houses, schools, hospitals, churches and so on. So vacant lots, following the demolition of whichever building was previously there, stay vacant. It's an odd sensation walking around.

This is compounded by the city's underground heating system, which sees plumes of steam rising from the bowels of the earth. Streets take on the appearance of something out of Gotham City.

Nearly forty miles of subterranean pipes carry super-heated steam to provide heating to downtown commercial customers in more than a hundred buildings. Essentially, it's like a giant version of a home central heating system, serving the inner core of the city. But if it has rained and cold water comes into contact with the hot pipes, or if there is a leak somewhere, then steam rises to street level through drain covers – or any gap – that might present a vent. That is no different to New York or other major cities which also have such systems, except Detroit's was installed over a hundred years ago and used to serve many times more buildings. It means the system leaks more than others, and as you walk around with plumes of steam rising as you pass another vacant lot, it all starts to feel a bit eerie.

It's a shame, because many of the buildings that have survived are spectacular, reflecting the days when Detroit was one of the richest cities in the world. The Guardian Building is known as the Cathedral of Finance, a nod to its initial owners and its impact once inside. When it opened in 1929, it was the world's tallest masonry structure, but unlike most art deco buildings of that time, its steel frame was covered mostly by bricks, rather than granite or limestone. A unique brown, orangey type of colour was even mixed for its 1.8 million bricks. In the flesh, it is about as unappealing as it sounds. In fact, with its harsh face and blocky rectangular shape, it is reminiscent of a lot of Soviet or East European government blocks.

To be fair, that is from a distance. As you approach the building, you can see its base is finished in a more fetching granite, on which sit twenty foot high art deco carvings. Step inside though and you enter a different world, as well as a cavernous one hundred and fifty feet long lobby. With its ceiling three stories above ground level, I challenge you not to be impressed.

The ceiling is arched in a shape similar to those in a real cathedral, whilst being finished in a multi-coloured mosaic reminiscent of Aztec designs. The supporting columns are travertine marble, topped with ziggurats edged in solid gold leaf. If this weren't enough, Numidian marble, not quarried anywhere in the world at that time, was used solely because of its unusual colour. It was so rare that a North African mine, closed for thirty years, had to be reopened especially. (And even then only long enough to extract the sufficient marble required for the building). You start to appreciate how rich Detroit once was.

As you pass into what was the main banking hall, again you find the cathedral-like high curved arch ceiling and Numidian marble floor. It is so big that bank clerks were once stationed at eighty counters within. They flanked a floor to ceiling mural painted by Ezra Winter, depicting the state of Michigan and a native American princess holding horns of plenty. A staggering five stories high, it is the first thing customers will have seen. It is spectacular.

Times may have changed and the bank clerks have today been replaced by small retail units, but the mural endures. A symbol of prosperity, security and industry, she still surveys all who enter. She was designed to awe and impress. She still does. It is no surprise that the Guardian Building is now a National Historic Landmark.

Leave the Guardian Building and within five to ten minutes walking you will pass innumerable grand buildings from the first half of the twentieth century.

Buildings such as the Beaux-Arts styled Old Wayne County Building – its lower floors encased in granite; its upper in contrasting sandstone. Complete with Corinthian columns and a 247 foot high central tower guarded by copper statues of Roman goddesses in horse-pulled chariots, it is as grand as you would expect from what was formerly the county seat of government and Court of Justice. Or the art deco Penobscot Building; forty-seven stories of limestone and granite which, when opened in 1928, was the eighth tallest building in the world and fourth tallest in the United States. Or the thirty-three story Book Cadillac Hotel, which in 1924 was the world's tallest hotel. And so it goes on. Detroit is a veritable cornucopia of architectural treasures.

Nor are all the grand buildings old. By the waterfront, The GM Renaissance Center was built in 1977, as a city within a city. When finished, it also housed the tallest hotel in the world at the time. Although built over forty years ago, you could imagine it was only completed recently, so modern is the mirrored glass cladding the buildings and the spherical shape of the tallest centre tower.

And it's massive. Seven interconnecting skyscrapers, the tallest 750 feet high, encompass a staggering five and a half million square feet of offices, restaurants, cafes and shops. That's over twice the size of Manchester's Trafford Centre, one of the UK's biggest shopping malls.

Its size and circular design mean it is easy to get lost, however. Something, we could certainly attest to. Initially, as we passed the same units and got that feeling of déjà vu, I put it down to our age. At the third pass, I started worrying about early onset Alzheimer's. Luckily, by the fourth I had worked out it was because we were walking around in bloody circles. It is so confusing, they even have an app to help you navigate round. Unfortunately in our case, this also took some working out as we hadn't realised the sensor on my phone was out by ninety degrees which meant the app kept thinking we were going north, when really it was east. As you can imagine, this didn't help matters.

In the end we aimed for the one structure we couldn't miss, its 103 feet tall Wintergarden, and escaped that way. That brought us out onto the riverfront and its views across to Canada. On a fine day, it makes for a lovely stroll. In the interests of time, we decided not to push onto Belle Isle, Detroit's answer to Central Park and the country's largest city owned park. Although its aquarium (America's first), conservatory (the oldest continually running in the US) and half mile swimming beach were tempting, we headed for the Fisher Building instead. Detroit's greatest construction from the 1920s, it is considered the finest work of Albert Kahn, America's preeminent architect of his time.

It isn't all living in the past though, and there is a lot of new investment now going into the city. As we walked up Woodward Avenue, we saw both sides of modern day Detroit – the vacant lots with ghosts of glories past, alongside the redevelopment of the comeback kid.

Near the downtown end of Woodward Avenue, at the corner of Gratiot Street, once stood the famous Hudson's department store. At four hundred and ten feet high, with twenty-five stories, it was the tallest department store in the world. It had over two million square feet of space (approximately 30-35 football fields) – only the world's largest department store, Macy's in New York, was larger. It was so grand, that it had a world record 705 fitting rooms; three electrical generators (enough to power a city of 20,000 people); and the biggest American flag in the world. When the stars and stripes were unfurled on important occasions, it took a team of fifty-five men to handle the seven storey tall, 3,700 square foot flag. They needed a mile and a half of rope.

But in January 1983, following the downturn in Detroit's economy, Hudson's closed. Sadly, despite ideas to re-purpose it, the building was demolished on October 24, 1998. The plot lay empty for over twenty years – until recently. In a sign of Detroit's regeneration, the site was acquired with plans for an ambitious $900 million mixed use development of shops, offices, apartments, hotel and events space.

Continuing up Woodward, we walked past the Fox Theater. With over 5,000 seats, it is the largest surviving movie palace of the 1920s and still one of the largest theatres in the United States. From the outside it doesn't look much, it's bland and nondescript. Step inside and try to prevent your jaw from dropping though.

You enter an eighty-seven foot deep, six floor high entrance lobby, with striking red columns that support an intricately carved, gold-coloured ceiling. Inside the main theatre is a rare Moller organ. Step in there and you are nearly overwhelmed with the colours and opulence in front of you.

Deep red seats complement the golden ceiling – a ceiling with a royal blue skylight from which hangs a thirteen foot diameter chandelier, weighing 910kg and containing 1,200 pieces of glass. Everywhere – every nook and cranny; every available surface – is adorned with some form of decoration, be it a statue, bezel, fresco or just more ornate carving. In the way that I described a bustling city not letting any spare piece of land go to waste, so it is in the Fox Theater. It's exhausting to look at. It's also stunning. You can imagine what it was like to live in the gilded age.

We passed Little Caesar's Arena next door, home to Detroit's NHL team, the Red Wings; its NBA team, the Detroit Pistons; and a venue for concerts. Opened in September 2017 at a cost of $863m, it would take a brave person to bet the good times aren't coming back.

As we continued away from downtown, we passed more vacant lots, but also more signs of Detroit's revival. This time in the guise of new premium priced condominiums along with a new Wholefoods store. Wholefoods, the bricks and mortar grocery chain now owned by Amazon, is an upmarket version of Britain's Waitrose. It's like a retail chain version of Harrods Food Hall. Shopping in there is a sensation for all the senses, if not the wallet. It feels akin to going out for dinner. Similar to Waitrose, you also tend to encounter it in the more well-to-do areas. Clearly Wholefoods believes the comeback kid will soon be home.

Eventually we arrived at the Detroit Institute of Arts (DIA). Set back from the road, elevated, it is a grand building for a grand art museum. Clad in white marble, it could almost be a piece of sculpture in its own right. Fashioned, in the Beaux-Arts style, it opened in 1927 and encompasses some 65,000 pieces of art. Whilst it may not be as extensive, or at the same level, as the Metropolitan Museum of Art in New York or the Smithsonian art museums in Washington, it is still ranked in the top six art collections in the United States. It could grace any leading world city.

Walk through its thirty feet high entrance arches and you're almost wafted to its star piece, Detroit Industry Murals by Diego Rivera; the artist later dismissed from his commission in the Rockefeller Center. The murals are in an internal courtyard, again in white marble, and line all four of its walls.

Set across twenty-seven panels, these are enormous works of art. Although you can look at them as a whole, they are also pictures within pictures. Little sub-scenes, each with their own meaning, that together form a larger picture and message. The murals portray man's progress through industry, but whilst nodding to the ingenuity of what mankind could create through complex factory production lines, they focus heavily on the negative consequences as well. Working in these factories is depicted as akin to something from hell. As is the destructive impact on the environment from plundering nature's valuable resources, whilst belching out vast quantities of unpleasant pollution.

Rivera's Marxist beliefs illuminate the work repeatedly. He portrays workers as long suffering, downtrodden heroes, toiling away, whilst depicting managers and supervisors as shifty, weasel types. Sneering and scowling as they subjugate the masses and profit from their labour. Not recognising that those portrayed negatively may have risked their wealth to create the enterprise which provides work for so many, or that they might feel a personal responsibility for the welfare of their employees. Which is an interesting strategy, particularly when the guy paying your commission is none other than Edsel Ford himself. And you decide to paint him in as one of the bosses.

What do they say about not biting the hand that feeds? Perhaps it was being allowed to paint his political views into the Detroit Murals that emboldened him in his work at the Rockefeller Center?

To say the work was controversial is an understatement. Decried by the clergy as blasphemous for the coded messages and figures painted, there were strong calls for it to be destroyed in the McCarthy era. It survived only after the Institute, (one wonders whether as part of an agreement), posted a sign stating, "Rivera's politics and his publicity seeking are detestable. But let's get the record straight on what he did here. He came from Mexico to Detroit, thought our mass production industries and our technology wonderful and very exciting, [and] painted them as one of the great achievements of the twentieth century."

The DIA lends you an iPad and audio guide to the murals, and it's so detailed that you could spend an entire afternoon just looking at and understanding those. As the DIA was the first art museum in America to acquire a genuine Van Gogh and has originals by Canaletto, William Hogarth and Thomas Gainsborough, and much other wonderful art, that would be a waste though. Of course, as seems almost de rigueur, there is modern art as well, which here looked like it had been painted by a trained chimpanzee. However, we had both learned from our debacle in the MOMA to better control ourselves and so moved swiftly through this section to avoid any complications.

That said, we still managed to get our money's worth in this area. This time by indulging in a bit of people watching. There was a late twenty something couple, clearly on a first date, and the woman kept asking the guy what he thought of such and such a piece. Whether she was teasing him, or testing him out, I don't know, but as she probed, you could feel his pain – the contorted expression repeatedly wrought across his face revealing his inner dilemmas,

"Should I be honest here? This is terrible. Or might she really like it?"

"She seems enthusiastic about this one. Surely not? Maybe she is just tricking me? This could be a trap."

"How did I get myself into this?"

"How do I get myself out of this?"

Boy, did you feel for the bloke. But his tormentor – sorry, date – wasn't letting up, turning the screw time and time again, as they approached yet another work where it looked like someone had accidentally knocked a bucket over whilst doing a spot of decorating. It made for compulsive viewing. Maybe we need to reappraise these parts of art museums in future.

After passing more vacant lots, we completed our tour of Woodward Avenue and Midtown by turning left onto Grand Boulevard and wandering up to Cadillac Place. When opened in 1920, Cadillac Place was the world's second largest office building. It is imposing enough, but pales alongside the Fisher Building across the road. Known as Detroit's largest art object, the Fisher was built on a scale of luxury that is hard to fathom today.

Within the building, there are 430 tonnes of bronze and forty different types of marble. Indeed, it is the largest marble clad building in the world with over 300,000 square feet of exterior marble. And they say the Taj Mahal is impressive. Its builders, the Fisher brothers, intended to build something that everyone could visit, admire and be proud of. Accordingly, they specified that 25% of the cost should be allowed for art.

It was why the building was built with four entrances, facing north, east, south and west. So it could welcome citizens from whichever direction they came. It's why no two of the sixty cherubs that grace its halls are identical. It's why intricate reliefs and etchings grace its 641 bronze elevator doors. Elevators designed to be both the fastest in the world at the time and automatically stop at the appointed floor. Indeed, the papers of the day described them as "a thrill ride for Detroit" as you whisked up twenty-nine stories at eight hundred feet per minute. It might not match today's speeds at The World Observatory, but imagine its impact in an age when elevators still needed an operator to align internal and external doors before passengers could alight.

The ornate frescos that adorn the ceilings in the main foyer were hand washed in buttermilk to prevent them from fading with time. Before being adorned in gold leaf. Gold leaf was even used on the building's roof tiles, leading to it being referred to as the Golden Tower.

Similar to the Fisher Building, the ceilings are also barrel vaulted, like naves in old cathedrals. With its frescos, murals and fifty feet high curved ceilings, the effect is again similar to entering a real place of worship. But the Fishers weren't fools, and, as well as building something special, they wanted it to pay its way and allocated space for shopping, offices and leisure. Hence, like the Guardian Building, the Fisher was also referred to in ecclesiastical terms, in this case as the Cathedral of Commerce. Again, it is easy to see why.

Sadly, the golden roof was lost during the Second World War. (It was covered with asphalt, over concerns its gleam might help enemy bombing raids, and in the process ruined). Fortunately, many of the building's other original features remain and, with five hundred thousand dollars spent restoring the frescos in the last three years alone, it's on its way to being as good as ever.

It seems ironic now, but when built, the Fisher brothers had wanted it constructed in downtown Detroit, but couldn't find enough suitable vacant land. So they had it built two miles away in what is now Midtown. How times change. As they did when the Wall Street crash occurred within a year of the building's opening. An event which prevented completion of the plans for it to be the largest office building in the world with two more towers. Nevertheless, a lot of what they had also intended to be a city within a city was still created, with underground walkways linking it with the Albert Khan Building and also the former General Motors Building, Cadillac Place, on the other side of Grand Boulevard.

As well as being wowed by the amount of opulence and beauty whilst you tour the building, one other thing strikes you – its resemblance to the Rockefeller Center in New York. Not in the building's shape, but with respect to its grandeur, art deco inspired architecture, vast quantities of adorning artwork and the concept of a city within a city linked by underground passages. Even the ornate reliefs on the elevator doors. But perhaps that is not surprising. Because the Fisher Building preceded the Rockefeller Center. Once upon a time, Detroit led the way in certain areas and New York followed. How times change indeed.

We didn't know what to think as we left the Fisher Building; there were so many competing emotions. The beauty and grandeur of what we had just seen. The poignancy in Detroit's fall from being one of the world's richest cities to its present, comparatively sorry state, rammed home. The irony that, had this been New York, the tour we had just undertaken would have been trumpeted from the rooftops as a major tourist attraction and we would have had to battle with hordes of onlookers on our way round. As it was, we'd had a free tour with a handful of others, despite it being available to anyone, courtesy of Pure Detroit, an organisation devoted to helping Detroit develop. It was uplifting, yet tinged with sadness at the same time.

By the end we needed some soul food, so what better way than sampling local specialities. We hopped on the Q-line, Detroit's fledgling tram system (it broadly only runs along Woodward Avenue connecting Midtown with downtown), and alighted at a restaurant known for Detroit's deep dish square pizzas. Whilst NYC is famous for pizza full stop and Chicago is renowned for the deep pan version, prior to coming to Detroit we'd never heard about their claim to be unique in creating the deep dish, square pan iteration. All I can say is it was different again – more a soft bread, almost focaccia style base, covered with a deeper topping. It was almost like a pizza casserole. But it was very good and definitely a go to when in that part of the world.

Uplifted and re-energised, we made our way back to our hotel, via the Q-line again and via a quirky music bar that in many ways summed up the essence of Detroit. To start with it only opens Thursdays, Fridays and Saturdays, despite it being in the heart of downtown. Maybe Detroit's lack of people means it doesn't pay to open other nights. I have seen that before, but in provincial towns to the north of Manchester, not one of America's larger cities.

Secondly, I know Detroit may have once led and New York followed and that those positions have reversed, but I'm not sure Detroiters have yet fully cottoned onto the concept of a speakeasy. As you know, in New York you have to work hard to find those elusive, hidden, hipster bars. Here they actually go as far as putting the word *speakeasy* in their sign above the front door. Still, I guess if you can't even get enough customers to open for over half of the week, it would be a hell of a ballsy marketing strategy to disguise matters even further.

That said, the welcoming Midwest charm was in full flow as we entered – on the door they asked if we would like to put on a fake moustache. Strangely enough, I don't carry too many of these around with me, but no matter as they kindly supplied us both with a pair.

At first I thought this moustache business was some form of theming from the bar where in line with the speakeasy concept we had to attempt to disguise ourselves, but it turned out it was a tribute to the resident band's guitarist whose birthday it was that day. Actually, as a stunt it worked quite well and it gave everyone in the bar a kind of camaraderie. But maybe that was just the beer.

It must have been in my case, as I decided I would try and schmooze Alison like I was Clark Gable. Sadly, she decided my efforts were more like Charlie Chaplin. It was clearly going to be a long night for me. Still it might have been worse – given my height at least no one mistook me for that despicable little German whose name I will not even grace these pages with.

A little slice of America

Today it was off to the Henry Ford Museum, an extensive collection of some of the most iconic items in America's history. For various reasons that seemed to make sense after last night's drinks though, we decided to go via public transport. Even though the museum was about eight miles out in a place called Dearborn.

We started by taking Detroit's Downtown People Mover. Something as hard to find the entrance to in the morning, as it was to say its name after a couple of drinks yesterday. Certainly at the Greektown station where we needed to get on. Try as we might, we just couldn't find the entrance to the monorail system's elevated platforms. What looked like the only feasible way – an enclosed walkway leading up to the platforms from street level – was an exit only ramp. Completely flummoxed, we were looking obviously lost, which isn't great in a strange city, when approached by a down and out.

"Here we go," I thought, but was astonished at what happened next. After asking if we needed help and guessing correctly it was to do with accessing the People Mover, she explained how to get in. Then she asked for help, not in the form of money, but that we might buy her a sandwich for breakfast.

Now everyone, including the help-the-homeless type charities, always recommend not giving people on the street money. They advise that if you feel you should give something, you should buy a drink or some food. Of course most people still give money, but that is what official groups and charities say. Never in my life though, has someone ever actually asked for anything other than money.

I have been asked for spare change to go towards something, such as a meal or a bed for the night. But regardless, I have always been asked for cash. Yet here in Detroit, with its terrible reputation for crime and despair, we were being asked for help in a positive way. Now, please don't misunderstand me. I am not trying to eulogise about Detroit or its people. Like anywhere, Detroit has its share of bad'uns. I'm just saying things aren't always as they seem. Sometimes the dog doesn't deserve a bad name.

Anyway, it turned out that to enter the system we had to go through the doors of the Greektown Casino and into its foyer. Before then taking an escalator to where we could buy our tickets and access the entrance turnstiles. All without any helpful signs on the casino doors to even hint at a clue. Even Sherlock Holmes might have struggled to find it. New York's speakeasies would have been proud.

It's about as unhelpful and illogical as the Mover's official website. Which, by the way, in its not-so-handy station by station guide lists the restaurants and attractions near each station, but not how to get onto the blessed trains and platforms themselves. I know, I tried whilst still flummoxed.

But then there is a lot about Detroit's People Mover that is illogical, full stop. Like the way it only moves in one direction. Clockwise, as it turns out. It means that if you want to go to a station two or three stops in an anticlockwise route, you have to travel ten or eleven stops in a clockwise direction to get there. By and large you would be quicker walking.

Indeed, for a lot of journeys on the Mover, by the time you factor in accessing and leaving stations, waiting for trains and so on; unless you have mobility issues or the weather is poor, you would be better off walking. Which kind of defeats the purpose of a mass transit system in the first place. Consequently, it is not used anything like the extent you find in public transit systems in other cities. Which means the system loses money and so has to be subsidised by city authorities; who are strapped for cash, and so the cycle continues. (As an aside, Miami's People Mover actually executed the bright idea of having trains running in both directions).

It's a shame, because with a little more thought and planning it could be a great system. With trains every few minutes and it only taking a quarter of an hour to cover the 2.9 mile loop, it's a great way of seeing the key bits of downtown whilst getting your bearings. Especially, as its monorail track is twenty feet above street level, and so provides good views. In fact it was so good, we stayed on for a couple of loops. Tell me how many other cities offer hop on, hop off tours for 75 cents.

Up there also offers another way of seeing Detroit's fall and rise. From its elevated vantage point, you get a different sense of scale and perspective on Detroit's grand buildings and vacant lots. Suddenly Detroit looked like the old man whose suit no longer fits. But whilst, sadly, an old man can never regrow into his younger clothes, a city can renew. Detroit has a chance.

We enjoyed a second helping of the great views across the Detroit River to the city of Windsor in Canada. Along with the strange sensation of seeing a Canadian flag flying whilst standing in an American city. After alighting at Michigan station to catch a bus, we then travelled down Michigan Avenue and saw yet more reminders of the rise, fall and rebirth of Detroit.

Michigan Central Station, when opened in December 1913, was the tallest train station in the world. It now lies isolated, looted and vandalised. Arguably, it's the one site that encapsulates Detroit's story. Except for the Packard Factory, all the other buildings I've mentioned – even the site of the former Hudson's department store – still had *some* properties around them. This 230 feet tall former transit hub, however, was not so much in an urban prairie as an urban desert.

Designed by the same architects that built New York's Grand Central Terminal, it was added to the National Register for Historic Places in April 1975. As with most buildings in Detroit's heyday, everything was done on a grand scale. With marble floors, bronze chandeliers, Corinthian columns and arched ceilings sixty-five feet high, the main waiting room was reputed to have been modelled on Rome's ancient public baths. Ninety-seven feet wide and two hundred and thirty feet long, it ran the length of the building. Apparently, it *was* awesome.

Reflective of the feelings when it opened, the Detroit Free Press commented, "The grandeur of the interior is something that will be lasting, for it is of marble, brick and bronze, all of this is set off by one of the best lighting schemes ever installed in a building." Sadly, no one told the vandals who progressively gutted and wrecked the building in the years following its closure in 1988.

But in keeping with Detroit's comeback, the Ford Motor Company bought the building in 2018. They plan to convert it into their hub for Autonomous and Electric vehicle research by 2022. Along with other buildings in the area they have acquired, Ford's intention is to create a campus in the Corktown area of Detroit. Something which will generate five thousand jobs.

They say you can't turn back the hands of time, but in Detroit maybe things really are different. This time.

A community, which has seen so many tough periods and false dawns, seems to have been touched by Ford's attempts to revitalise one of their shattered icons. So much so that a kind of reverse looting is now happening. Items thought lost forever are now suddenly reappearing.

Like the large, iconic clock that once hung over the ticket booths. Returned after an anonymous caller told the construction team where they had left it. The caller told the team that they loved that clock and they loved the station and now was the right time to return it. Following Ford sharing this in a press conference, the floodgates opened and streams of items have since been returned on a no questions asked basis.

As the bus continued down Michigan Avenue towards Dearborn though, it was clear the revitalisation of downtown and midtown still needs to spread out to the more outlying areas. Some areas were so desperate that you could see that the strategy of tearing down to start again in some parts might be the only feasible alternative. Still, you have to start somewhere and that always has to be at the heart of the matter. When you throw a pebble into a lake, it's from the centre that the ripples radiate.

Like the bus we took – clean, on time and reliable. Something that, by accounts, wasn't the case when the city hit bankruptcy. Tragically those most affected then – for instance, by not being able to guarantee to get to work on time – were also those that had the least. They used buses because they couldn't afford a car. And, as we soon found out, buses are the only realistic public transport across the wider city.

We got off at Dearborn Transit Center, which is an interchange between several bus routes and an Amtrak train station. We then went inside because I had thought it provided a quick back route to the Henry Ford Museum. Whilst it might not surprise you that, as usual, I was wrong (the station did not provide a shortcut to the museum), what shocked us was the lack of trains on the arrivals and departures boards. For the whole day there would only be three trains going Westbound and only four Eastbound. As one of the Westbound departures had been at 6.51a.m., with an Eastbound one at 5.20 a.m., it meant although we were there before ten in the morning, the rest of the day would see only two more services heading East and three more West.

Nor think that this was because Dearborn might be a provincial station, the situation was similar in Detroit. Now whilst three or so services a day might be all that is needed to link Detroit with the trains' ultimate destination of Chicago, this was a route also linking Michigan's other cities. Cities that included Ann Arbor (home to the University of Michigan), Battle Creek (home to Kellogg's worldwide headquarters) and Kalamazoo.

Even accepting that America is so much physically larger than the UK; that its lower population densities, mean the economics of train travel will not be as favourable as in the UK; that the better state of their interstate system compared to our motorways, means car travel in the UK is not as appealing as in the US; the difference between America and Britain was still staggering.

By comparison, Piccadilly, the main train station in our local city of Manchester, somewhere with a lower population than Detroit (both as a city and as a metropolitan area), sees 28 million passengers per year. An equivalent of 76,000 people per day. And that is only entering or exiting the station. It doesn't include those not boarding or alighting the train there, but en route to somewhere else. And we criticise our rail system. Maybe it's a Michigan thing, because New York's Grand Central has around 70 million passengers per year, but even so. One thing is for sure though, with only half a dozen trains a day, it must be great working behind the ticket counter.

A twenty-minute walk, now in the right direction, saw us arrive at the museum. Although, we then blew the system by explaining we had walked to the museum and therefore didn't need to pay the $10 car parking charge. Something they automatically add onto the tickets and isn't possible to remove if you book online. Clearly, they weren't expecting many pedestrians. Anyway, system fixed, we then proceeded into the cavernous space that is the Museum of American Innovation part within the Henry Ford Museum.

On site there are two main museum areas. These require separate tickets or a combo ticket if you want to do both. The other, Greenfield

Village is a recreation of a typical American village, showing American life from when the country started, complete with actors going about typical daily tasks from those time periods. So you can see working farms, experience cider mills and visit schools, homes and general stores as they were in the nineteenth century.

Not only does it provide a taste of living history, but most of the buildings are also the real deal, transported from their original locations and replaced in the village setting. For instance, the original home and bike shop from Dayton, Ohio of Orville and Wilbur Wright, the founders of flight. Or one of the actual Illinois courthouses in which Abraham Lincoln first practised law. Where it wasn't possible to have the actual building itself, such as Thomas Edison's laboratory complex, they have been faithfully recreated using detailed plans from the original. Complete with replica fittings in their rightful places.

Greenfield Village sounded great too, and by all accounts is, but we had been to similar experiences in the UK, such as Beamish and Ironbridge. (Taking inspiration from Ford's concept of an outdoor working museum they also recreate life from a couple of centuries ago, albeit as it was in England). So in the interests of time, we prioritised the American Innovation part of the complex. If time allowed, we would visit Greenfield Village afterwards. We made the right choice.

The size of the American Innovation bit of the museum and the vast array and diversity of items it contains is almost mind-boggling. Whether Henry Ford was concerned that it would be easy for important items in humankind's development to be lost forever in his era who knows, but it is a testament to him that he used part of his wealth to collect for posterity all sorts of arresting and significant pieces from America's history. The collection hasn't stopped with his death though, and the museum continues to honour the sentiments behind its creation, whilst still evolving to reflect life's constant innovation, ingenuity and progress. Nor is it just about Ford – General Motors donated over $1m in 2018 alone, alongside important donations from many others. Quite simply, it is one of the best collections containing iconic, and often extremely rare, items of our times.

Appropriately we started with a display of a Model T, the invention that made the museum possible. Rather nicely, it had been separated into its constituent parts so that it was easy to see its engineering and how it was put together. We even got to try our hand at building one. We toured a Dymaxion House, a prototype from 1946 of how people would live in the future. Circular and full of sleek lines, it looks futuristic now, never mind then. It looked like a flying saucer. It never caught on.

In a section devoted to Lego models, we got to see detailed 1:200 scale recreations of today's buildings of the future, such as Dubai's Burj Khalifa, the tallest building in the world and Toronto's CN Tower, the tallest in the Western hemisphere. Although not the highest, one of the most impressive was the model of Kuala Lumpur's Petronas Twin Towers, which used over eighty-two thousand Lego bricks and took three hundred and sixty hours to build. All these were put in the shade though by a fantastic train set running around a similarly scaled model of downtown Detroit, complete with its historic buildings such as the Fisher Building, the Penobscot Building and so on. That took five man-years to build, used over a million separate Lego pieces and even went as far as including a replica of the People Mover.

Elsewhere in the museum, there were originals (or again where not possible, faithful replicas) of key aeroplanes from history. Such as a replica of the Wright brothers Flyer that flew from Kitty Hawk; a 1909 Bleriot XI, the first plane to cross the English Channel (and identical to the one that made that original crossing which resides in the Musée des Arts et Metiers in Paris); and a replica of the 1927 Spirit of St. Louis, in which Charles Lindenbergh became the first to complete a solo crossing of the Atlantic Ocean.

Of them all, the Bleriot looked the craziest. Large front wings and tiny tail fins, connected by a fuselage that was just a lattice framework of wooden squares joined by wooden poles and metal wires. There wasn't even any skin or cover on most of the fuselage. It looked nothing more than a very large dragonfly. I wouldn't have been confident going a few hundred yards in it, never mind the English Channel. I still remember thinking, "I know I have done some dumb stuff in my time, but flying in that really takes the biscuit." That and, "*If I did that*, everyone would say I had shit for brains." People were clearly made of sterner stuff in those days.

As with the planes, so too there were key trains, ships and other important machines from history, such as early steam engines and so on. As you might expect, given the museum's founder, there was a huge section on automobiles. And not solely Ford vehicles either.

So whilst there was every key Ford model, onwards from a 1901 Ford Sweepstakes (a predecessor to even the 1903 Model A), there were also priceless treasures such as a 1931 Bugatti Type 41 Royale convertible. Only six were ever made. Described as, "the ultimate automotive expression of style and luxury," it looked like the car Cruella De Vil drove in the Disney classic, *101 Dalmatians.* Indeed, many believe it actually was the inspiration for her car. Sleek, curvaceous, with a bonnet that seemed to go on forever. Beautiful.

And yes, there was even an Edsel, the car named after Ford's son. It is regarded as one of Ford's worst cars of all time – a commercial disaster that cost the company $350 million and ceased production after only 27 months. For car nuts, there was enough to keep you there for days.

Other areas were themed so that they dealt with key things by decade or tackled important issues such as race, segregation and its impact on society. Nor were some of the abhorrent incidents that occurred glossed over. It was stark, chilling and made you reflect.

The diversity of topics coupled with the sheer quantity of items was staggering. Some made you reminisce, some made you think, others you simply enjoyed.

The two exhibits that left the biggest impression with us were *the bus* that Rosa Parks sat on and *the car* in the collection of presidential vehicles. To sit in *the seat* where her rightly defiant act sparked the Montgomery Alabama bus protest, ignited the civil rights movement and became a key moment leading to the repeal of the Jim Crow laws, was sobering and humbling. To say the least.

As it was when we stood by the limousine in which President J.F. Kennedy was assassinated as he toured Dallas in November 1963. Sobering and poignant.

The museum has five presidential vehicles. These span from Teddy Roosevelt's Brougham, a two passenger horse drawn carriage (circa 1902), to a 1972 Lincoln, which remained in service until 1992 and President George H. W. Bush. The latter was used by Presidents Nixon, Ford, Carter, Reagan and ultimately Bush.

It was also the car off which John Hinckley's bullet ricocheted in 1981 hitting President Ronald Reagan and causing life threatening injuries in a failed assassination attempt. Amazingly the same car was then used for another decade afterwards. Apart from thinking what a dangerous job it is to be an American President – of the 45 US Presidents to date, 4 have actually been assassinated and a further 13 the subject of failed attempts; some repeatedly – wouldn't you think they might retire the cars after an assassination attempt? Whether or not successful? Like it was a jinxed car sort of thing?

Apparently not though, as Kennedy's car was also used for a further 14 years after he was killed by Lee Harvey Oswald. Clearly Congress likes to get its money worth out of these vehicles. As did we in our tour of the museum. We used up every moment of our allotted time in the American Innovation area and never even got close to going to Greenfield Village. Good job we didn't buy the combo ticket after all. And, to deploy correctly another overused American phrase, it was awesome.

Franken Uber Alles

For various reasons that I won't go into here – not least of which is that it's a real shaggy dog story, and frankly dear reader you deserve better – we needed to catch a taxi across town. Believe it or not, Miami had been the first time we had ever got in an Uber. And then only because Josh arranged it. But, realising that you got a nicer car for a fraction of the price, we decided to try and do it ourselves.

Now, this may sound a little odd to seasoned Uberites, but despite our previous positive experience, I was still a bit nervous. It's one thing getting in an Uber that somebody else has ordered (and will pay for, on *their* credit card, with *their* details stored in the great ubersphere), but quite another altogether to have to do it yourself. Would it even turn up? Or would I end up paying for a ride that never arrived with no knowing how I would get my cash back? Not to mention would my credit card get hacked and it take weeks to sort things out, if ever? These were some of the thoughts troubling me.

Sadly, the older you get – or at least the older I get – adapting to new technology just seems to get harder. I don't know at which point it happens, but where once your parents asked you to program the video recorder*, suddenly you're the old fogey asking the offspring to sort out the Netflix, Firestick or Alexa. Or whatever confounded contraption is the latest development.

That said, irrespective of whether it's new technology or not, I'm still not sure I can see the point of an Alexa, or "Hey Google" machine at all. It seems they are either used for pointless requests because people can't think of anything better to do. Or you would be better and quicker

---

* For the pre-cable box/pre-tv-on-demand generation, the video recorder was a device used to record programs from one of only four TV channels we had available, so that you could watch them later. You used to have to schedule your recordings in advance, which required the programming skills of a NASA computer scientist. Or at least that's what my parents thought.

yourself, doing whatever it is you want Alexa to do. In fact, I am becoming increasingly convinced that these machines will be the single biggest cause behind our modern society's escalating obesity crisis.

Apart from regularly seeing people use them to issue inane commands like "Hey Google – bark like a dog!", I often hear "Hey Google, what will the weather be like today?" To which I reply, "Hey fatso, why don't you get off your sofa and have a look out the window." Or to the "Hey Alexa, turn the heating on," how about "Hey chubby, why not get off your increasingly large backside, walk five steps across the front room and turn it on yourself." But that is probably why these days I am now considered an old gimmer.

Anyway, with that off my chest, back to my inaugural Uber. It was wonderful. Easy to use and cheap, as you probably already know. Of course it was, that's why they have been so successful and grown so spectacularly. But the best bit was our driver. He was beyond wonderful and might have spoiled us for the future because I truly believe we had the best Uber driver ever. (No one has yet beaten him – nor do I think they ever will). Oh, and need I point out, we were still in Detroit.

He was honestly the most upbeat, cheerful guy you could ever imagine meeting, with a wealth of stories. It was like being driven by John Candy from the film *Planes, Trains and Automobiles*. Rather bizarrely, he even looked like him. His build, his curly hair, his cherubic face – even down to his bigger frame, bear hugging the steering wheel.

The only disturbing bit could have been when he kept glancing back over his shoulder, as he talked to us sat in the rear. (And I kept having flashbacks to that scene in the movie when Steve Martin falls asleep in the passenger seat whilst John Candy gets distracted and inadvertently joins the highway on the wrong side of the road, before getting to play dodgem with two oncoming trucks). But in reality, it wasn't disturbing at all. One, because he wasn't smoking (unlike John Candy in that film, which is the start of his character's problems); and two, because we were just laughing too much to be worried. As an aside if you haven't seen the movie, cue up that scene on YouTube and enjoy. It is priceless film making.

Anyway, it turned out that our driver had, in his former life, been a long distance truck driver in Michigan and, based on some of the stories he told us, my had he driven through some conditions in Michigan's infamous Winters. A bit like Malcolm the Mountie though, he swore he had always made it through. "And," as he told us, "that was before global warming made things easier!"

He also told us that he had retired, but had gone back to work because his son was at college. As well as helping with his son's fees and rent, he was specifically saving to buy him a car. Despite him being at a campus university. Despite being able to walk pretty much everywhere, his son felt he *needed* a car. Such was modern day America said our driver.

Perversely, it was the same with us. I didn't get my first car until I was twenty-one, when I bought one because I needed it for my job. Even then, it was an old wreck of a thing. (A Vauxhall Chevette for those curious, which was so unreliable we knick-named it the Vauxhall Shove-it. And yes, it was painted in the same dire brown colour as, for some bizarre marketing reason, all British Vauxhall Shove-its were. Perhaps it was a subliminal way of reflecting the underlying quality of that particular make of car).

Anyway, here we were, now having to search for a car for our son, also at college in Michigan, because "Dad, I'm telling you, in America you have to have a car." The irony that Josh, the captain of his university soccer team – and believe me a very fit guy – cannot use his legs is not lost on me. Same too with his girlfriend, also an athletic student who plays centre midfield for their university women's soccer team. A position that can see her cover over six miles in a match. Yet, despite their respective houses being less than one hundred yards apart, when they go round to each other's they drive. Seriously.

All the time. Even if they're not going out afterwards and you might have the excuse that one is picking the other up along the way. Even when they are just popping round. They drive. They don't even have to cross a major road or anything. It's less than one hundred yards, on the same side of the road. Perhaps they need to save their legs for more important things like playing for the university, or maybe it's a bit like Alexa and "Hey Google," and this is just modern life that I can't fathom, because I'm a gimmer.

Given his vast knowledge of the state, we thought we would ask our driver what he knew about Frankenmuth and test out whether what we'd heard in Boston was right. Especially, as we were still struggling to believe the biggest Christmas shop in the world could really be in the middle of nowhere.

I know Michiganders might bristle at this comment, but relatively speaking Frankenmuth *is* in the middle of nowhere. It's not in New York, the most populous city in the US, and easily reached from an innumerable number of destinations worldwide. It is not in the heart of bustling California. Nor is it in Florida, holiday capital for the US and large parts of the world. It's in a rural setting, two hours' drive north of Detroit, which itself is not easily reached from outside America. Michiganders may like things that way, which is fine, but the facts are that, relatively, Frankenmuth is in the middle of nowhere.

"Ah Frankenmuth," said our driver, "It's a pretty little Bavarian town," before continuing rather matter of factly, in that understated way that's such a part of people from the Midwest. "Oh, and they've got the biggest Christmas shop in the world. It's nice. You should go there."

"Well, we were torn between there and Ann Arbor, and we've probably only got time for one of them."

"Well, Ann Arbor is nice too, it's like a college town, but you guys already said that you'd visited Harvard, I'd go for Frankenmuth."

"What's the Christmas shop like?"

"Ooh, it's amazing. It's the size of several football fields, packed full of all sorts of Christmas stuff. We go every year and spend a whole host on crap we don't need. Each time I say to my wife, 'Honey, can we give it a miss this year, our house is already full of junk,' but no, we still go. And we come back having spent two hundred bucks on even more pointless ornaments. I love it! It's great!...... But be careful, once you're there you won't be able to help yourself."

Well, that sealed the deal, because when Midwesterners start gushing about something you know it must be good.

Going to Frankenmuth is a rather strange experience. To start with, you are suddenly transported from middle America to a little outpost of Bavaria. And I mean pretty suddenly.

One minute we were running around Birch Run, the big outlet mall in central Michigan, that shares the same interstate junction as Frankenmuth. Full of the usual sports shops, suitcase stores and retail brands that populate these centres, it also had the necessary obscure cooking accessories shop. We might have been in any modern outdoor shopping district. There was even the obligatory drive-thru milkshake bar, complete with server with a drive-thru brain.

We had detoured into Birch run for a quick check over for any bargains when, seeing Super Speedy Shakes (or whatever it was called), I suddenly developed one of those insatiable cravings. As we don't have any drive-thru milkshake bars that I am aware of in the UK, I thought why not give it a whirl.

Now, this was a serious set up. They must have had about twenty stations where you could park your car and place your order. It was like going into one of those massive motorway petrol stations, only to get milkshake from an intercom rather than petrol from the pump. The Americans must love their shakes I thought, even if we were the only car there. With it being a spur of the moment call though, I wasn't sure exactly what I wanted. Something that is not a recommended strategy when you are faced with an all-encompassing operation as slick as this.

When the server asked me what I wanted, I just stammered. He tried making suggestions, but there were too many to take in. From chocolate and strawberry to wild berry and lavender with seemingly every flavour in between. I was a drowning man. I decided I needed to see a list and choose, rather than having fifty shades of shake rapid fired at me. The trouble was, there were so many options I'm not sure they could fit them onto the little board at the stations where you ordered. I guess they just assume people will know what the choices are. Perhaps they do if they're American and used to these sorts of things. Anyway, I thought sod it, I'm going inside so I can have a better look. These places always have their full menu inside.

This was clearly a departure from what was expected of me. Certainly from my server.

"Can I help you?" he asked.

"Yes, I'd like a milkshake please." To be fair, I accept that wasn't the most enlightening comment I could have made at that point.

"Well, you need to order from the order point outside."

"Yes, thank you. But I don't know what flavour I want and I was hoping to have a look in here first, decide and then order."

So far so good, and I eventually opted for a regular vanilla. (Although you might reasonably ask here why I couldn't have decided that much in the car, but that is another matter). Where things started to breakdown though was when I then made the mistake of trying to order it.

"Right, I would like a vanilla shake please."

"Well, you have to go outside and order at the order point."

"Well, now I am here, can I not just tell you that I would like a vanilla shake please?"

"No, you have to go to the order point."

"Oh … ok. And if I do that, who am I going to speak to?"

"Me."

"Ah … and where will I pick it up from?"

"Around the back here at the pick-up point."

"Ok … and who will hand me the shake?"

"I will."

It was a good job there weren't any customers, as I am not sure how he would have coped with all this multi-tasking.

"Well, why don't we save everyone a bit of hassle and I ask you for a vanilla shake, here; give you the money, now; and you hand me back the shake?"

"I can't do that. You have to go to the order point, sir and tell me your order from there."

"But I'm only going to end up speaking to you through that intercom."

"Yes, sir. You have to go to the order point to place your order."

"So you're going to make me walk back across the lot to speak to you and then make me drive around the block to pick up my shake, when we are standing three feet away from each other?"

"Yes, sir."

I swear I am not making this up here.

Had other cars been pulling up, I might have had some sympathy. No one wants to be a queue jumper after all. Well, not this side of Cuba anyway. But there weren't. There was no one around. Perhaps this was the reason. Maybe the state of Michigan had been here before and had also lost the will to live.

So I also thought sod it and decided to leave for Frankenmuth. Although on my way out I made sure to ask Mr. Braindead if there was any chance they could do the vanilla in a double custard, triple concrete version.

At that point, I'm sure I saw sparks fly and his internal computer start to overheat.

Anyway, within ten miles of the I-75 motorway, and Birch Run, we entered Frankenmuth and were instantly plunged into a world of timber-framed buildings and sharp pitched roofs. Often with little turrets or spires. There's even a glockenspiel tower with wooden figures depicting the story of the pied piper of Hamelin that pirouette around the clock each day at noon, three p.m., six p.m. and nine p.m.

An old style covered wooden bridge crosses the river that runs through the centre of town. Should you fancy an hour's river cruise, you can take the Bavarian Belle riverboat, an authentic Stern-Driven Paddlewheel riverboat. It was all idyllic. As well as Teutonic.

Even the main restaurants in town serve hearty German food. Then, if all this wasn't enough of a shock for your senses, on the edge of town there is the Christmas wonderland spanning seven acres that greets you with a seventeen foot high Santa Claus and a fifteen foot tall giant snowman. Not to mention one hundred thousand outdoor Christmas lights that light up every evening of the year. Its showroom alone covers ninety-six thousand square feet. That's almost two football fields.

It was there we headed first. When we first pulled up at Bronner's, the Christmas store, with the weather a still unseasonally warm 27°C (81°F), the last thing I could contemplate was Christmas. Hearing all the Christmas songs playing and seeing all the Christmas trees, not to mention elves, gnomes and snowmen, I just kept thinking, "What are we doing? This is naff. We should be out getting some rays, not thinking about Christmas, let alone going inside a Christmas shop." (For those who have not been to the North West of England, I'm not sure I can ever emphasise enough how sun starved it is).

After five minutes though, we were grinning like children. You couldn't help it. The happiness was just so infectious. The Christmas songs, the genuine friendliness of the elves (sorry getting carried away again, I meant store staff), the overall Christmas feeling, all just put you in a good mood and a happy place. Honestly, we went from grinch to great in five minutes.

The sheer amount of choice of, strangely enough, Christmas themed goods was overwhelming. With tens and tens of thousands of products, from over seventy countries, pretty much anything you could imagine had been given a Christmas slant. From Christmas tree baubles in the shape and colour of your favourite NFL team's helmet; to baubles and items with shapes and slogans based on hobbies, "Golfers never have enough balls"; or jobs, "Accountancy is a balancing Act" and so it went on. The options were endless. They ranged from the pretty awful through to some of the most beautiful glass creations I've ever seen. And no, that wasn't the accountancy thing, thank you.

Not just baubles of course, but all manner of decorations, lights, gifts and trees. You name it, they had it. For sure not everything was to our taste – beauty is in the eye of the beholder after all – but the sheer variety, creativity and imagination of the various products was staggering. They will also personally engrave for you any decoration that you buy. For free. In our case that proved exceedingly good value as we asked them to inscribe the names of all four of our children onto a decoration that we had purchased. Not to mention that our daughter also has a rather long and complex name. I do try to get my money's worth.

I asked the lady personalising our decoration whether she ever got sick of Christmas, working here day in, day out. "Not at all," she said, and from the warmth of her smile and general demeanour, you could tell she meant it. Was it because there was so much happiness in there, it rubbed off on everyone else? Or was it because the friendliness of the people in there made it such a happy place? Maybe a bit of both. It probably also says a lot about the genial nature of many of the people from the Midwest. Perhaps they should send Bostonians there on some sort of mass de-grinching programme.

As an aside, it's not just Bronner's where the Christmas spirit lives in Michigan. Less than an hour up the road, in the city of Midland, is the Charles W Howard Santa Claus School, the oldest Santa Claus school in the world. Not only that, but the non-profit school is situated within a building that from the outside looks like a gingerbread house. Amazing, but true. Quite why Michigan seems to have this obsession with Christmas, who knows? Maybe, it's because it is so perishingly cold during their long Winters. Or maybe it's that these Midwesterners just like a bit of fun. Either way they certainly brought a lot of smiles to our faces.

After spending an inordinate amount of time in the Christmas shop, not to mention, as Mr. Uber had warned us, an inordinate amount of money, we went into the town itself to eat at the Bavarian Inn. One of the biggest independent restaurants in America, it specialises in chicken dinners, but of the Bavarian variety rather than the Southern fried. The town's Germanic assault continued here as well. Not just with the architecture and the internal decoration, or the food and drink, but with the waiters clad in Lederhosen shorts and the waitresses all dressed up in traditional Dirndls. (Wide, long skirts with a corsage over a white blouse, topped off with a colourful apron). All of which was accompanied by a man playing oompah music on an accordion.

I've been fortunate enough to eat in Bavarian restaurants in the Fatherland itself, as some refer to it, and my have these guys nailed it. Truly, it was like being transported several thousand miles and across a continent into the heart of Franconia.

Perhaps that's not as surprising as it seems, as when Frankenmuth was founded in 1845, it was by German Lutheran missionaries from Bavaria's Mittelfranken region wanting to bring Christianity to the native Chippewa Indians. What is surprising though, is that they ever got there at all.

To say their journey, which took nearly five months, was arduous is probably something of an understatement. The boat they initially sailed on in Germany was run aground by a drunken ship captain. Their voyage was then elongated by several weeks and hundreds of miles, due to stormy conditions forcing them badly off course. In the end they went the wrong way around the British Isles. Then, when eventually making the Atlantic Ocean crossing, their ship collided with an English trawler.

Things didn't get any better when the next leg of their journey saw the train taking them from New York collide with a coal train, leaving many injured. Safe to say their faith was being tested by this point. Finally, on arriving in Saginaw, they had to walk the last twelve miles of their voyage, with all their worldly possessions on an oxcart, through dense forest and thicket. Trailblazing. Although, having endured all that had been thrown at them until then, that was probably a breeze in comparison.

Their luck wasn't about to turn yet, however. Typifying the way things had gone, by the time they settled in Frankenmuth and started constructing their new village and church, most of the local tribe had left. They had decided to move to different hunting grounds, away from the areas now being cleared by America's new European settlers. It meant that in the end only about thirty-five Chippewa were baptised.

One thing you can say about these people though is that they were resilient. So instead of saving souls, they turned their attentions to harvesting the land. This proved more successful, and soon they were being joined by friends and relatives from Germany. Before long Frankenmuth had grown, and garnered a reputation for flour, sawmills and the production of beer, cheese and sausages. And now Christmas.

Wunderbar. As was our food in the Bavarian Inn. Not just in quality, but also in quantity. Perhaps rather greedily, or maybe because we had now been in America some while and were getting used to the bigger portion sizes, we had gone for their ultimate family style Bavarian dinner. When it arrived, my goodness, it comprised fried, breaded chicken, a pork schnitzel, some smoked pork loin, bratwurst smoked sausage, sauerbraten (a type of marinated roast beef). All of which was accompanied by homemade white bread, stolen (a kind of fruit bread), noodle soup, coleslaw, pasta salad, cranberry relish, a Michigan seasonal salad, vegetables of the day, buttered noodles, mashed potatoes and gravy. Followed by homemade ice cream for dessert.

Even by American standards, this was a massive meal. To say we were stuffed doesn't do things justice. To say we were in pain, probably does. We lay there groaning, but this time not in a Harry met Sally way. Instead, more like two beached whales slowly expiring.

At least, on the plus side we had so much left over we would be able to eat for a week with the carry out from the food left over. On the downside, we had to work out how we were going to make it to the car.

What do you mean Big Mac ain't a Burger?

You only truly appreciate the size and sheer vastness of the United States once you step out of its cities. For sure when you are in New York you are dwarfed (and overawed) by the size of its skyscrapers, but in terms of landmass, it's actually quite a lot smaller than London, Rome or Berlin. So too Chicago. Away from the cities and metro areas though, things are significantly different.

Michigan, which is only the eleventh largest state by total area and tenth largest in terms of population, is bigger than the entire United Kingdom. It is almost twice the size of England, yet only has a population of ten million compared to England's almost fifty-six million. Even allowing that a combination of the Great Lakes and its 11,000 inland lakes means much of its total area is under water (Michigan has a higher percentage of water to land than any other state in the Union) the size of its land alone is still bigger than England.

This was something that really became apparent as we journeyed up the middle of the Mitten State – one of Michigan's nick-names, because its lower peninsula is shaped like a mitten glove, complete with thumb. (Indeed, one of the other charms of Michiganders is that when meeting someone new and asking where they're from, the responder, whilst saying their town's name, often points to a certain place on their right hand).

Although I was aware of the size and population comparisons between my country and Michigan before I went, it still doesn't prepare you for the actual sense of space until you get there. At home we would regard a journey of fifty miles plus to be a decent distance, whilst most American's would just laugh at that as pitifully small. Many would consider that akin to a trip to the corner store. For some, it will be.

That said, our fifty miles will involve bumper to bumper traffic almost the whole way. Even when we're moving, and even if that's at 70 mph. Not to mention a good chance of a holdup on the motorway network somewhere. Whether that's due to a crash (a rather frequent occurrence somewhat unsurprisingly when people drive bumper to bumper at 70 mph), a broken down vehicle or serious roadworks. Or as often as not, some other random occurrence sent to try our patience as we sit there stationary, contemplating the meaning of life. Or whether we will make it home before our tea has been given to the dog.

Here, however, as we sailed up the interstate, it actually became pleasant to see another car. It made you feel like you weren't the last ones left alive, as well as sometimes offering a point of reference and a change of view.

Now don't get me wrong, some of the scenery is lovely, as the grey ribbon of interstate cuts its way through a forest flanked by bushy green pine trees either side of you. But with roads so straight it makes you wonder if the Romans secretly discovered America before Columbus, sometimes another object helps the concentration. At times the road is so undeviating, and the surrounding landscape so flat, that the interstate will taper to a point in front of you somewhere on the distant horizon. You look in the mirror and it's the same image, only reversed. A long straight line of freeway narrowing to a point before it disappears in the middle of your field of vision.

Sometimes the road surfaces changes from tarmac to concrete, and the road changes from grey to beige. Sometimes you play try and spot the difference between the view from your windscreen and the view from your mirror. You drive like this, for approaching twenty miles, before the road curves, you ride the bend and are then presented with a replica image of what you had before the excitement that the bend conferred. Namely, the interstate once more disappearing in a straight line to some vanishing point in the distance just below the sky.

In the 175 miles from Midland, in the centre of Michigan's Lower Peninsula, to Mackinac Island, an island lying in the strip of water separating Lower Michigan from its Upper Peninsula and Lake Huron from Lake Michigan, we passed only five settlements of any note.

Even the largest of these, the rather unfortunately named Gaylord City, had a population below 3,700. City! City? We've got villages that size at home. When you compare it to a journey I regularly make from where I live to Newcastle upon Tyne – broadly across Northern England and 165 miles – and realise that along the way I will pass the cities of Manchester, Leeds and Durham. Not to mention the towns of Bolton, Bury, Rochdale, Oldham, Huddersfield, Dewsbury, Bradford, Wetherby, Darlington, along with countless others I've neglected to mention in the interests of space, you start to get the idea.

Huddersfield alone, which despite its size is still only regarded as a regional town – definitely not a city – has a population of 163,000. More than forty times larger than Gaylord. Indeed, Manchester's population (and I'm only talking the city itself here, not its greater metropolitan area) is larger than all the people who live in the northern part of Michigan's Lower Peninsula combined.

Yet, in terms of population density per square mile of land area, Michigan is only the eighteenth most crowded state in America. That makes thirty-two states out there with even more space. In short, there is a lot of room. No wonder house prices are so reasonable. Although, you would probably offset any savings in housing on the cost of petrol in your trips to the supermarket. Or maybe not, given US petrol prices per gallon are less than half those at home.

When we got to Mackinac though, it was worth it. You park in Mackinaw City (population 800), then board a ferry to take you seven miles across the Straits of Mackinac to the island of the same name. At $25 per passenger, excluding your vehicle because motorised transport isn't allowed on the island, it's certainly not cheap. In fact, it's probably one of the most expensive ferry services in the world per mile of water crossed. But as we didn't fancy swimming it, there was no real alternative and only two companies operate that route. Aside from choking and asking the lady selling us our ferry tickets why she wasn't wearing her Dick Turpin mask and outfit that fine morning, we decided we would make the best of it and treat it like an enjoyable boat trip.

Once on board, I felt bad for being mean to the poor lady who had to sell the tickets as she was as nice and polite as all the other Michiganders we had come across. Plus, to be fair she didn't actually own The Goldmine Ferry Company. (Not its actual name, although it bloody well should have been). However, I consoled myself that she probably hadn't understood what I had said anyway due to my accent and, like a lot of Midwesterners, had just thought I had some sort of speech impediment.

As an aside, although I haven't got a particularly strong regional accent, this part of the world sees so few visitors from the UK, and presumably so few British TV shows, that Michiganders struggle to understand what you are saying. Josh had told us as much when he first moved across and we refused to believe it, convinced he must have been mumbling in that way teenagers sometimes can, but no he was right.

Frustratingly as you repeat things slower and slower, until they either understand you or smile inanely pretending to, at some point they decide they will guess where you are from. Bizarrely, they invariably pick Australia.

Anyway, the lady had looked like some sort of college student looking to make a few bucks on the side. I just hoped it was medicine that she was studying, as with those ticket prices her summer job was certainly going to give her a lot of practice in first hand coronary care.

The boat journey was nice (as it should have been for the cost of it), but please don't let me build up anything grand in your mind's eye here. It was just a regular ferry crossing at the end of the day, not a fancy boat. Let alone a cruise which it should have been for the price. It didn't even have a bar on it which, apart from reinforcing my point about a no frills service, seems a carelessly missed opportunity by the Goldmine Ferry Company. They're obviously making so much filthy lucre that they don't care.

That said, there was an upper level with an open deck and plenty of seating and we climbed the stairs to properly experience our trip across the water. After a toot of the ship's horn loud enough to finish off any customers who still hadn't succumbed to their now weakened hearts, we were on our way. (To be fair, they warned everyone of the impending sound blast beforehand – something Americans are sticklers at is paying proper attention to Health & Safety). Presumably it's to avoid the ensuing lawsuit for deafening somebody.

Once out at sea, we quickly realised why, on the upper deck, there were so many spaces ~~free~~ available. (It would not be appropriate to use the word free anywhere in the description of this boat crossing). As soon as we were away from the protected confines of Mackinaw's harbour, this lake that we were crossing turned into a ferocious monster. Soon, we were riding up and down on large waves and being pummelled by spray, as the water from the waves was thrown over us by a forceful wind. It was like going three rounds with Mike Tyson, both from the beating and the spray from his lisp. (I sincerely hope he never reads this, and if he does, that I don't get to meet him afterwards).

Actually, it was like a cross between those log flume rides you get at theme parks and the Big Dipper roller coaster at Blackpool's Pleasure Beach. The feeling of weightlessness as you went through a big drop, followed by a drenching of water, before you were pinned back in your seats as the ~~coaster~~ boat climbed its next ~~dip~~ wave. Over and over again. In fact, after a while it even became fun. In a masochistic sort of way.

Some people decided to retreat downstairs, but we Brits are made of sterner stuff. Well, that and our climate means we become pretty used to getting wet when we go outdoors. Plus, I wanted to ensure I got maximum value for the price I'd paid for my ticket, and the inclusion of this ~~free~~, sorry available, fairground ride gave me that opportunity. It was worth it though – enduring the wind and the water that is, not the ticket price – for the unobstructed view we got of the Mackinac Bridge as we sailed past. Mighty Mac, as they call her, is a spectacular sight.

Almost five miles long and with its roadway two hundred feet above water level, it was the longest suspension bridge in the world when it opened in November 1957.* Even today it still has the third longest suspension span in the US, and the twentieth in the world.

As a feat of engineering, it is quite remarkable. It is almost four and a half times as long as the Brooklyn Bridge in total, but with a river span that's almost thirteen times as long as the Brooklyn's over the East River. (The Brooklyn Bridge has a long run off at either end). It's almost three times as long as San Francisco's Golden Gate Bridge (although the latter does have a longer suspension span between its towers). At the bridge's centre point, the Straits of Mackinac are 295 feet deep (compared to the East River's forty or so). And its mighty towers sink 210 feet below the water.

---

* Between anchorages. Believe it or not, there is a lot of heated debate in bridge circles between distances calculated as suspensions between anchorages and those calculated as suspensions between towers.

These statistics also reinforce how, in reality, the Great Lakes are more like inland seas than the lakes people think of them as. In fact, Lake Michigan is 307 miles long by 118 miles wide, encompasses a shoreline that stretches 1,400 miles and has an average depth of 279 feet. Its peak depth is 923 feet. That compares to the English Channel's 571 feet at its deepest point.

Lake Huron, on the State of Michigan's northeast coast, might only be 206 miles long, but is almost as wide as it's long at 183 miles. It covers a whopping 1,850 miles of shore. And those shore lengths exclude the islands within the lakes. Lake Huron also averages almost 200 feet of depth, with, in its case, its deepest point at 750 feet.

However, both these heavyweights defer to – the clue is in the title – Lake Superior. Astonishingly, the five Great Lakes of Superior, Michigan, Huron, Erie and Ontario collectively contain more than one fifth of the World's surface fresh water. These things are vast.

As far as I can tell, the only things that stop the Great Lakes being called seas is that they consist of fresh water, instead of salt water; and, because they were formed from melting glaciers, they now lie trapped in glacial basins. (Effectively gigantic sinks scooped out by glaciers from the surrounding land). This means they sit at elevations from 243 feet to 601 feet above sea level. Certainly, as we sat there riding those big waves and getting doused and drenched with water all around us, they seemed like seas to me.

Mighty Mac is also engineered to cope with the huge winds that funnel down the Mackinac Straits. Winds so strong they are capable of blowing cars off it, as tragically happened on the 22nd September 1989, when a Yugo was blown into the Mackinac Straits killing its driver. These days the bridge is closed to traffic when wind speeds reach 65 mph, notwithstanding that it can safely sway up to 35 feet east or west, before returning to its centre point. That wind was certainly something we could attest to. Particularly, as when we reached the sanctuary of Mackinac's dock and disembarked, conditions, almost miraculously, reverted to a fine Autumn's day.

When we emerged into Mackinac's Main Street, it was like stepping into a theme park. You're confronted with wooden Victorian buildings two or three stories tall that line both sides of the compact street. Some of the buildings have pretty, galleried balconies, others are finished in attractive wooden clapboard. Either way, they are all painted beautiful pastel colours. The only things passing are either people walking, cycling, or in horse-drawn carriages.

You knew that already because of the no motor vehicle policy. But because we are so accustomed to seeing cars and trucks in our everyday life, when you're suddenly confronted without traffic in a situation where there are lots of people around, it still comes as a shock. The whole scene is like being transported back 100 years, were it not for the clothes that everyone is wearing.

Then, a moment later, as your nose catches up with your eyes, you're enveloped in the gorgeous sweet aroma emanating from the myriad of fudge shops around you. It's like being on the cover of a real life chocolate box. Or, should I say, fudge box. Everything is pretty much perfect. Even the downside of horse-drawn transport, road apples as they are sometimes known, are swiftly removed by Mackinac's modern-day equivalent of Tinker Bell.

It all seems too perfect to be true. Except unlike a theme park, this is all real. For sure the island will ham things up for the tourist trade, but this is a real life working island, with a year round population of 500. Yes, it gets busier in the Summer, with 15,000 visitors a day in peak season, but nevertheless there are businesses on the island that function all year round.

In Winter, these must be a lifeline, as the Straits of Mackinac freeze solid. The ferries can't get through and the only way to make the crossing between mainland and island is via airplane. Or by ski-doo, on roads that exist temporarily on top of the ice, lined either side by evergreen trees.

The trees help keep people on a track of thick ice, and because, when the ice starts to melt with the arrival of Spring, the trees either fall over or sink into the slush. Users then know that the route is no longer safe enough to support their weight. Sod Brits being made of sterner stuff, these are hardy folk. It also makes you realise how tough Michigan winters must be for bodies of water the size I described above to freeze solid. For months on end.

After a while, you also realise that every theme park you have been to is trying to recreate that perfect vision thrown up by Mackinac, as you enter their versions of Main Street, just after passing through their ticket barriers. Who knows, perhaps good old Walt himself visited Mackinac and did just that? Tried to recreate its look and feel into his parks – and then the others all played catch up and copy? They all seem to pipe that sweet home cooked fudge smell at you to get you in the right mood.

Back to Mackinac and the whole old-fashioned setting, combined with that oh so sweet smell started to make us feel young again, rather like when our respective Grandmas would let us lick the cake mix bowl out if we'd been good. So, somewhat rashly, we decided we'd relive our youth and hire some bikes to explore the island on. The sun and the sea/lake air must have gotten to us though, as we thought it would be nice and romantic if we hired a tandem, rather than two separate bikes.

For those who have not done it, riding a tandem is an altogether different experience from riding a bike. Like riding a bike, it's all about balance, except that on a tandem you and your partner have to be perfectly in sync. This is a lot easier said than done.

We were hopeless. One would start and the other wouldn't, leaving us in a heap on the floor with the bike above us. Or, if we managed to get the initial push off right together, we would invariably both lean too far to the left at the same time. Or on the next attempt, in an effort to correct things, both lean too far to the right. In each case the result was the same, with us and the tandem sprawled all over the place. All that changed was the manner in which we got there.

In hindsight, choosing to rent our tandem and start out from a place right in the heart of Main Street possibly wasn't the brightest idea and sadly we soon attracted a large crowd. We were so bad that some people thought we must be a busking act and started throwing coins at us. Their particular highlight came when in an effort to correct all this swaying too much to the left or right on the initial push off, I determined to stay in the middle at all costs – only to slip off the pedals and end up straddling the bike frame between my legs at an altogether unpleasant speed. Unfortunately, my nether regions didn't come to rest on the saddle.

Let's put it this way, the good news is by then I'd finished siring my family and fortunately have no plans for any more. On the plus side – there is always a silver lining in every cloud – I can now also easily sing the higher parts of the rock group Queen's song, "Bohemian Rhapsody." That and we also managed to raise $2.57 alone from that last trick. In the end I decided that the only sensible course of action was to continue our practice somewhere a little more quiet and, thanking and waving our well-wishers goodbye, we pushed our tandem to a more discreet spot. Well, at least we made somebody's day. Shamefully, it was quite a few.

I'm a firm believer that if you keep at something long enough, eventually you will succeed and after more prolonged practice, along with a few more bounces and pirouettes, we finally got there. I don't know which was more wonderful, the sense of achievement of conquering this and being underway or the excitement as we joyously pedalled along with the wind rushing through our hair. It was exhilarating. With no traffic on the road, as soon as you were away from the main centre there was hardly anything or anyone about, except for the odd other bike, and now that we had a rhythm going between us, we started to put our foot down and soon the scenery was flying past. This was great fun. We even started to get cocky.

Then I realised, with horror, that at some point we would have to stop this thing…… which was going to involve another coordinated, balanced effort. Like starting, but with different moves and weight shift. And I knew how many goes that had taken to master.

There was also another major difference. When you fall over when starting, at least you're not going at any real speed. I suppose I can only liken the thoughts going through my mind at that point to those of someone on their first flying lesson when they've got their plane off the ground (apparently the easy bit) and realise that they are now going to have to land it. The not so easy bit. At least they have an instructor sitting beside them.

I've also been a firm believer through the many years of our marriage that when we have to face a tricky situation together, it's usually best to talk it through.

"Alison, love," I tried to make it low key. Usually, when I start with "Alison, Oh love of my life," or something like that, she senses something is up and gets immediately suspicious.

"I've just been thinking."

"What about?" she said nonchalantly; she was enjoying the ride, the fresh air, the beautiful views.

"Well, we've got to stop this tandem at some point you know." Still low key.

"Yes, I know that, thank you," she replied. Still amazingly calmly. "Have you only just realised that?"

"Err, uhm, yes," said now through pursed teeth. And if I am honest, rather hesitantly.

"Well done Einstein. How do we do that then?" now said rather less calmly.

"Uhm." Pause. "I don't know."

I am not going to print the expletive here.

Perhaps this was one of those times when it wasn't best to talk things through together after all. Particularly, as she was sitting behind me and I had both my hands on the wheel. I think the only thing that saved me from a clobbering over the head, was that it would have meant her having to take her hands off her handlebars. Although I'm sure she tried with one.

"I've got a plan," I said.

Actually, I didn't have one. I was just trying to stop her from whacking me. Although she hadn't as yet figured a way to remove both her hands from her handlebars to get at me properly, I was sure it would only be a matter of time.

"What's your plan?" I love how after all these years of marriage, she still trusts me.

"We keep pedalling until we figure out how to stop!"

I soon found out – the hard way – that that was neither a helpful suggestion, nor a wise idea on my part to have made it.

"I know", I said, playing for more time, "Let's try gradually slowing our speed down and then when it gets near to stopping, if we can't manage it, I'll jump off and bring it to a halt."

Apparently this was a much better suggestion.

For one of us.

In the end I didn't do too badly and this tactic did have the advantage that at least, when we ended up in a heap again (which we did), Alison landed on something soft and bouncy. Albeit that that happened to be me.

Again after repeated practice, we also managed to learn how to stop, in a fashion – even if we never quite managed to perfect that particular part of tandeming – and liberated we explored huge swathes of the island.

There is a coastal road which runs the eight miles around the island's shoreline. On a fine day, such as we were fortunate to have, it makes for a lovely ride, taking in the beauty of the forests and rocks on one side and the dazzling blue water on the other.

Things were now going swimmingly, but as has often been the case in my life, when things are going well there is usually a cloud on the horizon somewhere. Sadly, today it manifested itself as a swarm of midges, or mosquitos, hovering nicely just at head height for those on a bike.

I had seen the first dark haze before we hit it, but for some reason that I still can't fathom hadn't processed the fact that there was this seething, swarming mass ahead. Nor that it didn't seem to be moving from its spot above the road. Or that we seemed to be closing on it rather quickly. Whether it is because my reactions are slowing with age, or because until that point in my life I hadn't experienced the pleasure of encountering a mozzie storm on a tandem going at 20 mph, I don't know. Whether I was still caught up in the moment, making the most of the surrounding beauty as we pedalled along, who knows. What I do know, was that as we hit the mozzie cloud with me still wide eyed and open-mouthed marvelling at the scenery around, it was akin to a whale scooping plankton on a deep dive.

It was horrible. Scratch that. It was beyond horrible. Even Ant and Dec's celebrity King of the Jungle would have struggled here. There were millions of the critters. They were in my eyes, my hair, my ears, my nose, my throat, my scalp, everywhere. Somehow, they were even in places that hadn't seen the light of day in many a good year.

I didn't know what was more likely to happen next. Us being maimed in a horrible crash, due to me having to keep pedalling whilst blind, or me choking to death from the few thousand little chums stuck in my throat. The only saving grace was that I had provided a windshield for Alison, who escaped most of the misfortune. Well, that and the fact that I had now consumed so much extra protein I didn't need to eat again for 24 hours. And they say insects are the future for humankind. Hmmm.

Eventually, with that well-known combination move of spit and swallow whilst wiping my eyes, I managed to get enough respite to regain control of the bike and bring us to a relatively stable halt a couple of hundred yards down the road. At least that was something, even if I was still covered in the blessed things. Although, my trauma was soon accompanied by a nauseous sinking feeling as Alison wondered aloud, "Other than humans, what do these mosquitoes feast on? After all," she said, "they have to put the road apples somewhere to compost down." This added information was not something I had wanted to think about.

Try as I might, I still couldn't get the blighters out of my being when suddenly I thought, "I know I'll just strip down to my pants, shake my clothes loose and then pile into the water. Have a quick splash and it'll soon be as right as rain."

Fortunately, somewhere inside me there is still some semblance of survival DNA left and at the last moment I realised that despite it being a warm Autumn day and the water looking invitingly beautiful, there wasn't another soul out in it at all. Not even paddling their toes. I then remembered that this was a lake that freezes solid for months at a time – indeed in all likelihood would in not too many weeks time – and that its current temperature meant I probably had a higher chance of death by heart attack from eagerly leaping in, than the risk of death by typhoid or toxic shock from having consumed so many shitty mosquitoes. Common sense prevailed, but I can tell you for the next half an hour every time I smiled it looked like I had eaten a whole packet of liquorice allsorts to myself.

You could see cyclists passing the other way thinking, "What a miserable guy he is. Never smiles back to us when we wave." So I started. Until those of a fainter disposition started screaming when my black teeth came into view, and I had to put that on hold as well.

That unwelcome incident aside though, it is a wonderful island for exploring. With an area of less than four square miles and several paths that cut through it, you can easily visit many of the island's attractions, such as Arch Rock, Fort Holmes and the Grand Hotel. Fort Holmes's claim to fame is to be the highest point on Mackinac, whilst the Grand Hotel lays store in being the hotel with the largest porch in the world.

Something, in both cases, we were once again about to find out the hard way.

Fort Holmes lies in land just over half a mile as the crow flies. Although it's a bit more by road, it involves a climb from shore level of over 300 feet. That would be strenuous enough walking.

Try it on a tandem.

The Grand Hotel, built to take advantage of the wonderful views offered by the height of the hill, is about a third of the way up. Now, you might be thinking this could be helpful in providing a useful staging post. I can tell you emphatically that this is not the case.

By the time you approach the Grand Hotel, you are already in dire need of oxygen masks and breathing apparatus; your legs have turned to a jelly probably only matched by when you've actually been hit by Mike Tyson; and your tandem, as you desperately try to get one more turn of its wheels up the hill, is now weaving and wobbling more than an inebriated drunk doing the Aztec two step on his way home from the pub.

All this would be bad enough, were you not to look up, in your final moments of submission, and see the longest hotel porch in the world, in all its glory. Its American flags flying. Its white paint gleaming brilliantly in the resplendent sunshine. The longest hotel porch in the world, absolutely packed full of people sitting out, enjoying the clement weather. All of whom were now looking at you as their latest entertainment and judging by their reactions had been for the last few minutes as you'd increasingly struggled up that bastard hill.

I swear I heard a cheer and saw the exchange of cash and someone high fiving another as he saw his bet come home upon us finally give up the ghost. Perhaps worst of all, I'm sure I recognised some of the crowd from our busking gig that morning. They must have thought we were mad, or idiots, or both. I know I did. Still, at least we helped reinforce the worldwide stereotype of the English being rather odd. Only mad dogs and Englishmen sort of thing. I do like to provide a service.

We declined to use the hotel as a staging post, partly because, after Boston, I couldn't face another standing ovation and partly because they have the temerity to charge you $10 each just to enter it. Yes, you read that correctly. $10 each just to be allowed to go into the hotel, even before you hit the bar. Must be a nice porch. Or they're getting their ideas from the Goldmine Ferry Company. Or both.

Instead, we wheeled our bikes up to Fort Holmes. Thankfully, the views of the Upper and Lower Peninsulas, Bois Blanc Island and the Mackinac Bridge made the effort worthwhile. On a clear day you can see about 35 miles. It was good, but not as good as the way back down again. This time we had the hill with us. Weeeeee is all I can say!

It was great, even if Alison was shrieking like a demented zombie. "Slow down, slow down, slowww down," she wailed, as I cackled away.

Now I know this might seem nasty on my part, but it was my little measure of payback for the pelting I had taken earlier whilst trying to first work out how to stop us. I also knew I was safe, because we were going so fast there was no way she would even take one finger, let alone one hand, off her handlebars to get me. Then……

"Alison, love. I've just been thinking."

"What about this time?"

"Well, I'm not sure our brakes are working properly."

"You are joking?"

"Yep!!!"

Nor can I print the expletive this time either.

Apart from being, as I was later made to understand, an unfunny joke, this also reveals that, like most men, whilst I am fairly good at solving the here and now, I am not always as good at the thinking one or two stages ahead bit. What if our brakes had been dodgy? Hmmm. It also became abundantly clear that whilst I could momentarily enjoy my fun; safe in the knowledge that whilst we were in full motion Alison couldn't get me. I hadn't thought through the bit ahead about what would happen when we stopped. I found out soon enough though and I promise you, I won't be doing that again.

God does have a way of levelling things up though, certainly where I am concerned. In my case, Karma was to be meted out to me shortly after Skull Cave. In my defence, by that stage we weren't going that fast, but we were going too fast to make the necessary turn needed to take us to our next port of call. Particularly, given the late call from my navigator. In her defence, Skull Cave is not worthy of the billing implied from the maps we had indicating it as quite a sight to see on the island.

A listing as blink and you've missed it would have been more appropriate.

Regardless though, it was a late call and one of the other things you discover at this point in your tandem education is that these things do not have the turning circles of bicycles. Indeed, given their lack of balance and manoeuvrability, they would do well to match the turning circle of a bus. I tried to make the turn, but realised pretty quickly that that was going to get messy. And quickly. So I reacted with a swerve to get the bike upright, and we shot down a patch behind some bushes opposite the infamous Skull Cave. It was at this point we found where they kept the compost heap of road apples.

It was also at this point that I realised the stopping distance on a tandem is also more like a bus than a bike. Realising we were not going to stop in time, I swerved the bike once more and managed this time to ensure that not only did we avoid parking ourselves in the compost pile, but the bit we rode through was only a few inches deep. Believe me when I tell you though, a few inches of squishy mud like substance can still make quite a splash. In fact, it has the capacity to pebble dash you enough for most people to think you look like a dalmatian dog afterwards. Sadly, in this case even smell like one. Fortunately for Alison at least, I had once again provided the role of windshield. Or perhaps that wasn't fortune, but Karma at work once more.

Rather amazingly, we managed to see out the rest of our tandem tour without any further major incidents. As a result, I don't know who was more surprised when we eventually gave our trusted tandem back with all three of us still in one piece. Ourselves or the guy who had rented it to us and watched our initial attempts at riding off.

At least, after a freshen up and our exertions during the day, we had the luxury of being able to walk guilt free into one of the many shops where they make fudge in front of you. That is an amazing process to watch as the liquid product slowly solidifies in front of you as it is beaten, stirred and paddled by the fudge masters. All while that lovely smell wafts over you. It's even more amazing when you get to taste it just after it has been made. A taste that is in a different league to fudge that is even a few days old.

We made our way back to the ferry's wharf, sad that our time in Mackinac was drawing to an end. We'd had a great day and just wished we could have stayed longer, but unfortunately for us time precluded it. You can stay on the island overnight in one of several accommodations, including the Grand Hotel of course. Many people had told us that to do so was an amazing experience. Reputedly, after the last boat leaves the cute, pretty Dr. Jekyll side of Mackinac is packed away and tucked up for the night. Then out comes its Mr. Hyde, and the place goes wild. With everyone effectively trapped on the island for the night. With no one able to get off and perhaps more importantly no one able to get on, apparently this tranquil place starts rocking. Seemingly many people stay for days at a time.

Even though, as we boarded the boat, we now understood why there was so much space available on the top deck, we decided to brave it for our return trip. Just so we could take at least one more good look of the beautiful island that we were leaving. Then, whilst chomping on our fudge, we made a promise to come back one day and make sure that next time we stayed the night.

I'm not ready to end it on a high yet

We had to be at Detroit airport for a 6 a.m. flight, to start our long journey home, which included a 12 hour lay-over at Boston. Ordinarily that would have been terrible, but for the wrong reasons, as you shall see, it turned out to be a good thing.

A bit like leaving Mackinaw, we weren't yet ready to leave Michigan. We'd had a great time, been enamoured with the charm of its people, and fitted in a diverse range of things from downtown in a large city to rural tranquillity, from 1930s art deco inspired skyscrapers to a Bavarian village winter wonderland, from traditional museums to the largest collection of Americana I think I will ever see in one place, at Dearborn.

Partly due to the size of the state though, it still felt like we hadn't scratched the surface. We hadn't been to Ann Arbor, not just a pretty University town, but also the location of Michigan Stadium, home field of the University of Michigan's American football team. No big deal, you might think, until you realise that American University sport is nothing like in Britain. Michigan Stadium has a capacity of over 107,000 and regularly fills it when the Wolverines (The University's first team) are in town. It's such a first rate stadium that Manchester United selected it when they played Liverpool on their 2018 pre-season tour of America. Over 100,000 turned out to watch.

When the University of Michigan plays Michigan State University, in their big college football derby, tickets are sold out weeks in advance. Even with official ticket prices ranging from $50-$100 a ticket. Millions more watch on TV. When they play their rivals from Ohio State, over 13 million people regularly watch on the pay TV channels. It's also worth remembering that these are student athletes and under strictly enforced NCAA (the National Collegiate Athletics Association) rules, colleges and universities are not allowed to pay their players or students.

It's no wonder that many American universities are so well endowed, with state-of-the-art sports and teaching facilities.

Indeed, in his book *Leading*, Sir Alex Ferguson, Manchester United legend and one of the most successful ever association football managers, notes (on touring another of the country's leading universities) that the sporting facilities rivalled many an English premiership club – the richest professional soccer league in the world.

Apart from a brief drive over the Mackinac Bridge and back, we hadn't made it to the Upper Peninsula, which is renowned for its walking trails, waterfalls and state parks. We hadn't visited Traverse City, cherry capital of the world and apparently awesome in May when the blossom is at its best. Also, despite Michigan having the fifth most breweries of any state in America, along with many thriving independent ones, we hadn't been to any of the summer craft beer festivals. Nor had we sunbathed on any of its beaches or had a few days stay in any of its beach resorts, let alone seen the 400 feet high sand dunes beside Lake Michigan at Sleeping Bear. Once voted by the viewers of America's breakfast TV show, *Good Morning America*, the most beautiful place in America.

I am willing to bet that a lot of people reading this would not have been aware of any of these beforehand. In the same way I am also willing to bet that if I said to any of my friends that we were off to Michigan for a sun, sea and sand holiday, they would think I had gone absolutely raving bonkers. Even more than usual. Yet, bordered by four of the Great Lakes, or should I say seas, Michigan has 3,288 miles of shoreline, including its islands. Whilst that is less than half of Florida's, it doesn't suffer from Florida's hurricane season or its daily dose of summer rains. Plus, it still regularly hits temperatures in the high twenties and low thirties Celsius (low eighties to low nineties Fahrenheit) throughout summer. Admittedly, it doesn't have Disney, Universal or Busch Gardens. Although I bet it's a lot less crowded.

Perhaps this lack of wider awareness of Michigan's sites is due to the nature of Michiganders themselves? Whilst part of their charm is their understated politeness, maybe it's what also stops them shouting about their attractions to a wider audience; marketing themselves in a wider arena. Certainly in Europe anyway. Perhaps it's because it's so blinking difficult to get to, with only London and a handful of other European cities providing direct flights to Detroit. Plus, even once there everywhere is still a good drive further. For time pressed people, as mostly everyone is these days, it's difficult. You would have to be extremely dedicated to go on a walking trip in the Upper Peninsula, given the hassle of getting there. Particularly when there is a big world out there and lots of other places offering great scenic adventures as well. For families, a direct flight to Orlando, or Tampa or California, and the lure of Mickey Mouse is hard to beat.

Perhaps things are changing. Detroit seems to be on its way back and makes a great city break for a couple. Indeed, Lonely Planet recommended it as their second best city in the world to visit in 2018. And once there – if you've got the time – it's not that much further to Ann Arbor, Frankenmuth, a summer beach trip or even, at a pinch, Mackinac Island.

It was with these thoughts in mind that we boarded our flight.

****

At this point I need to warn you that if you are sensitive to a fear of flying, you may want to skip on five pages to page 200.

****

I shall find it difficult to write the next few pages, as until now I have kept this boxed away in a little recess of my mind. But I know it's something I must do, or I wouldn't be being true to either myself or this book. A small digression here will also help me explain this comment.

Until we had the kids, I used to be fine with flying. Then – and I still don't know whether it was a subconscious thing to do with having responsibility for someone other than myself – I got very bad. It became quite debilitating with my heart raised through the roof, heightened breathing and seriously sweating palms every time I flew. It even got to the stage where that was happening a couple of days before each flight.

To get myself through a flight, I used to have to play little games with myself. I'd look at my watch – 15 minutes in, only 1 hour 45 to go; right

I won't look at my watch again until I have read the whole of the next newspaper article. Done. Ok, what's the time? That's good – 20 minutes in, now only 1 hour 40 to go. Right next article. And so it would go on and on, with me experiencing heart rates raised to the levels you would experience when you go to the gym. It was exhausting.

Then, rather bizarrely, after a management conference one day on motivation, I got talking to a guy who it turned out was a behavioural psychologist. He explained to me that whilst we all know flying is the safest form of travel, my brain wasn't thinking straight. "No shit, Sherlock," I felt like saying.

He went on to explain that the brain works by firing lots of neurons down pathways and this was the biological process behind memories and thoughts. For whatever reason, something had happened to my neurons, causing them to deviate from their previous "I'm happy with flying" path and get locked in some parallel track that wasn't. However, he said they could be trained back with repeated practice. Apparently the brain is like any other muscle and responds to a good workout.

He told me that I had to find something positive about flying – the ability to travel (or take my family) to destinations that I/we couldn't otherwise get to; the serenity provided by no one being able to disturb you for a couple of priceless peaceful hours; the pleasure of enjoying a lovely ice cold glass of gin and tonic, served by a charming air hostess; whatever, just find something – and then focus on that as much as possible for the next few months.

He explained, what we all know, that the media overplay the importance of things. It's always big news when a plane goes down (or even has a near miss), but they never trumpet Mr Jones was killed in his car on the way to work today. Even though thousands of people die every year in road traffic accidents. Tragically in Europe alone that is regularly over 25,000 people each year; in the United States 40,000. In 2019, only 257 people died in plane crashes. Across the whole world.

It's precisely because air accidents are so rare that they make the news. Except, our brains don't work like that and when we hear a bad news story, our survival instincts take over and exaggerate the likelihood of such things occurring in an effort to protect us from doing similar types of things. He said the best thing to do, on the rare occasions such a bad news story popped up, was to immediately turn off the TV, radio etc, and begin refocussing on the positive side of flying that by then I would associate with good feelings.

And you know, for me it worked. Slowly, but surely, over time I got better, to the point where I could fly anywhere, anytime. Yes, I still would always rather be off a plane than on one, but nowadays, I can fly relatively calmly, even when we hit turbulence. Even if, like most of us, I am happier when it has stopped.

Now, believe it or not, even that passage was hard to write, as it took me back to memories from the bad old days. Hopefully, you will understand why the next will be harder still.

As our flight was so early we both tried just to get our heads down and some sleep in after we took off. In reality though, it was more of a restless shut eye. You're awake from being up to get to the airport and all the processes before you get on the plane and your body's rhythm is disturbed. You try and get to sleep, but it's difficult. After some minutes though (I don't know exactly as I try not to look at my watch too often these days), I had the feeling something wasn't right. After our initial take-off and ascent, we just didn't seem to be climbing like we should. I looked out the window, could see Detroit in the background and that we were flying away from it, but could also see that we didn't seem that high given how long we had been going. I told myself I was tired and probably disorientated, but I remember thinking "I'll be a lot happier when the pilot says 'cabin crew released'."

I will never forget when the bong came across the loudspeaker for the pilot's announcement.

"Ladies & Gentlemen, I'm sorry to tell you we have a problem with this flight."

This is not what you want to hear.

"We have a problem with our landing gear."

This is also not what you want to hear.

In fact, of all the things you want to hear on a plane, this probably ranks third last after "we have lost an engine" and "brace, brace, brace." Even the engine point is debatable as they can fly most planes on one engine these days. They only have one set of landing gear.

He was calm and measured, and I shall be forever grateful for him saying what he said next.

"We don't know exactly the problem, but we know the landing gear has not retracted into the fuselage as it should have. It may still be down, but as you can understand for safety reasons, we are unable to continue our flight to Boston and will be returning to Detroit."

We had something to hang onto. "It may still be down."

I looked at my watch. We were 15 minutes into the flight. Bless him, he had known pretty much straight after take-off, which is clearly why he had curtailed our ascent. Presumably, he had then spent the subsequent minutes dumping fuel out over Lake Huron to make us lighter (and reduce the potential for flammable spillage for whenever we finally re-joined earth), sorting things out with Detroit airport and getting everything as straight as possible before he had to tell us. I rest my case about not over burdening people with unnecessary information needlessly.

Apparently in these situations they normally do a fly past the control tower for them to try and assess the state of the landing gear (half down, all down or can't see any at all sort of thing)*, but at that time of the morning it was still pitch dark, so I don't suppose that might have been a realistic option. All we knew was that it wasn't up.

Anyway, even if the landing gear was still down, there was no guarantee that it was locked in place and wouldn't buckle as soon as we touched down.

Nevertheless, we had something to hold on to.

The atmosphere on the plane was surreal. There wasn't wide panic, although people were, individually, in various degrees of nervousness. Instead, it was more of a case of shock. Maybe it was the time of the morning with people still being sleepy, but it was like collectively the whole plane didn't believe it was real. "Am I dreaming this?" sort of thing. Everybody was going through the same thought process.

---

* I had previously learned this useful nugget from my hairdresser who used to be an air stewardess. She was on a flight where the landing gear had gone up, but they couldn't get it down. In the end they used a wrench they have as a back-up in these situations to manually crank the wheels down. They were then diverted to a military airport, so as not to disrupt one of Spain's busiest airports in holiday season and instructed to do several fly pasts of the control tower, with the pilot wiggling the aircraft from side to side to check (a) that the wheels were fully down and (b) that they were locked into place. It was after that she decided to change career.

I remember talking to one lady afterwards who said her son worked in aviation and she had felt like calling him mid-flight to see if he had any suggestions, but somehow she couldn't believe it was actually happening, so didn't. Another said to me, "I just didn't know what to do. I wanted to call my son and tell him that I loved him, you know, just in case it would be the last time, but then I thought I'm not supposed to use my cell phone on a plane, in case it affects things and I figured the pilot needed all the help he could get."

As well as being the most surreal descent I have endured, it was also the longest. Not because time seems to slow down in these situations (a real phenomenon when the brain enters fight or flight mode), but because the pilot brought us in at the flattest possible angle and as slowly as he could manage. To give you an idea, we came in at an angle like you would run a plane (no pun intended) over a piece of wood when shaving it, or when skimming stones across a lake.

I had a window seat and I distinctly remember looking out and thinking that we were so low (with the airport still some way in the distance), going so slow that much less and the engines would stop and we would literally fall out of the sky. I actually wondered whether in the latter stages the pilot cut the engines all together and tried to glide us in. Maybe he did. Or maybe this is another example of where a little knowledge is often dangerous.

I also vividly remember our last moments on that flight, and will do to the day I die. I had one hand on Alison, trying to comfort her whilst she, like most other sensible people on that plane had their heads buried in their hands, leant forward in the brace position. Even though I don't recall that command being issued. I, probably foolishly, didn't and as I looked out the window all I could see was the runway, now a few yards ahead of us, flanked on its side, by fire engines all the way from top to toe, their lights flashing, waiting for us. Although better the fire engines were there than not, it was not a morale enhancing sight. Perhaps rather bizarrely, in that last moment before we touched down, I also clearly remember my final thoughts as being, "Well, this is going to be interesting."

Thankfully, everything was fine, and as the wheels locked in, and we all knew we were going to be ok, there was a cheering and deserved round of applause for the captain like I have never heard before. It even dwarfed those you used to get on the charter flights to Spain a few years back when it was people's first experience of flying.

Perhaps Michigan hadn't wanted us to leave her yet either.

* * * * * * * *

After hugging and holding Alison, I said a prayer of thanks to God and we disembarked – a line of passengers walking on auto pilot, still shell-shocked, to await what would happen to us next. After being given some food and drink, we were told that our plane was not in a state to take us to Boston, was being withdrawn from service and that they were flying in a replacement for us. Obviously, these things aren't just lying around and it was nearly eight hours later before we were ready to try again. As I said it was a good job, we had such a long lay-over at Logan.

Getting back on the replacement plane was a hard ask, not just for me, but for most of the plane, but of course you had no real alternative. Not if you wanted to get home. As you might imagine, Alison and I were apprehensive enough on our rerun Detroit-Boston leg, but the thought of our subsequent overnight Trans-Atlantic flight really weighed on us. I am not ashamed to say that when we got to Logan, we headed straight for the Wahlburgers and got absolutely smashed. And do you know what? They still didn't have any Sam Adams Boston lager! Unbelievable, but absolutely true. Talk about a crap day.

How am I with flying since? Strangely ok. Although until today, as I said, I had boxed this away. I've told myself that it was a rare occurrence, that as we know flying is still the safest form of transport and that if we want to go to all these amazing places, I would just have to get on with it.

Which is how we came to be in Washington DC next.

Washington D.C.

This can't be real!

If you love *The West Wing*, you have to go to Washington.

If you loved *House of Cards*, you simply gotta go.

If you want to try and understand America, and its history, you have to go.

In fact, Washington is so good...... just go!

Washington is everything New York isn't. Please don't misunderstand me, New York is great. But whilst New York is amazing, Washington is wonderful.

Although only separated by 250 miles, they might as well be poles apart. Where New York is dominated by skyscrapers and commerce, Washington is museums and politics. Where one is all high rise granite and steel, fissured with dark ravines gushing with people and traffic; the other is an undulating, low level backdrop set amidst wide boulevards and grand thoroughfares.

One is incessant noise, energy and mayhem. It's Warner Bros. cartoon bird, the *Road Runner* on speed. It's the loud child, screaming for attention. Exciting yet exhausting. Fun, but brash. Oh, and a little crazy. The other is refined, demure and elegant. The grand dame of the family.

One has the best theatre scene in the world, the other the best museums. One is such a melting pot of different cultures over two hundred different languages are spoken. You can eat food from pretty much any country around the world. Over half of its residents speak a language other than English at home. The other, whilst not without fine restaurants, is not in the same league.

Of the world's one hundred and twenty Michelin restaurants with 3 stars, New York has five alone; Washington has none. They will tell you they do have one, but it is in Little Washington, seventy miles away. But just because the District of Columbia has less than a quarter the number of Michelin starred restaurants of New York, doesn't make it Hicksville. Just because DC is by and large more traditional in its food offering, doesn't mean you'll starve. Besides, who has a desperate need to eat Kazakhstani besbarmak at two o'clock in the morning anyway?

Washington is still cosmopolitan, but it feels more European than American. It is more like London or other great European capitals, such as Madrid or Paris. Except cleaner and calmer. There isn't the smog, the noise or the pollution of those cities, never mind New York.

There is less traffic. Way less traffic. There are fewer people. It is simply, much less crowded. Whether it's because it's less crowded, or because we're starting to enter the South, with its more temperate climate, I don't know, but people are calmer. Calmer even than the Madrileños, in the famously laid back Spain.

We even had the case where pedestrians crossing the road waved us through as I made a right-hand turn in our hire car. Despite it being their right of way and me correctly waiting for them. They'd have been crushed if they tried that in London or New York. Either by a dozen cars seizing to take advantage of their naivety, or by the numbers of people crossing behind them, not anticipating anyone might be so stupid as to stop in such an unexpected manner. Or worse, both – swept by a tidal wave of humanity into the onrushing traffic bolting for the sudden gap. Whichever way, it would have been ugly.

Not in DC though. Indeed, crossing roads was not only possible, it was positively pleasurable. Instead of taking your life in your hands and professing deep gratitude to your maker every time you made it to the other side all limbs still intact, you had so much time you could sight see. As you crossed Pennsylvania Avenue and took in the grandeur of the Capitol from its middle, you had enough time for your very own photoshoot. If not full-length feature film. You had time to take advantage of the views its forefathers intended.

Designed by a Frenchman, Pierre L'Enfant, in 1791 it is perhaps not surprising it is reminiscent of his hometown, Paris. Just eight years after the war of independence, he envisioned a capital worthy of the new nation with grand avenues and boulevards and major monuments and buildings strategically dotted around the new city.

Great boulevards to march great armies down.

Grand avenues for grand processions. For all the pomp and ceremonies that great nations do.

L'Enfant, having the luxury of designing a new city from scratch, created a grid pattern that numbered streets from north to south and alphabetised them from east to west. On this he superimposed the wide avenues in a diagonal pattern, each to be named after a state, with grand circles at their intersections. Perfect for locating those grand monuments, buildings and other symbols of the brave new world. Emblems for a great new country, where all who travelled those thoroughfares could marvel at the masterpieces. And of course in those days there were no cars.

In a city dominated by politics and museums, where else could we start but the White House?

People will tell you it's smaller in real life than they imagined. They say the same of Buckingham Palace though. Maybe it's a function of our media obsessed, selfie crazed world these days where everything has to be the biggest, the best, the costliest, the greatest. What do people want? Big flashing neon arrows screaming this is where 'you know who' lives?

I thought it blended in perfectly. It was stately, serene and elegant. Like the rest of Washington. It had the strength and confidence to stand classy without having to shout about it.

Surrounded by its lawns, the graceful columns supporting its north portico and its simple neoclassical exterior, it quietly stated, "This is the capital of the free world." Rather like Marlon Brando in *The Godfather*, when you've got real power you don't need to raise your voice.

In terms of grandeur though, it is, somewhat surprisingly, upstaged by the building next door. Almost three times as long as the White House, and well over one hundred foot wider, The Treasury Building *is* imposing. Its East Wing frontage alone has thirty ionic columns, each thirty-six feet tall and weighing thirty tons. But then they say it's always the money people that pull the strings.

After a wander that took in The Ellipse, the fifty-two acre grass lawned area to the south of the White House, we arrived at the

Washington Monument. At 555 feet tall, it was the tallest structure in the world when completed, until overtaken by the Eiffel Tower in 1887. Apart from a couple of communications masts, it is still the tallest structure in Washington.

That is largely because of the 1910 Height of Buildings Act, legislation which limits building heights in the District of Columbia. But that is also something that has helped preserve Washington's unique feel amongst large American cities.

Aside from the height of the monument, you are immediately struck by the sense of space and scale provided by the National Mall and its surroundings. You are also struck by the way the monuments on the Mall have been placed with the Capitol, the Mall, the Washington Monument, the World War II Memorial, the Reflecting Pool and the Lincoln Memorial all aligning perfectly. It is impressive. It's arresting.

The next thing you notice, however, is that about 150 feet up (156 to be precise), the Washington Monument changes colour. Hard to believe now, but in 1854 funds were exhausted and its construction had to stop. Building didn't resume again until over twenty years later, by which time the marble from the original quarry in Baltimore had been exhausted. Despite every effort being made to find a suitable alternative source and match the new stone with the old, you can still clearly see a difference in shade. Washington isn't perfect after all.

We then made our way to the Smithsonian Institution Building. Built from red sandstone in a gothic style, it looks like and is now referred to as the Castle. Fittingly, as it is now home to the remains of the Institution's founder James Smithson, an Englishman. As they say, an Englishman's home is his castle.

Smithson was a chemist, mineralogist and member of the Royal Society – the United Kingdom's pre-eminent body for scientists. He bequeathed his wealth to create, specifically in Washington DC, "an institution for the increase and diffusion of knowledge." What is incredible though, is he had never set so much as a foot in America, let alone Washington, during his life. As is the fact that his estate of $500,000 in the 1830s has now grown into the biggest museum, education and research complex in the world. Quite why he bequeathed his wealth in such a manner, no one knows.

The breadth and depth of the Smithsonian museums are remarkable. From the National Museum of American History to the American Art Museum; from the National Museum of African American History and Culture to the National Museum of the American Indian; from the National Museum of Natural History to the National Air & Space Museum; from numerous other art galleries, including the National Portrait Gallery to the National Zoo. They even have a National Postal Museum. And these are just the ones in Washington. Anything you can think of, they probably have a museum for.

As London is a world-class city, with world-class museums that are free, so too Washington. And when I say world class, I don't use that term lightly. Like the Natural History Museum.

In addition to its collection of 145 million specimens and artefacts, it is home to the Hope Diamond, one of the most famous diamonds ever mined. Although not the biggest (that title belongs to the Cullinan Diamond, which sits in the Queen's Royal Sceptre) at forty-five and a half carats, it's still mighty large. An inch long and almost an inch wide, it was donated to the museum by Harry Winston, a renowned jeweller. But at the risk of sounding picky, whilst it is worth $250 million and is indisputably impressive, it wasn't our favourite.

Although, in a collection with over 7,500 individual gemstones, having a favourite is next to impossible. That said, the Pearson Diamond and the Whitney Flame Topaz would be right up there. The Pearson Diamond (a gift from Mrs. G. Burton Pearson, Jr.), whilst much smaller than the Hope Diamond at only 16.72 carats, shone with a haunting intensity. Nearly colourless, it was flawless. As for the 48.86 carat Whitney Flame Topaz, a gift of Coralyn Wright Whitney in 2018, its deep red sparkling colour (fiery is the term used by the museum) was simply captivating.

We were both so transfixed. I couldn't tear myself away.

Jaw dropping is an overused phrase. Not in the Natural History Museum's gallery of gems it's not. Amongst its 10,000 specimens, (the vast majority of which have been donated by individuals) were:

The 423 carat Logan Sapphire (a gift from Mrs. John A. Logan). Its crystal blue sapphire is surrounded by twenty diamonds, themselves totalling sixteen carats;

A demantoid, a gem favoured by Fabergé in his creations for the Russian Czars. It sparkled the most brilliant green I have ever seen;

The Cartier designed 98.6 carat Bismarck Sapphire Necklace (gifted by Countess Mona von Bismarck) – its deep blue surrounded by 312 diamonds;

A 22,892.5 carat (don't forget the .5) American Golden Topaz, one of the world's largest gems. Although, in my humble opinion, that was too big. It looked like a giant crystal punch bowl that hadn't yet been hollowed out. Besides weighing over 10lb, there was no way you were going to wear that.

On and on the displays went. Rubies, sapphires, amethysts, elbaites, spinals, aquamarines, quartzes, diamonds, sheets of gold. The list is endless. There were precious stones you had never heard of like a Hydroxyl-Herderite; although if you ask me that might need a name change if it is to catch on at Beaverbrooks.

It wasn't all polished gems though. The 253.7 carat Oppenheimer Diamond was still uncut, showing it in a more natural state, which was a nice touch. There was even a 147 kilogram copper sheet from Northern Michigan, one of the largest ever found. Rather bizarrely, it also appeared to us to be shaped like Michigan's Upper Peninsula, the area where it was mined.

I was mesmerised.

Your pupils involuntarily dilate when you are attracted to something. It's why the gem dealers of the old silk road used to wear dark glasses to conceal their feelings. I was enraptured. Sod my eyes being wider than saucers, I was starting to resemble Kaa, the snake from the *Jungle Book*. I even think mine had started to spin like his. Perhaps the gems were starting to exert some sort of hypnotic influence.

What else might explain me starting to contemplate that I might even be able to smash through a case, grab a precious, and hotfoot it out of the door, all alarms blazing before being brought down? Never mind the quick jog down the two mile long Mall or the wall to wall cameras with my pretty face all over them.

"Snap out of it!" I told myself.

"But you know you want precious......" came the inner voice.

"Even Usain Bolt wouldn't make it out of here without looking like a colander after Washington's finest had decided they needed a bit of target practice."

"Yes, but if you slips the ring on, you'll become invisible......"

"Hmmm. Good point......"

I knew I shouldn't have read J. R. R. Tolkien's *The Lord of the Rings* as a child.

Fortunately, at times like these I have an Alison to bring me back to my senses.

I should state here though, lest I never be allowed back through immigration, that I never seriously considered a smash and grab. But the vast array of gems and precious stones are so beautiful I am sure there will be plenty who have entertained that idle thought. The blues, greens, reds, aquamarines, turquoises, purples, golds, all so brilliant, all so iridescent, all so sparkling under the show cabinet spotlights...... it would be enough to tempt a nun.

From there, it was onto The David H. Koch Hall of Fossils–Deep Time, recently opened following a $110 million renovation. You can see over 700 fossils, including big hitters such as Tyrannosaurus Rex, Diplodocus, Camarasaurus, Allosaurus, Triceratops and Stegosaurus. The latter even being the specimen type for the species – when other scientists find bones that may belong to a Stegosaurus, they use the museum's as the reference for comparison. The Hall doesn't only look backwards though, it also tries to convey how life and ecosystems have evolved as our planet has changed. Boldly, it also tries to get us to think about the environmental implications of what we are doing now.

The museum was amazing, a veritable treasure trove of rare finds. But, having exhausted more than our fair share of prehistory from dinosaurs to diamonds, from bones to stones, it was time for the future and we jetted off to the Smithsonian National Air & Space Museum.

Once again, it was stuffed to the gunnels. Filled with all sorts of curios and memorabilia pertaining to flight – whether inside our atmosphere or out. From the original 1903 plane the Wright brothers flew that started the age of mankind flying (the one at the Henry Ford in Detroit is a faithful replica); to the spacesuit worn by Neil Armstrong when walking on the moon. Which also made you realise what an amazing century of progress the twentieth was. From that first lift from the ground in North Carolina, to the first steps on the moon inside just sixty-six years.

In keeping with the Institution's purpose to increase and diffuse knowledge, there was also a live feed from the International Space Station. Rather appropriately, that helped complete a circle – in 1899 the Wright brothers had asked the Smithsonian for any publications on flying the Institution could spare to help the Wright's research. Something which of course the Institution obliged. Standing there watching the astronauts go about their tasks, you could imagine it inspiring visiting youngsters, some who might go on to themselves become future astronauts, pioneers or shapers of our world.

Unfortunately whilst there, the museum was undergoing extensive renovations limiting the number of exhibits. But, there was still plenty to see, learn and poke before we finished the day's museum visits at the National American History Museum.

If the Natural History Museum had been a treasure trove, then the National Museum of American History was an Aladdin's Cave. There were all sorts of fascinating odds and ends. From dresses worn by America's First Ladies to the shoes worn by Dorothy in *The Wizard of Oz* ; from a Batmobile – yes that's right Batman's car – to Abraham Lincoln's Hat, the one he always wore. *The one* he wore to the theatre the night of his assassination.

There was a comprehensive collection of machines to do with the history of recorded sound. From the first Talking Machine invented by Thomas Edison to Alexander Graham Bell's Graphophone, to Emile Berliner's Gramophone, to Ray Dolby's noise reduction system, to today's Apple iTunes and MP3 players.

There were sections explaining how the legislature evolved and the history of the American presidency; areas on the great struggles and reforms throughout American history, from the abolition of slavery and civil rights, to universal suffrage. There were themes around transportation; about the economy; in fact, pretty much anything you might think of. They even had a numismatic collection that ranks amongst the world's largest. (As well as some of the oldest coins in the world, the museum also has two of the three most valuable. A double eagle $20 gold coin from 1933 for those curious).

And this only begins to hint at the amount of artefacts within the museum and its breadth. It was overwhelming.

As well as the sections on slavery, civil rights and the exhibit of Lincoln's Hat, the item that made the most impact on us though was *the* Star Spangled Banner. I'm not sure I can fully explain why, but seeing the actual flag that survived the battle between the British and Americans at Fort McHenry in 1814; *the flag* that was flying in the morning, that inspired Francis Scott Key to write what has since become the American National Anthem was a moving moment.

Whether it was because it only had fifteen stars reflecting the number of states in the Union at that time*; or because it was a bit bedraggled – as well as surviving the battle it only had fourteen stars (one star and other bits were removed over time as keepsakes); or whether it was the low lighting needed to preserve it, adding to the atmosphere is hard to say. But, standing there, at that moment, you just felt such a personal connection to history. Looking at the thirty foot by thirty-four foot cloth with its handful of stars and fifteen red and white stripes, you almost felt like you had been transported back two hundred years. It's hard to explain, sounds a bit crazy when you read it, but it was a really powerful sensation.

Overwhelmed, overawed indeed, the brain could take no more. You pack a lot into a day's museuming in Washington. So not knowing how to end such an awe-inspiring day, we did the only sensible thing in America when in doubt. We went for a beer and a burger.

---

* Actually there were 18 states in the Union by then, but when Mary Pickersgill made the flag in 1813, she used the official design approved by Congress. That had last happened in 1794, when there were only 15 states. The flag was next updated in 1818.

Panda Express

The area we stayed in typified much of Washington. Vibrant, but relaxing; cosmopolitan, but calm. People sipped in pavement cafés, whilst mothers pushed child laden buggies past. Athletic types jogged past delicatessens, French bistros and Mediterranean restaurants, before turning down tranquil side streets of well-tended brownstone houses.

Even when we had arrived at 8 p.m. and it was dark, young women still felt safe enough to jog or walk alone. On a Saturday morning, as friends caught up over cappuccinos, it positively screamed community. You could just imagine the dads and cubs throwing balls and scrimmaging in small-sided matches in local parks. It seemed the perfect place to raise a family. There was even a Wholefoods.

Yet Logan Circle was only one mile from the White House. And our Airbnb cost just over a third of a similarly located property in Manhattan. We were so imbued with the uplifting vibe that sunny Saturday morning, we decided what better than strolling the two miles to the zoo.

As we walked further out, the latte and literature scene thinned, and Wholefoods was replaced by Trader Joes. Still good, but we're talking Aldi now, not the love child of Waitrose and Harrods. Although some of the pixie dust thinned, it was still charming. For somewhere not two miles from the heart of one of the world's major cities.

We climbed up and into Meridian Hill Park, with its reflecting pool, lawns and stone monuments. According to the National Park Service, its thirteen basin cascading fountain is the longest such in America. Set on a hill 150 feet above the capital, it would have provided perfect views down to the President's House, as it was known, when used by Union forces in the Civil War. Sadly, apartment blocks built since have now obscured those sight lines.

Approaching from the east and cutting through a tree-lined ravine onto National Zoo Drive NW, you arrive at the zoo moments after crossing a charming arched stone bridge that affords views over the running water of Rock Creek. A tributary of the Potomac River, this part is at the southern section of surrounding Rock Creek Park.

Stretching about four miles north to south and a little under a mile wide, Rock Creek Park is a 1,750 acre oasis within the city. Over twice the size of Central Park, it was the third National Park ever to be designated, after Yellowstone and Mackinac. Replete with trees and trails, it also has a planetarium; a 4,200 seat amphitheatre, a soccer and tennis complex, an equestrian centre and an eighteen hole golf course. You can also find Fort Stevens and see where Abraham Lincoln came under enemy fire during the Civil War. It reinforces the charm and tranquillity that is Washington. Oh, and let's not forget the zoo.

Washington Zoo, or Smithsonian National Zoological Park to give it its proper title ranks as one of the top ten zoos in the world. Plus, as part of the Smithsonian institute, it is once again absolutely free to enter. Being a Smithsonian means you can also safely bet there will be some world class feature within it somewhere. In our case, that meant being home to three giant panda bears when we visited. Not just a mummy bear, not just a daddy bear, but a whole family of panda bears. We were fortunate though. Despite being born in the zoo in August 2015, Bei Bei, the baby bear, had to move to China as part of the international agreement for keeping pandas in captivity shortly after our visit. Mummy and daddy bear still remain, however.

What is it that captivates everyone about Giant pandas, or Ailuropoda melanoleuca to give them their correct name, though? Some say it's the eye patches and their round faces. Others say it's because we use them as cuddly toys. What's for certain though is as we stood there watching them munching their bamboo shoots, everybody around us was transfixed. Everybody was smitten.

"Aw, aren't they so cute?" cooed somebody.

"Look at those big eyes," another.

"Aren't they adorable?"

And so it went on.

Meet one of these 250 pound beasts, with claws that can shred a human finer than pulled pork, in their natural habitat and you might not think so. Sod that well known Chinese dish, chopped suey, if you had the wrong name you'd be chopped Huey.

Although preferring bamboo, their digestive system is more akin to that of a carnivore, rather than a herbivore, and they have one of the strongest bites in the carnivore kingdom. With no fence to stand behind and one of them hurtling towards you at 20 mph, suddenly you might not think they're so cute anymore. A bear is a bear, after all. The clue is in their name.

Plus, after a diet of sodding bamboo all day, every day, wouldn't you fancy something different? We'd probably make a tasty snack. Worryingly, as I've got older, I might even be regarded as a bit of a banquet.

You can just imagine the conversation between mummy and daddy panda bear now.

"Well, I know we're supposed to be vegetarian and all that, but once in a while won't hurt."

"Besides that one over there has got enough to keep the family going for a week."

Fences are there for a reason that's all I am saying. If you don't believe me, ask a guy called Zhang who in 2006, after a bamboo beer or two too many, climbed into the panda enclosure in Beijing Zoo. He made it out, just not in one piece.

Space constraints mean the zoo stretches in a 163 acre rectangular sliver, from northwest to southeast. It means you naturally progress through its many areas, rather than rambling haphazardly as you can in many other zoos. Which helps avoid the inevitable, "I'm sure this is the third time we've passed the elephants," type of comment that often plagues us when we visit our nearby Chester Zoo.

With it being mid-October and the run up to Halloween, the park was bedecked with all manner of themed decorations and displays. I know the Americans go for Halloween in a way that makes us look like we've never heard of the festival, but the zoo seemed determined to outdo everyone. Perhaps it was another Smithsonian attempt to be best in class. There were skeletons in cowboy outfits and hats, roasting marshmallows over an unlit camp fire; skeletons dressed up as a rock group (appropriately called the *Boo Band*); reindeer skeletons pulling a sleigh containing a Santa skeleton, which was rather odd; a skeletal bride and groom in front of a mocked up altar and pews, something that seemed a touch macabre; and even skeletal dogs out playing with a skeleton family, as they took a walk. Perhaps the British don't know how to embrace Halloween, or maybe we're just more reserved around the subject of death, but somehow the last two seemed just a step too far.

The real horror show was reserved for the Great Ape House, though.

"God in heaven above!" were my exact words after I'd opened the door and ventured precisely four paces inside.

The stench was beyond awful. It made my exploits in Boston appear like a trip to the perfume counter at Macy's. Having been in there, I now truly understand what the word putrefying means. Putrefy or petrify, not being very good at English at school, I always used to get them mixed up. Here the smell was so bad though, I don't think there was much difference.

Genuinely fearing that we might turn to stone if we stayed much longer, we beat a retreat. Indeed so hasty was our exit, rather embarrassingly, we didn't even get to see so much as a baboon, let alone one of the blessed gorillas we'd gone into see.

People say you have to be careful of sneaking up on gorillas in the wild. They are placid animals, but don't react well to being surprised. Surprise them and things can turn nasty apparently. Well, I tell you now, unless you have had your olfactory receptors surgically removed, there is not a chance you could unwittingly stumble upon these creatures. Honestly, the stench was so bad that try as we might, we just could not penetrate their lair. Standing outside Alison said, "Come on, we've got to give it a go. We haven't seen anything yet."

"After you then," was all I could muster in reply. My eyes were close to watering – and it wasn't from laughter.

Thirty seconds was the best we managed in the Ape House. Thirty miserable seconds. I know, I timed it. Twenty-five seconds advancing in, five seconds to make it back out again.

After the zoo, it was off to the memorials. To save time, we decided to take the subway. With us aiming for the Smithsonian stop, and having travelled on several underground systems, I made sure we were on the downtown bound platform. After the ordeal in the Great Ape House (something which I am still receiving counselling for), it looked like our luck had turned as our platform was crowded, whilst the other one was empty.

"They must have had a train, whilst we must be due one," I said to Alison, and sure enough ours arrived within moments.

"Wonderful, simply wonderful," I continued, "only three stops until we have to change at Metro Center."

It struck me as slightly odd when only a few from the platform boarded, with the majority waiting as the doors closed. I figured that maybe there was a split further down the line and they were waiting for the blue train instead, or the red one, or whatever, despite my map not indicating such a thing. Nevertheless, it seemed odd as I thought the Mall and the memorials would be more popular. Oh well. Three stops later, and we were due to alight. Looking up, I was rather confused to see Tenleytown-AU.

"That's odd," I mused.

Alison, smelling trouble, was onto me like a flash. Oh, that she could only sense the lottery numbers half as effectively as when something I am deemed responsible for hasn't gone as well as might be expected.

"What's odd?"

"Well, you know we wanted Metro Center. Well, that says Tenleytown. Either they've done a quick make over, or it's not our stop."

"Don't say we've missed our stop."

"Ok, I won't."

"Have we? Have we missed our stop?"

"I'm not saying."

"Ow!" That woman has a swat quicker than Oliver Hardy on Stan Laurel.

"Tell me if we've missed our stop."

"You just said, don't say we've missed our stop, now you want me to say we have?"

"Ow!" Is it any wonder men are confused?

Looking at the in-carriage map, I quickly worked things out. It's amazing how the threat of an incoming Exocet can do that for you.

"We've not missed our stop."

There was a peaceful pause.

"We're going in the wrong direction!"

"Ow!"

Now I know why Laurel had his bowler hat. It must have softened the blows. I think I might opt for a steel lined one.

"What was that for?"

"Because you must have stood us on the wrong platform."

"I didn't!"

"Ow! What was that for?"

"For lying to me."

"I didn't!"

"Ow! What was that for?"

"For lying to me again."

This process continued until we got to Friendship Heights, where we got off. Sadly, confirming we were indeed going in the wrong direction.

I was starting to worry about concussion setting in as once again only a few of the multitude on the platform boarded our now departing train, even though again there was no one on the other platform. Aside from my aching head, something wasn't right.

"Excuse me," I said, grabbing someone who looked both local and that they might know what they're about. "How do we get to Metro Center?"

"You need to catch the next train coming in."

"From which platform?"

"This one."

"Hey?" Boy, was I looking forward to trying to explain this to Alison, "But these trains are going away from town?"

"No, it'll go to Metro Center."

"But I've only just got off the one that arrived on this platform and it was definitely going out of town."

"Oh, that's because they're double-tracking today."

"Huh? Double-tracking?"

"Oh yes, it's where they close one track down and all trains use the other track."

"So northbound and southbound use the same track?"

"Yes."

It really is no wonder men are confused these days.

Aside from the obvious safety aspect, why the heck can't Washington do its maintenance in the middle of the night like other subway systems the world over?

Or perhaps that's also part of its Karma? No one's stressed because no one's doing night shifts.

Pointing in the right direction now, we eventually got to where we should have been half an hour previously.

Washington seemingly has more memorials than an undertaker who has stocked up for a buy one, get one free promotion. There are memorials for everything. Leave them a spare piece of land and I'm sure they'll find something to commemorate. There's probably a whole department at the Council of the District of Columbia (DC's equivalent of county hall), dedicated to this very activity. Brainstorming away as you read.

To say you are spoilt for choice is like asking King Solomon which of his seven hundred plus wives he wanted to be with that evening. Notwithstanding that though, there is a nice route which starts at Washington Monument, circles the Tidal Basin, taking in the World War II Memorial, the Thomas Jefferson Memorial, the Franklin Delano Roosevelt Memorial, the Martin Luther King Jr. Memorial, the Korean War Veterans Memorial, the Vietnam Veterans Memorial, before ending at the Lincoln Memorial.

Walking these is a humbling, even cathartic, experience. Often it's their grandeur and setting that provides serenity and peace, such as the Jefferson or Roosevelt Memorials. Others, such as the Korean War Memorial, provoke a sense of displacement with the sculpted soldiers in the bushes and shrubbery intending to pay homage to the fighting conditions experienced in that conflict.

The Vietnam War Memorial is particularly sobering. The names of all the fallen are inscribed on two polished black marble granite walls, each comprising seventy panels, that meet in the centre at an angle of 125 degrees to create a flat V or wide boomerang profile. The end of one wall points to the Washington Monument, the other to the Lincoln Memorial. Each wall is just under 247 feet long. Similar to the way that the deceased are commemorated with their name and date of passing on tombstones in cemeteries, so too here. Except the tombstone is a shade under 500 feet long and has over 58,000 names inscribed on it. The poignancy is heightened with the name of the deceased ordered, neither by name nor regiment, but by date of death. All lives lost are tragic, but you can't help feeling an extra sense of pain for those lost in the last few days or hours of the conflict.

Rather cleverly, the memorial inclines down from its start, before rising from the middle to return to ground level at its end. The incline increases the emotional impact. Not only as you walk along are you enveloped by more and more names – more and more people lost – walking down the slope subtly adds to the sense of despair. More and more dying as we're pulled down into an abyss.

At the start of the memorial you dwarf its eight inch high panel and you can see all around. By the time you're in the middle, the wall towers over you, more than 10 feet high. All you can see is black. Polished black, in which you can read your own face, through the names of the departed. It makes you contemplate. It also cocoons you from the city around, rightly, in a private place. As you reach the end, you're once again taller than the last marble and you appreciate your wider surroundings.

Some come to find the names of relatives. Some to find and remember comrades from their regiment. Others simply to pay their respects and reflect.

At the Jefferson Memorial, etched into its white marbled walls, is an extract from the Declaration of Independence. Rather than simply snapping away at the nineteen foot high bronze statue of Jefferson, or the Tidal Basin, or the white marble rotunda, everyone should read it, pause for a moment and then reflect. Whether it's enhanced by the lakeside setting, or the majesty of the ionic columns surrounding it, or simply the quality of Jefferson's drafting, it gives the perfect insight into the morals and principles that drove America's founding fathers.

The Roosevelt Memorial is also imbued with wise words. To an extent all the memorials are, it's just that his seems to have more than most. Perhaps a function of having served for a record four periods of office. Across its seven acres of space and interspersed amongst its many water features are some of his quotations such as,

"Men and nature must work hand in hand. The throwing out of balance of the resources of nature throws out of balance also the lives of men."

"We have faith that future generations will know here, in the middle of the twentieth century, there came a time when men of good will found a way to unite, and produce, and fight to destroy the forces of ignorance, and intolerance, and slavery, and war."

"The only limit to our realization of tomorrow will be our doubts of today."

"The only thing we have to fear is fear itself."

I have only listed four; in total there are twenty-one. It is almost impossible to provide a synopsis – they are all worth reading and contemplating. Insightful, profound, they are also timeless. They could as easily have been uttered today as seventy-five years ago.

We ended at The Lincoln Memorial, dedicated in honour of America's 16th President and most revered of the forty-five to date. The grand man sits upon a grand chair, thirty feet high. With America being a republic, it can't be a throne, but it's probably as close as you can get.

His statue is surrounded by a building in the style of a Greek Doric temple, fashioned from white marble. It is supported by thirty-six columns, each forty-four feet high, representing each of the thirty-six states in the Union at the time of his assassination. It's vast. Not only are you dwarfed, you start to feel as though you might just have arrived from Lilliput.

Inside, the sense of grandeur is completed with an area seventy-four feet deep, sixty feet wide and sixty feet high; Pink Tennessee marble for the floor and Indiana Limestone for the walls. In a chamber to his right, is his address for the fallen at Gettysburg. Instead of taking selfies and pouting by the reflecting pool, once again everyone should read it and reflect. The photos can follow.

The fourth side of the memorial is open, save for the columns that support the roof. It leads out onto 87 steps, referencing the "four score and seven years" that started his Gettysburg speech. They lead down to a reflecting pool over a third of a mile long, filled with 6.75 million gallons of water. In my opinion, it is the best view I have seen in any capital city in the world. Indeed, any major city in the world.

From the top of the stairs, the two thousand foot long rectangular reflecting pool tapers to the fountains of the World War II Memorial, behind which stands the Washington Monument. That is flanked either side by the green of the Mall before the scene is finished with a glimpse of the Capitol, staring back; itself also standing majestically astride a hill.

For us, those grand monuments all perfectly aligned; the sentiment and meaning of Lincoln's words at Gettysburg; the sheer sense of occasion that comes from sitting atop a two hundred feet wide staircase at Abraham Lincoln's feet. It truly was a money can't buy moment.

After leaving Lincoln's memorial, we headed towards a recommended burger joint in the student district of Foggy Bottom, but Washington couldn't stop giving. Not even on our radar, we stumbled onto the Albert Einstein Memorial. Although not a great American politician, or war hero, it was nice that the committee for memorials had found space to honour one of the greatest minds of the twentieth century.

Sited, rather appropriately, outside the National Academy of Sciences, it was almost as clever as the great scientist himself with a star map centred on the north star at his feet. In it, 2,700 metal studs depict planets, stars and galaxies in their positions at the time the memorial was dedicated. They are even different sizes to reflect how they appear to us here on Earth.

Walking through the student district was also symptomatic of Washington. Normally characterised by gardens overgrown with vegetation, booze bottles or just plain rubbish, students traditionally live in the poorer parts of town. Throw in a boom box wailing through an open window and a few undergraduates staggering home after a drink or ten and the picture is complete. Not in D.C. however. Whilst the buildings weren't quite manicured, all was neat, tidy and remarkably placid. It was as though the Swiss, whilst visiting on holiday, had taken responsibility for organising student affairs.

Whilst the wags at MIT would have found an inventive way to blow up any sign placed in Boston that read along the lines of No Hell Raising Here (probably along with anyone who had the temerity to erect such a sign in the first place); one suspected here that the students from George Washington University would have polished it.

There was even a nice, orderly queue when we arrived at the burger joint. Maybe they should run an exchange visit programme with the guys and girls from Havana University.

As to the burger joint, well the burgers were every bit as good as we had been lead to believe. From their build your own seven buck chucks to their signature special big daddies. Not only that, but they had a craft beer selection so extensive you couldn't have got through it in a weekend, let alone one visit. It would have probably taken the local students all year.

The best bit though, was their line in alcoholic milk shake desserts. Or were these alcoholic custards, I'm still not sure. They were sinful, indulgent, decadent and delicious. I do love America.

Let it rain, Let it rain, Let it rain!

"What the hell?" I had just opened the curtains.

Ever since we arrived, it had been sunny and warm. Today, God had clearly decided it was time to balance things up.

The rain was biblical. Sod the scenes in movies where someone out of sight pours a watering can for the camera, here they would have needed a fireman's hose. Looking around, I could see animals were starting to form pairs and search for a large boat. This would have been bad enough anyway, but today we were scheduled to see Washington's Redskins play San Francisco's 49ers.

To make matters worse, aside from having to get there (and back), the eighty-two thousand seat stadium helpfully has no roof. That, and our tickets said we couldn't bring anything in – not even umbrellas. The same tickets that cost upward of $150 each. And they were only mid-range tickets. On average, teams pay their starting quarterbacks around twenty million dollars per year. Some, over thirty million. It's a shame they can't stretch for a roof.

Retractable roofs run between $100 million and $150 million extra than the cost for an open stadium. Or about the cost of a top quarterback over their contract. A contract that's significantly shorter than the life of a stadium. Even then, that's the cost for a *retractable* roof in a fully enclosed, domed stadium. I'd have been plenty happy with cover just over the stands and spectators.

Puritans will tell you the glorious game is all about muck and bullets. That the best games are those where you stand on the sides in the wind and the snow, as your team grinds out a hard-fought victory. Well, if that's the case, how comes Houston, Miami, New Orleans, Arizona, Indianapolis, Dallas, Seattle, Minnesota and Atlanta can all run to shelter? Even the city American's love to diss, Detroit, has found the wherewithal to provide an enclosed stadium.

It's because franchises like Washington, ostensibly one of the top quartile most valuable teams, see those that turn up as fans, not customers. An unusual outlook in a country where the customer has long been regarded as king. Fans who will turn out whatever. They'll turn out for the team regardless, so let's put the money there and not into the environs. Sure, fans want a matchday experience, so let's jazz up the cheerleaders and music. Besides, they're a lot cheaper than a cantilevered covering.

Short sighted thinking. English football suffered the same blight in the 1970s and 1980s. The curse of taking their fans for granted.

Frightened by examples where teams had suffered a few years bad form after modernising their grounds, owners concentrated their monies on the team and let their stadiums crumble. And where did it all end up? Even die-hard fans will only put up with so much. Decent folk stayed away, and those that went were treated like animals. And as they say, treat people like animals and they just might start behaving like animals. Our national game became blighted by hooliganism, so more decent people stayed away and the vicious cycle continued. Ultimately, a succession of disasters inside stadiums saw hundreds of innocent people needlessly lose their lives.

Forced to act – by the government, sadly not from within – the industry (because let's be honest, sport at that level is a business) saw the light and changed. Investment in modern safe stadia, that now rank amongst the best in the world, attracted women and children and persuaded the traditional football fan to return. Fathers felt it safe and pleasant enough to take their families. To share their love of the game, or the love for their team, with the other loves in their life.

Attendances soared, lucrative TV contracts were secured and soon legions of foreign players arrived; also attracted by everything on offer. Decent stadia, decent playing facilities and decent teams. Something good crowds can fund, along with the associated TV contracts. (TV only pays a premium when it's a popular sport; football without crowds isn't as attractive). Now English football is the richest and best association football league in the world.

In America, people talk about world series championships. Well, with stars from many countries across all the world's continents, the best teams in the English Premier League are now better than even the national teams that win the FIFA World Cup. They contain the best players in each position in the world, irrespective of which country they're from. From the real prospect of the death of the English game, to UK government legislation, to now the best soccer product in the world. And it all started with that most American of beliefs, treating fans like customers and putting them first.

Whilst this may be so, chunnering away on that given Sunday wasn't going to alter the situation inside the next twelve hours. Having planned and packed for every eventuality, save a monsoon, we spent as much of the morning as we could, frantically searching shops for something suitable. This was not helped by an early kick off, stores opening later on a Sunday and, strangely enough, a run on wet weather gear. I am not proud to say we were waiting in a queue for the doors to Macy's to open. That sort of antic should be reserved for Black Friday bargains, not soggy Sunday scuba wear. Unfortunately, our efforts were in vain though and bedraggledly, we made our way to FedExField.

Alighting at Morgan Boulevard Metrorail station, there was a chink of light when we spotted enterprising groups of guys selling disposable plastic ponchos. Until we heard how much they wanted for them and that ray of hope reverted to mush. Much like the surrounding day. Paying over the odds is one thing, being robbed another.

After a brief interlude where I pointed out that I wasn't prepared to pay Saks Fifth Avenue prices for a piece of plastic tat (honestly, a bin bag with three holes would have done just as well), Poncho Pete looked at the sky and reminded me we were going to get wet. Soaked, in fact.

"No offence mate, but we're from Manchester, UK. This is what we call summer." I don't suppose was the answer he had anticipated.

"Seriously, we think Boston & Seattle are tropical paradises."

I'm not sure whether the look of bemusement on his face was our inability to grasp that supply and demand wasn't in our favour at that point. Or whether anywhere could actually have worse weather than Boston or Seattle; other than Canada. Or that he just couldn't understand my accent – as I have said, something that happens with remarkable regularity in America as soon as you get away from the main tourist areas.

And whilst I'm on the subject, why when American's can't understand your accent do they always assume you're from Australia?

Our population is almost three times theirs, and we're a six-hour flight away, not twenty. It makes no sense. Perhaps it's because, whilst they can't understand you, they can still recognise the words as English and the perception still exists that all English people must talk like Prince Charles. Or Dick Van Dyke.

Canadians are easily identifiable to Americans, so if we're not Prince Charles or Dick, then I guess that must leave Australia by default? Until we went to America, I used to think this was a caricature, inspired by the legendary British sitcom *Only Fools and Horses*. It's not.

Indeed, only once I have been asked if I was anything else other than Australian, when I was asked if I was Scottish. (Please, no cringing or looks of horror from Scottish readers here – disbelief is appropriate enough). Even then, that was only as a precursor to a wider conversation about the ancestry of the American asking me.

Anyway, with Poncho Pete temporarily speechless, I went for the jugular.

"Seriously buddy," I had been learning to talk American you see, "Manchester is nearer the North Pole than Montreal, Vancouver or Winnipeg. It's even nearer the North Pole than Calgary."

Whether it was that that sealed things or Alison's, "I'd do the deal. He's stubborner than a mule and tighter than a duck's rear end. I should know I've been married to him for thirty years," is hard to say.

Sealed it, it did though, and we secured two ponchos at Walmart rates, rather than something requiring a loan from the Federal Reserve. Anyway, Walmart prices were still a good deal for Pete, given they'd probably been nicked from there in the first place. Although, I'm still not sure she needed to add the bit about the mule and the duck.

We followed the crowds in a twenty-minute squelch to the ground and, after mandatory security checks completed, we were soon in our seats. Or should I say more accurately, standing in front of them. Whether it's because it's tradition to stand at American football games, or whether it's because by this stage the seats now resembled something that ducks might take up residence in, I'm not sure. What I am sure though, is where we were, almost everyone stood for the whole game.

Rather like our fateful ball trip to Miami's Marlins, things did not start well. It took over halfway through the first quarter for Washington to gouge enough yards to be able to attempt a field goal. It was still the first drive. Although only on the San Francisco 21 yard line, their attempt was no good. Given that I had told Alison how these guys routinely make these kicks from ten yards further out, this was disappointing. To be fair, these guys don't routinely kick in driving rain. Neither side then did anything except being forced to punt, and the first quarter ended 0-0.

In the second quarter San Francisco managed to claw their way up the pitch sufficiently for them to be able to attempt a field goal from the Washington 27 yard line, but like the home team they also couldn't convert their opportunity. After that frisson of excitement, both teams then reverted to type. And punting from end to end. I wasn't sure we weren't watching a tennis match.

The first half ended 0-0. By this stage you might have been forgiven for thinking it was a soccer game. Other than you would have had a roof over your head.

After reassuring Alison that it had been over seventy-five years since an NFL game ended scoreless, even I was starting to think our forays into American sport might be cursed. Especially when, after managing to intercept a 49ers pass, Washington failed to take advantage and ended up having to punt again after three more plays.

Then, with just over 5 minutes left on the play clock in the third quarter; with two-thirds of the game gone, came the big moment. A field goal attempt for the 49ers on the Washington 10 yard line. They almost never miss from this distance. He couldn't miss. Could he?

This time they scored. Halleluiah! Not a touchdown, but Halleluiah, some points. Although, that's not what the fans around us were shouting.

By this stage, only one team looked like scoring, and it wasn't Washington. So, in an attempt to increase the chances of the crowd seeing a touchdown, they generously fumbled the ball on their next drive, in order to give it back to those that might. Although, by this stage it was moments before the end of the third quarter, which ended 0-3. Standing there soaking, you couldn't make this up.

The 49ers still couldn't do anything meaningful with the ball though, but at least they had now got the hang of kicking these field goals and added another, this time from the Washington 4 yard line. 0-6 and nine minutes left on the play clock. Things didn't get much better, but at least with 23 seconds of the game remaining we got to see another field goal. This time San Francisco converting from the Washington 11. And that's how it finished, Washington 0-9 San Francisco.

Talk about unlucky. Not only had we been drenched to the skin, we also seemed to have had the worst weather in the NFL, if not the country, that day. Even those in Green Bay and Buffalo, famed for their bad weather and playing matches with snow banked up by the pitch, had had sunshine. Not only had we not seen a touchdown, we were the only game that week without one. In fact, we had paid good money to watch the lowest scoring game of the regular or post season.

Never mind Super Bowl, Richard Sherman, cornerback for the 49ers, joked after the game that his team had just won the Mud Bowl. ESPN called it "an underwater rock fight." What with the disaster in Miami and now this, I wondered if we might have a new sideline in announcing which sporting event we are planning to attend and watching the contributions flood in from fans paying us to stay away. Either that or from betting companies. What price a 0-0 draw when we get to a basketball game?

Despite the washout, in more senses than one, I was still glad we had gone. Tourist haunts are usually good – they often become popular for good reason – but as I've commented before, it's through food and sport that you get under the skin of a nation's culture. When you get to appreciate the nation's psyche.

Prior to going, part of me had been concerned about the amount of stoppages that occur in an American football game. It's bad enough having to endure an interminable amount of adverts when watching on TV, but what would it be like in the ground? It was never an issue. Even with the relentless lashing of the rain making seconds feel like an eternity, there was always something happening. From the cheerleaders, to the scoreboard, to watching an eleven man, 240 stone defensive unit try and jog seventy yards and be replaced by their corresponding offensive players or special team, before the play clock restarts.

Even though the weather was terrible and we'd done our best to catch pneumonia; even though it had been a touchdown free zone and the worst game of the season, it was still really good. Would we go to another game? Definitely, I'd just make sure it was somewhere sunny with a team that knew where the goal was.

By the time we got back to the apartment, we were so wet that we didn't so much take our clothes off for a drier set, as unwrap ourselves. Our jeans were stuck tighter than a tight thing in a tight squeeze.

Things were so bad that Alison even asked me to help her get out of hers. Quick as a flash – these opportunities seldom arise these days – I was there. Tugging, pulling, heaving, gnawing, as though my life depended on it. Anything that would get the job done.

"Easy tiger," she said, "you'll pull my leg off."

"I'm doing my best. Believe me, I am *really* doing my best. I'm going as fast as I can."

"You're acting like a man possessed."

"Hmmm."

Anyway, any sense of ardour – which sadly was probably one sided anyway – soon evaporated. In the end the only solution was to peel our clothing off. At which point we realised that our legs were now a less than fetching shade of blue.

Whether that was because the dye from the jeans had stained our skins or because we were both so cold it was hard to say. But in the end, there was nothing to be done other than have a nice warm shower and treat ourselves to a mug of hot chocolate whilst watching the Sunday night football round up programme. At least that way we could get to see what a touch down looked like. Oh, what it's like to be a raver these days.

I Only Wanted a Doughnut Ring

"What the heck?"

I had opened the curtains once again, prior to making our compulsory cup of tea. English breakfast blend, of course.

"Tell me it's not raining again."

"Ok, it's not raining."

Duck. I've got pretty good at avoiding the flying objects over the years. Especially when I'm several feet away.

Why I haven't managed the next step and cut out the sarcasm still eludes me. It baffles Alison as well, maybe that's why she keeps reminding me with her version of carrot and stick. I'd prefer a bit more carrot.

As it so happens, it wasn't raining. The storm had passed and left us with glorious sunshine. Why it couldn't have passed through a day later when we were in museums, and not the mausoleum FedExField became as most home fans left with a few minutes to go, is beyond my pay grade however.

Today, we were off to the Capitol for a guided tour. Like a lot of Washington's offerings, it was once again completely free – not even a tip for the guide. We'd applied for our slot several weeks in advance. In theory, you could rock up on the day, but you will be put in a standby queue with all the extra hassle, waiting and risk of not getting in.

Like a lot of Washington's buildings, the Capitol is also suitably stately. Given that it must accommodate The House of Representatives (with 435 voting and 6 non-voting members) and The Senate (with 100 senators, all voting), not to mention the necessary support staff, it is much larger than The White House; that being reserved for The President and their support team. In fact, it is almost thirty times larger at one and a half million square feet; compared to the White House's fifty-five thousand.

The tour was fascinating. We learned how the legislature worked and about the roles, duties and powers of the House of Representatives, the Senate and the President; each of the three branches of U.S. Government.

Our tour started in the Rotunda. If you asked people what one thing comes to mind when imagining the US Capitol building, it would be the great white dome atop and in its centre. The Rotunda is the room directly under the dome – geographically, as well as metaphorically, at the centre of the Capitol. It is even more impressive on the inside than you might imagine from looking at that great dome when outside. Perhaps because the scale is concentrated when you're underneath it.

With a diameter of 96 feet, and a 48 feet high circular sandstone wall encompassing the polished stone floor, you are immediately captivated. Light floods in from the 36 large arched windows above the walls and at the base of where the dome starts to form. (Not to mention the 72 smaller windows further above as the dome curves in). Your eyes are drawn upwards. Then, 180 feet above you, you see The Apotheosis of Washington. Covering an area of 4,664 square feet, Constantino Brumidi's creation depicting George Washington ascending to heaven surrounded by figures representing Liberty, Victory and the original thirteen colonies that formed the Union, would be worthy of a place in many great European Cathedrals.

Beneath the arched windows, at the top of the wall, is a frieze depicting scenes throughout America's history. It was completed in 1953, seventy-six years after painting first began. Hanging near the base of the wall are eight giant paintings. Four, painted by John Trumbull, depict events from the American Revolution, the others detail earlier scenes from America's history such as the Landing of Columbus or the Embarkation of the Pilgrims. Things are completed with statues of several former presidents such as George Washington, Dwight Eisenhower, Ronald Reagan amongst others.

The Rotunda is as impressive as you would expect from a room that America uses for former senior politicians and members of its armed forces to lie in state, or for distinguished citizens, such as Rosa Parks, to lie in honour.

From there it was to the Statuary, which is another impressive neoclassical designed room. Albeit this time semi-circular. It was built for the House of Representatives, but is now used to display the greatest number of the Capitol's statues. Each state is allowed to contribute two statues of prominent citizens to the Capitol, which all have done. They all used to be displayed here, but as the collection grew someone realised that their weight would be more than the floor could bear and so an appropriate number have been redistributed around the Capitol into other areas such as the Visitor Center, Hall of Columns, Crypt, Rotunda and other various other corridors and wings.

Although the statues here aren't former presidents, a lot of them were senior politicians within their respective states. Some states, however, have chosen to honour other special people, such as Thomas Edison (Ohio); Standing Bear (Nebraska), who pursued – and won – a court case in 1879 that established Indians were also persons under law; and Dr. Norman E. Borlaug (Iowa), who for his work on modifying crops to suit their local environments dramatically improved yields. As a result, he saved millions upon millions from starvation. According to the Architect of the Capitol (the agency responsible for the maintenance, preservation, operation and development of the Capitol), Dr. Borlaug "is only one of seven people awarded the Nobel Peace Prize, the Presidential Medal of Freedom and the Congressional Gold Medal." His statue bears the inscription, "The man who saved a billion lives."

As you continue to tour this great building, with its Brumidi Corridors (named after the same artist who painted the Apotheosis and so many other pieces in these walkways around the Capitol); with its Hall of Columns (the 100 foot long marble and scagliola corridor that houses much of the statuary collection); and all its other passageways, corridors and halls, you can't help but be impressed. The Capitol is a worthy testament to the power, wealth and values of the world's most successful democracy.

Keen beans can also sit in on a session of Congress, in either the House of Representatives, or Senate, subject to appropriate security checks. Even foreigners like us. It was wonderful.

America, rightly, is proud of her democracy and it seems this is their way of sharing it with everyone.

By the people, for the people.

For their people and for others in order to shine a beacon for the world. An example of how democracy can work. A beacon of hope. If you think that sounds grandiose and a bit far, consider that 39% of the world's population still don't live in a completely free society. Something we learned to our horror when we visited the Newseum the next day. Sure, some people will bitch about America and think I have rose-tinted glasses on here, but some people will bitch about anything. And besides, nothing is ever perfect. Look at the alternatives, most of them are a damn sight worse.

Our tour of the Capitol (and session of the House of Representatives) complete, we walked the underground passage to The Library of Congress. Wow!

People say you shouldn't keep putting, wow, amazing, wonderful in books, but describe the scene instead. Fine, and I'll come to that, but sometimes a picture paints a thousand words. Where I'm from, when you're faced with the largest library in the world, "Wow", does just that.

It is also what I blurted out, involuntarily, when we walked into its Great Hall. Visit yourself, and I challenge you not to do the same. No cheating, though.

From its marbled floors to the marbled pillars that support its ornately painted ceiling it is once again, overwhelming. There is almost too much to process, similar to when surfacing at Times Square. Except here it's not noises, smells, insane amounts of people and huge buildings, but instead ornately painted, arched and curved ceilings; a forest of extravagantly carved supporting pillars; elaborate floors, inlaid with beautiful mosaic patterns; sculptures; tableaux; it goes on and on. After a while in Washington, you run out of superlatives.

We both stood there gaping.

We weren't the first. The Architect of the Capitol says that when the building first opened in 1897, "the grandeur of the building, its size and scope, the noble artwork and fascinating sculpture left many Americans breathless." They tell you that one writer at the time opined, "Not until I stand before the judgement seat of God do I ever expect to see this building transcended." Truly, it is beyond impressive.

Amongst the collection of 39 million books, 72 million manuscripts, 14 million photographs, 8 million pieces of sheet music and 5.5 million maps are also some incredibly rare items. You are able to look at a perfect vellum copy of a Gutenberg Bible, one of only a handful surviving. Or you can examine one of Abel Buell's New and Correct Maps of the United States of North America from 1784.

The first map to be copyrighted in America, it shows the United States as it was in 1783 after the Treaty of Paris ended the War of Independence. The country stops in a line on the western edges of Georgia, South Carolina, North Carolina, Virginia and so on heading northwards. There is a clear border between the thirteen colonies and Louisiana, Arkansas etc. as those territories hadn't yet been purchased from France. It is fascinating. It is also one of only seven copies known to exist. The copy on display in the library, deposited by Mr. David Rubenstein, is regarded as the best.

We ascended two floors to the Visitors' Gallery and looked down at the vast reading room. One hundred feet in diameter it is another vast rotunda, topped off with a dome one hundred and twenty-five feet above the floor. Crammed alongside its books, desks and endless marble are once again myriads of columns; statues; ornate sculpted frescos and balustraded galleries, atop arched marble landings. Above, eight arched windows are filled with stained glass depicting the Great Seal of the United States, and the seals of each of the forty-eight states of the Union at the time the library was built. At the apex of the intricately inlaid dome is another exquisite mural, Human Understanding. It's a wonder that students can concentrate for all the distractions. Once more it was breath-taking.

After our fill of literature and constitution, we decided we needed to concentrate on our constitution and fill our tummies, and Alison knew just the place. A speciality doughnut shop about twenty-five minutes walk away. I don't know how she does it, but when it comes to seeking out doughnut shops, she's a better tracker than Davy Crockett. Although, as it turned out, we could probably have done with Mr. Crockett as well.

As we walked southeast from The Library of Congress, things weren't as well to do as the other parts of Washington we had so far seen. No Wholefoods here. Within ten to fifteen minutes walking, things no longer felt as calm and sophisticated. It was nowhere near the scale of deprivation, we had seen in parts of Miami or Detroit, but it was clear this was not Washington's best side.

Passing a Metrorail station, it appeared that many people we encountered were on the verge of passing out. It seemed that many of those around had been taking a serious amount of illicit drugs. Not substances that had made them hyper, or conversely super chilled, but instead had turned them into a zombie like state. We passed a succession of people who were either standing catatonic; or you could see from looking into their eyes as they walked past us in the opposite direction, there was nothing there at all. Nobody was home. It was very disconcerting. It was the closest thing to walking through a real-life scene from *Dawn of the Dead* as you could imagine. Certainly something I hope not to experience again.

We didn't feel as directly threatened as we had in Miami – as in "we have to get out of here now," but truly it wasn't good at all. Perhaps that was because it was daylight and busy with people, but even so it was still pretty awful.

A discreet check of Google Maps told me it would be a further ten minutes walk to the doughnut shop. After confirming with Alison that she still wanted these doughnuts – sadly, yes – we pushed on.

"This might be interesting," I muttered to myself.

"And she says it's always me that gets us into trouble," I muttered even quieter.

As we continued our trek, whilst there were plenty of signs that this neighbourhood wasn't as salubrious as others we'd been to in DC, there were also plenty of indicators of gentrification. Hipster coffee shops rubbed cheeks with chic eateries. The taste for exotic, pricey alcoholic milkshakes had also gained a foothold. The area had clearly reached the bohemian stage of up-and-coming neighbourhood. Give it another five to ten years and it will probably be overrun with wholefoods and wholesome families.

But which comes first? And what happens to the former, more economically challenged residents then? Perhaps that's why they were taking so much stuff.

We didn't have time to dwell on this though. Google's route took us through a succession of side streets. Although they were lit by today's strong Autumn sun, each turning still brought a new sense of excitement. Would it be a leafy cut through? Or would we encounter a character from *Shaun of the Dead*?

Sadly, as we made our last turn into Doughnut alley, it was the latter. Although, truth be told, even the most imaginative of script writers would have found it hard to pen this character.

Standing a couple of hundred yards right ahead of us, we saw a deranged man in the middle of the road. In the process of stripping.

"Didn't know Newcastle were in town," I quipped, referencing my beloved football team – England's most northerly – whose more diehard fans are famed for going to matches topless. Even on a February night in sub-zero temperatures.

"This isn't funny. Be quiet, he might not have seen us," was the response.

Clearly, my attempt at humour to diffuse the situation had been as well received as always.

Over the ensuing minutes, the guy continued to strip until completely naked. Trying to enact dance moves as he went along. Although he had a relatively athletic build – certainly not like the Mediterranean chunkers I've previously described – it was still awful. There was no way could you regard this as good. His dance moves needed far too much work.

He was clearly enjoying his moment on stage though, as by this point, although the police hadn't yet arrived, there was a small crowd gathering. To be fair, the crowd hadn't assembled to watch the show – as I said it wasn't that good – but because they had also wanted to go down the street. And, like us, they were also now adopting a wait and see approach.

Whether he felt he wasn't getting enough positive appreciation from his crowd, or whether taking off all his clothes hadn't cooled whatever was burning inside him, who can say, but he suddenly started to get angry. Very angry.

He started shouting obscenities, which will add nothing to the story by reprinting here, and careering and flailing around. Sometimes he would run in a circle; sometimes he would jump up and down; sometimes he simply ran in the crowd's direction before stopping as though at the edge of an imaginary stage and hurling his invective.

"Maybe he thinks he's King Lear?" I tried again.

"It's ok love, I'll skip my doughnut today," Alison replied.

Sod's law meant that his average position was in the middle of the street, ten yards opposite the doughnut shop.

"Listen honey, we've made it this far through Zombieville, we're not going to give up on getting you your doughnut now."

"You just don't want to come back tomorrow."

I thought I might have got a few brownie points for compassion, maybe even some for valour, but no. Rumbled again.

However, I had spotted on the other side of the road, also about ten yards from our stripper, that there was a marine barracks. Standing outside were several soldiers in uniform, who were the subject of the worst of his vitriol and antics. They were displaying remarkable composure and not reacting in the slightest. Particularly as they had guns.

Anyway, I figured that should things go pear-shaped, and Stripper Steve attack us as we tried to go about our daily business of walking down the street and buying a doughnut, the soldiers would shoot the right guy. Probably.

As we approached the shop, there was a slight bum clenching moment when Steve, temporarily bored of taunting the guys in uniform turned, charged in our direction and started knocking seven bells out of a car parked on our side of the street. At this point we were about twenty-five yards away. Fortunately, the car's windows withstood his battering palms and after a few seconds, frustrated, he resumed his verbal assault of the soldiers on their side of the street.

By the time we got inside the bakery, I thought these doughnuts better be good. Particularly, as it was now clear we were going to be in there some time. I then realised getting served was to be our next challenge. All the staff were at the window, riveted.

"This is awesome," said one.

"You're not the ones who have had to walk through it," I thought. "Do you think so?" is what I said.

"Oh yes. Nothing like this ever happens around here," came the reply.

"Really?" I said. "Finding this hard to believe," is what I thought.

We ordered a Cranberry Crumble flavour as well as a Vanilla Bean Crème Brulee type and sat beside the girls, munching whilst watching the show. It was a surreal experience.

Steve, who had been working himself up to a crescendo, saved his encore for when the police arrived. After stopping for some time and helping himself to enjoy the moment, shall we say, Steve then lay on his back and raised his legs straight in the air in a move worthy of an Olympic gymnast. Before spinning round and round like the best of break dancers. Unfortunately, the view was not as attractive as his technical proficiency.

It was a good job we hadn't chosen the chocolate ring doughnuts, let's put it that way. Indeed, I am still not sure I can eat one of those without some form of flashback.

By this stage, I'd had enough and turned inwards so I could focus on my food, leaving the girls – Alison now being an honorary member of the sisterhood – shrieking and giggling by the window.

The police must also have not wanted putting off their food, because it was at that point they decided enough was enough. To be fair, I think they only tolerated the earlier milkshake moments, if we're continuing the food analogy, because let's face it, tough job or not, would you want to intervene at that point? You can just imagine the conversation.

"Come on John, off you go. You know this one's your turn."

"Hold on buddy, I bust the last looney. It's gotta be yours."

"Shit, you're right. Where's Jim? He's new. Let's get him. This is a rookie's job all day long."

The show hadn't entirely finished though as a medic, or perhaps a detective, attending the scene came into the shop asking the staff if they had any spare refuse sacks.

"Sure. Why?"

"We've got to put the guy's clothes in them."

They say holidays are about the memories and experiences. You certainly get a lot for $3.50 in the Southeast end of Capitol Hill.

Two for the price of one

Today was our last day in Washington. Tomorrow we were due to pick up our hire car and head down towards Memphis. Rather like New York though, there was still so much to do – five days simply isn't long enough here, you're only scratching the surface. You need at least eight, ideally more, to do the city justice.

Our first visit was the Newseum, a museum dedicated to journalism and its role in spreading freedom around the world. It was good and thought provoking, as well as explaining the harsh realities of being a journalist on occasion. (Particularly when unearthing stories on oppressive regimes or organised crime syndicates). It also highlighted the role news and independent opinion can play in freedom defining events.

For instance, all the newspapers in the colonies collectively warning of the death of newspapers, and so liberty, when the hated Stamp Act was introduced; John Adams sensationalising the Boston Massacre of 1770 in the Boston Gazette. Something that lead 10,000 people – half of Boston's then population – to attend the funerals of the five victims.

Pieces such as Thomas Paine's 1776 pamphlet *Common Sense*, which called for the establishment of a separate democratic nation. It is considered critical in turning the tide of public opinion towards independence and regarded as one of the most important pieces of writing in American history. Reprinted by every newspaper in the colonies, it was read by almost every American able at that time.

Or the publication by the Pennsylvania Evening Post of the full Declaration of Independence. Within a month, thirty American newspapers had reprinted it and enraged mobs started to attack and destroy British property. The news didn't reach London until the middle of August, by which stage the British were already on the back foot. Never mind the time to organise and deliver a response in the days when the only way to cross the Atlantic Ocean was in boats under sail.

Sadly, the Newseum is no more, closing its doors on New Year's Eve, 2019. It had been losing money for years, and could no longer continue. Unlike most attractions in Washington, it was a museum you had to pay to enter. Presumably, it was crowded out from a market where the competition offered world class products much cheaper. Even freedom has its price.

From there, we headed to the Ford Theater, scene of Abraham Lincoln's assassination on 15 April 1865. As well as touring the theatre, you can also visit the Petersen House across the street, and see the room where Lincoln died. In what is a familiar refrain for this city, both are free to visit. That's especially notable here, as the Ford Theatre is still a working theatre with a full programme of performances. Something that can curtail visiting hours at times.

As well as seeing the actual places where those momentous events occurred, both also have museums exhibiting precious artefacts and detailing the history. (Although, the chair in Lincoln's theatre booth is a copy; like so many other pieces of valuable Americana, the original resides in the Henry Ford museum in Detroit). The developments and context leading up to the assassination are also explained, as are the aftermath and ramifications.

In a tragic example of how even the best-laid plans can go wrong, you also get to learn how bad Lincoln's Vice President Andrew Johnson was. The museum never explicitly says so; that would be political and non-objective. But it is remarkable how many of the things that Lincoln fought for, and ultimately gave his life for, his successor let slide. Or shall we say failed to pursue with a notable lack of vigour. Besides, the museum doesn't overtly need to criticise Johnson; he is regularly voted amongst the worst of all US Presidents when periodic rankings are undertaken.

Our next stop took us to The National Portrait Gallery, which has some wonderful paintings, sculptures and photographs of famous Americans from all walks of life. Actors and actresses, comedians and comediennes, sports stars, authors, musicians, artists. They're all there. It's a who's who of *Who's Who*. Too many to list or even attempt to whittle down into must sees, it is a worthy detour in its own right. Although the one of Muhammad Ali shadow boxing, whilst standing at the bottom of a swimming pool filled with water, is particularly good.

To capture that moment when Ali has one foot flat on the floor, the other curled on the ball of his foot, his back straight in a classic boxer's stance, whilst the pressure of the water will have been forcing his body upwards is special. Not to mention Ali holding his breath throughout.

The gallery is best known for its collection of America's Presidents, however. Outside the White House, it is the only place in the world where you can see a portrait of every single US President. The good and the not so good. It's like an American version of the Downing Street staircase. Except there is no staircase, and anyone can visit. Their collection also encompasses a lot of first ladies.

Everyone will have their own favourite, but the one that stood out for us was Chuck Close's portrait of Bill Clinton. It's a mosaic, made up from all sorts of abstract pieces in each of the tiles, that together look striking. Perhaps because it nails the eyes.

People say that the one thing that you always noticed about Bill Clinton was his eyes. Those that met him said he had an incredible ability to make you feel extra special. Apparently it was the eyes that made the difference. With these types of compositions, the further back you stand, the more lifelike it gets. That's also true here, but the one thing you're drawn to no matter where you stand are Clinton's eyes.

The need for sustenance combined with the two birds for one stone school of planning took us next to the Willard Hotel. Close to the White House's South Lawn, it has hosted many notable events since the 1860s. From the Peace Conference of February 1861, and its failed efforts to seek compromise and broker a deal to avoid the Civil War; to over one hundred years later, Martin Luther King putting the finishing touches to his "I Have a Dream" speech. Abraham Lincoln even moved in for ten days prior to his inauguration in 1861 due to fears over impending assassination attempts.

You can sit in its lobby and enjoy a drink, in the same way that President Ulysses S. Grant used to. Only you won't be plagued with continual interruptions, unlike him. Something that, allegedly, lead to the popularisation of the term lobbyists – as he called those constantly after his attention or help.

By now it was dark and after a beer and a bite to fortify us, we again toured the monuments we had visited three days ago. Plenty of people were doing likewise, and it was safe; something that had concerned me prior to going, when someone had recommended we see the memorials at night. Seeing the memorials in the dark was a different experience to during the day. Washington was giving a two for the price of one experience, which given it's free to visit the memorials anyway, is like a super bonus.

At night the memorials are illuminated with spotlights. All background distractions are removed, it's like going to watch a show. Or a floodlit sports event – all your focus is on them. Impressive in the day, at night they are elevated to a new level.

The one which underwent the biggest transformation was the Korean War Veterans Memorial. With the temperature dropping, moisture from the bushes surrounding the soldiers starting to condense. Under the lights it started to appear misty and murky around the bases of the soldiers. You would not have been surprised if the Hound of the Baskervilles had appeared at any moment. From paying tribute to the conditions the soldiers experienced when fighting, it was now distilled into something even more sensorial. You could literally feel the hairs rising on the back of your neck. Oh, what it must have been like to actually have been out there during that conflict. Thankfully, we will never know, but at that moment we were starting to have a vague inkling.

Finishing at the Lincoln Memorial once again also made us reflect. We were standing at the same memorial where, in 1963, Dr. Martin Luther King had given his most famous speech to a crowd of 250,000 people. We considered the words of Thomas Jefferson, Abraham Lincoln, Franklin Delano Roosevelt and Martin Luther King. Words that revealed a time when many leaders had the utmost morals, allied to a huge sense of duty. When leaders, even if they didn't always get it right, did things for the right reasons and for the greater good. Rather than their own personal interest. Even when that meant great personal risk.

It is what enabled the overthrow of powerful tyrannical regimes, whether that was the scourge of slavery or twentieth century European fascism. That commitment to liberty, even at the ultimate personal sacrifice, is one of the things that has made America great. Free and true. Oh, that some of our leaders today could walk in their shoes.

The Blue Ridge Mountains

Asheville not Nashville!

We still had so much to see of Washington. We hadn't seen the National Archives for instance – home to the Declaration of Independence, The Constitution and the Louisiana Purchase amongst many historical documents. Amazingly, there were also many museums, as well as many parts of the ones we'd been to, untouched. Nor had we visited the Kennedy Center, or paid our respects at Arlington.

Washington is a city that has so much to offer. Sure some areas, like any metropolis, are challenged, but for the most part Washington is a clean, welcoming, charming city. We'd be back.

In the meantime though, we had a date with the King and we needed to push on. More pressingly we had a date with Crappo Car Hire from whom we were collecting the vehicle that would take us the one thousand miles to Memphis. After our experiences with Detroit Alamo, you'd have thought we would have stuck with them, but it wasn't so straightforward because we only wanted a one-way rental. (We would be flying back, rather than reversing the drive). Whether Crappo blew them out of the water with their pricing I can't remember, but what I will always remember now is the saying, "You pays your money, you takes your choice."

We got to Crappo's in good time, but I knew trouble was ahead, given the time it took to serve the solitary customer in front of us. Keen to get going, after several minutes of thumb twiddling, I started becoming inwardly impatient. Externally calm, and polite, but inwardly irritated.

In much the same way as when you're in a hurry at the supermarket checkout and it seems God has deliberately set out to test you that day with the person ahead updating the cashier on their lives, their children's lives – in fact the lives of the whole family tree. And then they decide to pay for their week's groceries with the coppers they've saved in the change bottle by their bed.

Here, God must have fitted Crappo's clerks with a man-in-a-hurry detector, because they actually slowed down their previously languorous service. If that were possible.

Things peaked, or perhaps troughed would be the better word, when they started reading a magazine in front of me. I kid you not.

Lack-of-speedy Gonzales 1 was doing her best not to process us anytime this side of Christmas, when her compatriot Lack-of-speedy Gonzales 2 appeared from the back office, wandered past, and caught sight of *OK* magazine or *Hello* or whatever was on the desk.

"Well, would ya look at that?" she said, pointing to whichever lurid headline it was.

"Oh, I know. Who'd a thought it?" said number 1. At which point, they thumbed to the story and became lost in whatever constituted a world in their minds.

With my blood pressure now boiling more than a bubbling geyser in Yellowstone, I considered exploding, like its Old Faithful but decided against it as (a) some people in America have guns and we didn't; (b) apart from minor irritants like these buffoons I quite like America and didn't fancy deportation; (c) I hadn't ruled out the possibility that there was a hidden candid camera type device somewhere, and sometime soon I would be featuring on a Saturday evening prime time practical joke programme.

In the end, I concluded this must be a test from God, and that now was the time to practise my Zen like deep breathing skills. Loudly.

Crappo shared their offices with a premium car rental brand. Complete with premium prices. Consider that for a second. Different sticker on the car, but same fleet, same offices, same staff, vastly different prices. I wonder if you book with them whether you also get the same shit service from Crappo's staff. Or does the computer flash a sign saying premium brand chump and the staff suddenly switch their delivery.

Perhaps they have two patterns of communication, depending on who you've booked with. A premium service for the premium brand customer and a conscious effort to treat you like the name implies if you've booked with Crappo. Maybe when the computer flashes premium, the staff go into the back office and change into a premium suit to deliver the premium experience. I somehow doubt it though.

When the car finally arrived (with it being a city centre location, they bring it to you from their underground car park instead of you walking to it across a big lot) the Crappo theme continued. A cracked windscreen and so many scuffs and scratches that even in Detroit they would have sent this back.

However, by this point, we'd been there forty minutes, we needed to get on and I just couldn't face whatever tortuous process I would need to go through to try and sort things out with the Gonzaleses. Let alone whether any replacement car would be better. Besides, they had upgraded our car from an economy wreck to an SUV wreck. (Although I don't want any sympathy for them here. I reckon that because they knew this was a one-way rental, they were just looking to dump a problem car on another office's books).

I must admit I was rather nervous when first getting behind the wheel. It's one thing driving America's interstates – even the six lane ones that skirt Western Miami. (In each direction. Eight in places, if you include joining ramps and merges). It's quite another navigating one of their major cities.

If this was New York, I'd have been mincemeat. But it wasn't New York, it was Washington, and I could virtually mince my way through the traffic. As I've already said, pedestrians were even letting me pass when it was their right of way. Maybe it was my mincing.

Within minutes we were in Virginia and, a few miles further down the interstate, the scenery started to open up. Wide vistas, leading to rolling hills, it was beautiful.

In many ways, it was reminiscent of northern England as you start to enter the Lake District. Except much brighter. Nor is that a gag about how much rain the Lake District is famous for. Rather, it reflects that Washington is almost eleven hundred miles due south of Cumbria, and so the sun's rays strike the Earth more directly. The light is more concentrated, more intense. To put in context, DC is further south than the Spanish city of Valencia. Because of the gulf stream, it's easy to forget just how far north the United Kingdom is. Until you're there in December and the sun sets at three thirty in the afternoon.

It was a splendid, relaxing drive. As you progressed from the foothills to the Blue Ridge Mountains proper, it simply got better and better. Over the course of a few hours, the scenery slowly grew more and more impressive. The height of the hills, the tree cover, the backdrops. All became more striking, more vivid, more alluring.

We broke our journey at a Cracker Barrel restaurant. Loved by many British visitors to Orlando, Florida this is a national chain with over six hundred and sixty locations, predominantly in edge of town or interstate locations. Themed as though they were country restaurants from the late nineteenth and early twentieth centuries, their menu is similar. Good, old-fashioned, wholesome country food. Wonderful and good value too, they are worth detouring for if you are in the vicinity of one. They also make great pancakes.

I know it sounds silly, them being not much more than a simple chain of solid restaurants, but we always try to include a stop somewhere at one every time we go stateside. Many British people I've spoken to say the same. Having been a few times now, I also know the rules and manage to avoid making a fool of myself in a Mighty-Quinnesque fashion or in some similar way. Somehow though, I always forget about the portion sizes.

I blame the menu. It's better than blaming Alzheimer's. Instead of describing favourites such as Old Timer's Breakfast or Grandma's Sampler better names should be Belly Buster or in my case Pig Fattener. At least they would give you a clue. Yes, I know I should read the detailed description of what comes with each meal or look at the number of calories helpfully listed aside, but I'm sorry, for some reason the brain short circuits at this point and even if I do read the detail, it doesn't process. Probably, because by this stage I am usually salivating like Pavlov's dog and just want that maple syrup pancake hit.

By the time the waitress has finished asking whether you would like your eggs poached, over-easy, over-medium, over-hard, hard-boiled, soft-boiled, sunny side up, soft scrambled, hard scrambled, perfect scrambled, baked, or basted, (a process that still bewilders British visitors for whom the options at home are usually fried eggs … one or two?), I am willing to sign up for anything. Virtually screaming, "Just bring me the pancakes...... NOW!", I am stabbing at the menu like it was a bingo card. Something I usually regret once my craving has been satiated and I still have to plough through a plate that would feed an African village for three days.

And Alison doesn't help here. Not only does she not hoover up any bits left, like I do for her, I also have to endure the,

"Eat up. We're not leaving until you're done. You ordered it, you can jolly well eat it."

Maybe it is her way of helping. She's thinking, "Right, surely he will be in so much pain after this, he must remember next time we come."

But I don't, and sadly, the process repeats each time we go.

Lying there, loosening my belt, I just wanted to die. But we needed to push on, so, making sure I'd refastened my belt – I told you I was a Cracker Barrel pro – we waddled back to the car.

Our one thousand mile trip to Memphis was too much to do in one go, so we had chosen to break it into manageable sections. Besides, getting off the interstate gets you into the heart of America. Our first detour involved driving the Blue Ridge Parkway.

The Parkway is wonderful. It's not dubbed America's favourite drive for nothing. A speed limit of forty-five miles per hour enables you to leisurely take in its majestic views. Often the volume of traffic will slow you to a crawl and you are compelled to appreciate its scenery. Even though you don't need much compelling.

Better still is to stop at some of its numerous viewpoints and look out at the rolling landscape of hills and peaks covered in chestnut-oak, pine, beech and hickory, amongst many others; its trees a million shades of green through to blue. When we went, the blue green blanket was interspersed with the hues of autumn, with the deciduous trees that had already changed colour dabbing dots of gold, brown, russet and red across your view. Hanging over it all was a slight blueish haze, a product of the isoprene omitted emitted by the plants. It had the effect of finishing the scene with a soft pastel edge, whilst allowing odd peaks to pop through in the far distance for added variety.

It's not just the beauty of the colours though, or the pleasing way the terrain undulates between its peaks and troughs as tips of the trees accentuate points of interest. It's the scale. It's vast.

Your whole panorama is taken up with trees, hills and sky. Blues, greens, reds, golds, as far as the eye can see. Sometimes in the Mediterranean, when you look from the top of a cliff, all you can see is sea; you can even make out the curvature of the Earth. Here, from the elevated position of the Blue Ridge Parkway, it's the vegetation that seems to continue to infinity. You are literally looking at millions and millions of trees. As well as over 20,000 species of plants and animals.

Somewhere around the Linn Cove Viaduct, Alison said it was the most beautiful view she had ever seen. I was mildly disappointed. Not because I had been hoping for that honour, but because I was driving at that moment and unable to look away. It was between designated lookout posts, and so the opportunity was not there for me to stop. It didn't matter too much, however, for there are so many places to park up; and at each the views are repeatedly wonderful.

Like at Craggy Gardens. At that point of the Parkway, the Blue Ridge is so narrow you can look out at both sides. To Tennessee or to North Carolina. It literally is a ridge within the Appalachian Mountains. Better still, you can walk to the summit of Craggy Pinnacle for uninterrupted 360-degree views.

As well as numerous opportunities to stop at viewpoints, one of the splendid things about the Parkway is that there are also plenty of attractions along the route to tempt you into longer diversions. So, as well as Craggy Pinnacle, we had earlier stopped for a prolonged stretch at Linville Falls. Home to a waterfall that steps in sections, culminating in a forty-five foot drop at its last, it is accessed by a choice of trails that lead from a visitor centre. These range from a relatively easy stroll allowing you to view the top of the fall, to a more challenging 260 foot descent which takes you to the pool the fall plunges into. Of course, that route also means a strenuous 260 foot ascent when returning.

The park service tells you to be aware of bears and take sensible precautions such as making lots of noise as you walk along trails so as not to startle one; to dispose of your food at proper visitor centre bins and so on. I will admit to being slightly nervous prior to setting off for our first trek – bears aren't high on your list of worries as you wander around Manchester after all. But we needn't have been. There were so many people clomping on the trails we took, that any bears would have already left town in search of a bit of peace.

The Blue Ridge Parkway runs 469 miles from end of the Shenandoah National Park at Afton, Virginia to Oconaluftee Visitor Center near Cherokee, North Carolina. As there was no way we had sufficient time to see it all, we focussed on the stretch many believe best – from Blowing Rock at milepost 292 to Asheville, North Carolina at mile marker 385. It was excellent, but we made a mistake in breaking our journey from Washington overnight at Roanoke.

Nothing wrong with Roanoke, a town with an eighty-nine foot star overlooking it for some reason (the largest, free standing one in the world incidentally), but we would have been better pushing onto Boone and staying there. Boone, a quaint, vibrant mountain town, might have made for a longer drive the day we left DC, but would have meant that we got much more time on the Blue Ridge Parkway the next day. As it was arriving in Roanoke late afternoon, it was too late to use the extra time profitably, and the trade-off meant that the next day we later ran out of time on the Parkway and had to skip Mount Mitchell due to the failing light.

At 6,684 feet, Mount Mitchell is the highest point east of the Rockies and tragically, the weather that day had been bright and clear. It couldn't have been better for its views. Still, always good to leave a reason to go back I suppose. It is a beautiful part of the world.

That night, our second after leaving Washington, we stayed in Asheville. A charming town of 90,000 people it is home to numerous wine bars, fine restaurants and a bustling arts scene. It regularly features in lists of America's most romantic towns, or great places for a couples weekend away. Home to a thriving craft beer scene, including many local breweries; craft markets, with merchandise actually made by the stall holders (instead of identikit artisan looking items that, in reality, are produced en masse around the world); and all sorts of niche and unique shops selling genuinely different items, it was the sort of place where you could spend days ambling aimlessly.

One of the best examples of the Asheville difference was its former Woolworth's store. Sensitively restored, complete with original working soda fountain, it now houses 160 distinct local artists who both display and sell their work. Quirky, different, memorable. It's a marvellous place to lose a few hours.

Perhaps I just needed a break after two solid days in the car, albeit that the Parkway had provided breaks where we got our hiking boots on. If so, Asheville was the perfect place for such a break.

Asheville is also home to Biltmore, America's largest owned private house and estate. It is the closest thing America has to an English stately home. Given that we have lots of those at home though, we decided to give it a miss and spend our time instead on its other treasures. Besides, after the freedom of Washington, ticket prices in excess of $70 (including tax) came as a bit of a shock.

Anyway, we got our fix of history through our accommodation. To change things up a bit, we had decided to stay at a proper American B&B. Asheville has plenty of historic houses within its centre, and many of these have now been converted to bed-and-breakfast establishments. It promised great home cooking in a traditional old-fashioned house and delivered on all counts. Even if we had our misgivings on arrival.

One of those old Victorian houses with more stories than Enid Blyton, it ascended all the way to where crows nested. With a facade of broken weatherboards (in that shade of peeling paint estate agents call rustic) and turrets in the roof, I thought we'd stumbled onto a set for *The Addams Family*. All we needed was a streak of lightning and a cackle of thunder.

Tiptoeing up the gravel drive so as not to disturb any passing phantoms, I honestly thought I saw two dead people sitting in the rocking chairs on the porch. Well, in chairs. They were sitting so still they weren't rocking. It was like one of the Halloween tableaux at the zoo. I had to check carefully to make sure they were still breathing.

I realise my eyesight has deteriorated with age, but even so. The setting must have gotten to me. Compounding my embarrassment of having peered too closely, I tried to introduce myself to cover things up, but sadly mistook them for the owners when it turned out they were guests too. Boy, was I now looking forward to sharing breakfast with them in the morning.

On entering the house you knew it would have no elevator, which was to be expected, but you also knew by this stage we would also be in the eyrie. You also suspected it was probably haunted. Eyrie by name, eerie by nature. Still, at least we'd get to cuddle up close in bed that night.

After a long day's driving and walking, by this stage we both just needed a drink. Tea would have been fine, although given we might have to share our room with Casper later, something stronger was calling. Either way, it would have to wait, as we were then treated to an excruciatingly detailed tour of the property by the proud owner. Moving even slower than the couple on the front porch, I asked him if he didn't have any relatives in Washington.

"Your surname isn't Gonzales, by any chance?"

He looked at me as if *I* was the weird one, whilst Alison booted me in the leg. It wasn't the best of starts to our time in Asheville.

Our room though, just about finished me off. After a quick infusion of oxygen, required from lugging our suitcases up to what must have been the roof, I opted for a shower. Meanwhile, Alison unpacked on the envelope he had told us was our bed. You are probably thinking why didn't the owner carry the bags up and not the guest, as is usual in most American establishments. The truth is he did offer, but I declined as I didn't fancy giving him mouth to mouth resuscitation at the top.

Anyway, I hit the shower. To be more accurate, I limboed. It was the only way I could get the hose above my head. Small? There was no way I could stand up and, as you know already, I am not the tallest.

As to the shower, it was one of those over the bath types where you have to tuck a shower curtain in around you. Actually, bath was stretching the description a bit. Sink would have been more appropriate. I did tuck in the curtain as requested by Mr. Gonzales on our tour, but it was like being wrapped in clingfilm, things were so tight. After a couple of pirouettes to wash my hair, it felt like I had been shrink-wrapped. At that point, I thought sod it and got out. Unbelievably, despite my best efforts, I had still turned the bathroom into a swimming pool. Such are the charms of period houses. Now you know why we didn't need Biltmore.

In the morning, sitting at the same antique breakfast table as eight other guests was an intense experience. Particularly with us being from across the pond and a bit different. At times there were so many questions it felt like we were being interviewed by panel. The other guests were great though and it provided a great opportunity to meet people from all over the States as well as pick up useful tips for future trips.

Sadly, our itinerary only allowed for two nights in Asheville. With lots to do in the surrounding area, as well as its quaint downtown, it really is a hidden gem if you'll forgive an oft used cliché. Had we known just how good it was beforehand, we would have doubled the length of our stay. As it is, it is has now joined the ever lengthening list of places we need to return to.

Tennessee

How Long until we're there?

At this point American geography needs a bit of explaining. By this stage we were in Tennessee, which is in the South. Some people say it's in the Deep South. Even though if you look at a map, it's in the Midlands. Except America doesn't have a Midlands.

Unlike England, where we have the North, (helpfully subdivided at times into a North West and North East); the South, (also helpfully divided into a South West and a South East); and a Midlands. Sometimes the Midlands are also divided into the East Midlands and West Midlands, but that isn't as common as when splitting the North and South into their respective sides.

We do have some smaller areas, such as East Anglia (as its name implies to the east of England); the Black Country, (part of the West Midlands, that got its name from the amount of soot generated and coal mined in the dark days of the Industrial Revolution); Geordieland, (part of the North East that refers to the Newcastle and Gateshead area); and Cornwall, at the extreme tip of the South West.

Although, these are mostly sub-areas of the North East, South West etc., the latter two get a special mention because some Cornish don't regard themselves as English and even have a small band campaigning for secession. And as for my beloved Geordies, most people think they don't need a separate country as they already speak an incomprehensible language anyway.

I won't dwell on these as they are not much bigger in size terms than an Average American county, let alone state or region. Even if being as squashed up as we all are over here, their populations are either side of a million; half a million for Cornwall. But apart from these exceptions, we have a generally sensible zoning based on the traditional compass.

We even put signs on our motorways saying "The North," "The South" etc. For reasons we shall come to, I can't imagine those existing in America. Yes, on Interstate and highway markers they will add a clarifier to the number of the road so I-95 South, I-95 North, or 60 West, but that's different. In England, you see signs just saying things like "The North", "The South West" and so on. American signs state cities and compass directions, English ones state cities and regions.

I know it seems I am going on a bit here, but from talking to people as we travelled up and down the country, it seems regional classifications in America are a state of mind, rather than geography. And there was never agreement, although it was certainly emotive. Nowhere was that more evident than when we discussed it with those at the bed and breakfast who were from California, Michigan, New York, Ohio, Illinois, Vermont and South Carolina.

As best as I can understand it – and please don't flame me here – there is a West Coast, which comprises Washington State, Oregon and California. So far so good, even if people mainly have California in their mind, when they say West Coast. There is an East Coast, but things start to break down here. This seems to start only halfway up the country at Washington and continue through New York to Boston. Apparently the Carolinas, which are unarguably on the East Coast, are in the South. As is Georgia.

As well as being on the East Coast, Boston, being special, is also regarded as being in the North East. Although interestingly, despite there being a North East made up of the six states also known as New England, there doesn't seem to be a North.

There is a Midwest, which geographically is in the Mideast being between the centre and the East Coast. The Midwest doesn't run the total length of the country in its Mideast corridor, however. Whilst starting at the Canadian border, like the East Coast, it too seems to end somewhere in the centre.

It covers Michigan, Indiana, Ohio, Illinois, Kansas, Wisconsin, Iowa and Minnesota – on that pretty much everyone agreed. It seems that the Midwest is kind of a Midnorth. If you thought that was tricky though, south of here, things get a lot blurred.

Missouri, whilst officially defined by the US census Bureau as a midwestern state and roughly smack in the middle, seemed to be either a southern state or a midwestern state depending on who you talked to. Nebraska and the Dakotas got support for being in the Midwest, but we were sometimes told they weren't and were Great Plains states, instead. The Census Bureau includes these in the Midwest though. Perhaps it's trying to drag the Midwest to a more sensible location in the mid rather than the Mideast?

Kentucky and Virginia, which are both on the same middle strip as Missouri, are definitely southern, however. Even though they are both north of the middle. Even though they both have large tracts of land north of the southern parts of Indiana and Illinois, which as we have seen are midwestern states.

Tennessee, it seems, ranged from a southern state in East Tennessee to a Deep South state by the time you got to Memphis. Quite where that leaves Nashville is anyone's guess. Although, how the heck a state can change midway I don't know. That said, they manage to change time zones as you drive across Tennessee, meaning those in Nashville are one hour behind those in Knoxville.

Mississippi and Alabama to the south of Tennessee and Arkansas to its south and west were definitely in the Deep South. What the heck that makes Louisiana, heaven only knows. Antarctica? French, one wise guy said.

Florida and Texas, which are further south than any though, we were told are not in either the South or Deep South. Texas is well, Texas. Big enough to be a country on its own, and kind of regarded that way as well. And as for Florida? Aside from Floridians feeling they're not really American, even Americans will tell you that Florida is not like the rest of America anyway.

The rest, and I sincerely apologise here if I offend any citizens of these states, we were told are the fly-over states. How Americans understand their country is beyond me. I'm not sure I ever will. Although, to be honest, I'm not sure they do either. One thing that was clear though was boy does this generate a lot of emotion.

Armed with this information and the sensitivities it may cause, we entered Tennessee. After the arts and crafts, indie nature of Asheville, the town of Pigeon Forge delivered a major shock to the system.

A built up resort town, it is Tennessee's answer to Blackpool. Whereas Nashville has its strip, that's concentrated around bars and bands. Pigeon Forge, however, goes the whole nine yards. Complete with the roller coasters, crazy golf, go-karting, amusement arcades, cheap T-shirt shops, evening shows and the ubiquitous too-incredible-to-be-true display type attractions you expect in family resort centres. It even had stores boasting the world's biggest knife collection, and gun ranges where you could fire machine guns if that's what you wanted. Not even Blackpool offers such delights.

Not two hours before we had been in a city renowned for its peace and love hippie scene; the contrast could not have been greater. Nor did driving down through the Great Smoky Mountains prepare us.

Perhaps it was its setting at the edge of one of America's great National Parks that surprised us so much – rollercoasters and rivers, amusement arcades and hiking, normally being worlds apart.

Or perhaps it's just that our experience of built up mega family holiday resorts invariably involves seaside locations, Blackpool included. Notwithstanding that Blackpool provides a lot for stag and hen groups as well. I suppose you could say Orlando, Florida is an exception. Over forty miles from the sea it isn't on the coast. Although it is very hot there, and, to the British, hot usually counts as seaside anyway. Although, I accept I may be stretching a point there. Either that or my brain works in odd ways.

That said, people who live inland need family resort destinations too, and in a country the size of America getting to the coast isn't always practical. I suppose if you've got to put it somewhere, picking a place within a day's drive of two-thirds of those that live east of the Mississippi isn't a bad idea.

As with all these things, where some are trashy, others are terrific. Falling into the latter camp was the Titanic Museum. Owned by John Joslyn, who co-led the mission that explored the wreckage, retrieved items and filmed the ship's remains, they have tried to recreate as faithfully as possible the story of the doomed boat and those who sailed on her. They have done it very well.

You can walk a one million dollar exact replica of the ship's Grand Staircase and view over four hundred genuine artefacts throughout the museum. Guides in period costume add to the theatre, as well as being a mine of useful information. The museum is even housed inside a half-scale replica of the front half of the boat. Something that's quite arresting when you see it as you drive up Pigeon Forge's main parkway.

They have also added a little twist as you enter, when you are given a mocked-up boarding card of someone who was actually on the real ship, whether passenger or crew. At the end, you find out the fate that befell them, or indeed whether they survived. Although it may have seemed a little macabre – certainly for some English sensitivities – it added an extra level of interest as you toured the exhibits and saw photographs or mock-ups of the living quarters and state rooms. It was certainly something different, and we were glad we had visited.

From there it was on to Nashville. But not before a detour back to nature and Falls Creek, a 256 feet straight drop waterfall; the tallest single drop vertical waterfall east of the Rocky Mountains. Loud, powerful, dramatic, it was worth the one and a half hour diversion in the drive and subsequent fifteen minute descent to its base. Even if we needed breathing apparatus to get back to the top. From Pigeon Forge's chalk, it was back to cheese again. Nature at its rawest, a beautiful state park and solitude. In the 29,800 acre state park, we ran into less than a dozen people in our three hours there.

Having burned some calories, now it was time for Nashville. Just a couple of hours until we stashed the car and we could have a beer and a boogie. Or that's what we thought. We hadn't bargained on the remnants of Tropical Storm Olga ripping through central and Western Tennessee.

Although it had dissipated since making landfall in Louisiana, it merged with a cold front in Mississippi leading to a small band of powerful winds between 70 and 90 mph. Blissfully unaware what we heading into, we were marvelling at the imaginative names of many of the hamlets and small communities we drove through. Names such as Turkey Gobble Creek and Pork Scratching Valley, or something similar. I dare say their inhabitants think some of our villages have equally unusual names.

Parts of Tennessee are still mountainous and very rural though, and as darkness fell, you thought I wouldn't fancy breaking down here. It was the sort of place, where you are lucky if your next-door neighbour is in the same postal district as you, let alone the same street. If you could see their property, even with binoculars, it would be a bonus sort of thing. Pretty much everyone would own at least one gun, if not an arsenal. Clearly unaccustomed to passing people knocking, I certainly didn't fancy being one who had to ask for help out of the blue. Standing on someone's porch in the pitch black, looked like a sure-fire recipe to risk getting your stomach pumped full of lead.

But then we hit Olga. I have never been so frightened in my life while driving. The wind buffeted the car, whilst the rain thrashed it. It was like being hit with a left hook, followed by a right hook a fraction of a second later. Followed by the left hook, then the right over and over again. If it had been a boxing match, it would have been stopped inside seconds. Even the one throwing the punches would have gotten tired. But storms don't tire that easily, and we had no referee in the corner to put a stop to things. On and on it went.

I slowed to a crawl, but I still couldn't see a thing.

"Maybe we should stop?" said Alison.

"Where?" I responded. By now we were in the middle of nowhere. Even Farmyard Goat Fold, or whatever it was called, ten miles back now looked like a positive metropolis.

"Besides, if we do the car will probably fill with water and we'll drown." I quipped. More seriously, I was worried that just stopping might leave us more at risk of something piling into us, unable to see or anticipate a stationary car in their path. Although, with sod all on these roads at the best of times, that may have been less likely than feared. Especially, as unlike us, locals would have had the benefit of the weather forecast and storm warnings and wisely stayed in. And this part of Tennessee didn't seem the sort of place for lots of tourists.

"Anyway, double besides, we don't know how long this thing is going to last. We might be here all night until a wandering bear finds us and decides it's time for breakfast. Have a look at Google Map and see how far the nearest town is."

"Don't be silly," Alison said. But the way our luck had turned it was clear she hadn't ruled out the bear argument and I could see her frantically swishing for Mr. Google out of the corner of my eye.

"Six miles!"

"As the crow flies or of these wretched twisting roads?" That was the counter hazard to stopping still – falling off the side of the tracks that pass as roads around there.

"Oh. Nine then." Bloody Google, why does it always do that?

Then the yellow low tyre pressure warning lit up my dashboard.

This was either a faulty sensor – they usually are – or we were in big trouble. At this point I had two options. One, get out and, not withstanding my previous comments about any sensible thing being inside in these conditions, risk death by bear, being run over, or blown down a hillside. Or two, push on even more gingerly and pray for no wheel or tyre damage. What would you have done?

I pushed on. Although, I did a few tests to see if the wheel was pulling – it didn't seem to be. They rank amongst the longest nine miles of my driving life. It was as though the odometer had stopped moving.

Eventually, we got to civilisation, only to find the power was out. It was as dark as where we had come from. Still, at least the roads were straight and wide and I was able to pull into a parking lot, get out and inspect the tyres. They were fine – it was a faulty sensor. Bloody Crappo Car Hire. The wind had also started to subside and the rain began to ease. Soon things improved to what passes for just a dreadful weather day and tentatively we threaded our way on.

It had been bad though. We later found out that seven lorries had overturned on Interstate 40 in Western Tennessee, causing its closure in both directions. There were a quarter of a million power outages across Tennessee, Mississippi and Louisiana. It made me think back to the Keys and those poor folk in the Labour Day Hurricane. This was nothing on the scale of what happens when a hurricane hits. Nor is it something I want to experience again. Thank goodness the Gonzaleses gave us the SUV.

Eventually, some three hours later, the car was parked and we were suited and booted. It was time to hit town. I promise you I hadn't enjoyed a beer as much, since we hit Wahlburgers at Logan airport after our horrific flight from Detroit.

Nashville - Tumbling in Tennessee

The morning didn't start well. Kindly our Airbnb host had left a selection of hotel style toiletries. These even ran to a mint mouthwash aside from the usual shampoo, conditioner and bodywash. Sadly, though as we get older, our vision degenerates to the stage our arms are no longer long enough to be able to hold things and read them. Something I also found to my cost when I picked up the mouthwash, believing it to be the shampoo.

I knew something was up when I first smelt the mint, as it's not normally a smell you associate with shampoo. The next clue things were wrong was the tingling sensation on my scalp. Tragically though, I didn't switch on at this point. I was too busy enjoying the luxury of a shower that I didn't have to make like Quasimodo to fit under. I may even have thought it was a premium product. Like something from a spa therapy.

Stretching out, relaxing as the powerful hot water jetted away all my aches and pains, I made the mistake of opening my eyes and looked around. As you tend to, when you start thinking something's not right.

"Aaaarrrgh!!!" is about the only word I can print here.

It's a wonder the neighbours didn't call 911.

It was like somebody had gouged my eyes out with a hot spoon and dropped them into a bath of sulphuric acid. Before replacing them, wrapped in sandpaper for good measure. If I'd had the option to chop scotch bonnet chilis for an evening and then rub my eyes with my hands as an alternative, I might have taken it.

Knowing the only way out of this was to rinse my eyes until all residues of the mint monster had gone, I stood there for what seemed like an eternity, head back rubbing my eyes frenziedly. Until the hot water was exhausted and out gushed something similar to what the *Titanic* sank in.

"Aaaarrrgh!!!" is all I am able to print for the second time.

It's also a good job the neighbours weren't on the ball or we would have had a whole SWAT team outside by the time I finished. Plus, we'd have lost our security deposit as I know how these guys open apartment doors. On the plus side, at least I was now wide awake.

Touring Nashville, they will tell you they were the last state to join the confederacy and the first to re-join the Union. They will tell you how it was their state that was the key one in ratifying the nineteenth amendment giving women the vote across the nation in 1920. Perhaps it is their way of saying they're a southern state, not a deep southern state. (Mississippi was the last to ratify the nineteenth amendment. In 1984). What they don't tell you though is that prior to Nashville, thirty-five other states had already voted to give women suffrage. Or that Tennessee's legislators tied 48-48 when first voting on the relevant resolution. It was only when their youngest representative, Harry T. Burn, changed his mind and voted in favour – ironically following a letter from his mother – that the necessary legislation passed.

In terms of architecture and things to see, Nashville isn't on the same scale as New York, Washington, Boston, Detroit or even Miami Beach, but there is plenty to keep you distracted for a few hours. Particularly, if you are into country music and its history. The Ryman Auditorium is well preserved and the Grand Ole Opry, and the Country Music Hall of Fame and Museum are great destinations for those who love that genre. The former Union Station, built in 1900, has been sympathetically converted into a fine hotel that highlights its sixty-five foot barrelled ceiling lobby. There is also a full-scale replica of the Parthenon in Centennial Park, built in 1897 for the Tennessee Centennial Exposition.

Perhaps reflecting the party atmosphere, there are also lots of fun, or even just quirky, items dotted around. From artful murals on building walls through to a 1956 former Greyhound bus parked on top of a hotel (where it serves as a pretty cool bar). Their tallest building – in fact the tallest building in Tennessee – even looks a bit like Batman.

The Nissan Stadium, home to the Tennessee Titans football team, is in the centre of the city, as all good stadia should be, even if it hasn't got a roof. It's something that helps generate a good atmosphere, especially being just a short walk across the Cumberland River from the plentiful downtown bars.

Nashville is also famous for its boot shops. Or cowboy boots as we call them back home. I've always been partial to these and not just because they add a couple of crucial inches to my height. I can't explain why – I just think they look nice. Well I can tell you, that if you like your boots Nashville is where to go. They have pretty much every shape style and pattern you could ever think of. Along with an interesting pricing strategy. Sod the buy one, get one free deals you see the world over, here it is buy one get two free. Pairs that is, not boots. Of course the boots are probably three times the price of anywhere else and the deal means in reality you get to buy three pairs of boots instead of one to break even. That said, you're so spoilt for choice it probably saves people all the heartache angsting between options and makes their lives easier anyway. "Sod it, I'll take all three," kind of thing.

It's hard to stress enough how seriously these folk take their boots. In what is a fairly macho, where men are men, sort of town I even had an American guy start a conversation with me by asking me where I'd got my boots. I was delighted as they were quite a snazzy pair Alison got me for a special birthday.

When I told him England though, he point blank refused to believe me.

"Not possible," he said.

"Seriously," I replied.

"No sir, no way are those English boots. They can't be."

"Honestly, they are. My wife bought them off e-bay."

Even if it reinforced his point, it did leave him speechless for a while. It turned out she had had them specially imported.

Make no mistake though, Broadway is the focus of Nashville's downtown. It is literally, as well as geographically, its beating heart. It's what Nashville is famous for. Plus these days, with the Broadway area having undergone dramatic growth over the last decade or so, Nashville is now also famous for the quality of all of its live music scene. Not just country.

Rightly so. It's brilliant.

In the one hundred or so acres covering Broadway, Printers Alley and related streets, there must be a hundred bars and I can't think of any that didn't have a live band on. I'm sure there will be some, but for the life of me none spring to mind. Some of them have several floors, with a different group – and even a different style of music – on each level. Competition is fierce. Meaning, not only are the bands free to watch, but the standards are also high. Rather like Key West, you end up choosing your bar based on which band you like, as opposed to other considerations such as the décor, range of beers, or the crowd inside.

There is also a league pyramid to the bars. Broadly, the bigger and better the bar, the bigger and better the band. Along with usually a dollar or two on the drinks. But hey, it's more than covered by the step up in quality of the music. Some of the bands we saw – in particular at Kid Rock's place, or later in the evening at the Wildhorse Saloon – were as good as if we had paid to go to a concert.

The area, particularly later on and at weekends, is insane. The noise from the bars. The sheer amount of people – all staggering, squawking, and shrieking. Everyone, excited and twittering. It's like pigeons in Trafalgar Square. And even though it's crammed and people are loaded with drink, it never gets out of hand. Or not that we saw anyway.

But that was to come later. First, we had a line dancing class to get to. If you're going to line dance, Nashville is the place to do it. Whilst I admit to not being super enthusiastic, this had been on Alison's bucket list for ages, and so that was that. Besides when in Rome……

As it was so important to her, this time Alison had done the research and we bowled up at a place called the Wildhorse Saloon. A large dancefloor, (the biggest in Tennessee); a good stage and sound system, (so the instructor could take you clearly through your paces); and a big bar and seating area. It was perfect.

The lesson was free, and when we arrived, the bar was holding its happy hour promotion. What could possibly go wrong? I had even put on my lucky cowboy boots, especially for the occasion.

Things started smooth enough. The instructor would talk the class through a move, show us it, and we would then all copy it. Or attempt to copy it in some of our cases.

After learning how to stomp, stamp and sashay, we progressed to shuffles, stepovers and even some fancy thing when you did a combination of these, clapped your hands and culminated the move with a turn to your right. Or left, I still can't be entirely sure. Maybe they used both directions, and the direction selected depended on the exact move?

You can probably tell here that dancing isn't my strong suit. To be honest, I even struggle with old man dancing at weddings. You know the sort, when you broadly just have to shuffle your weight from one foot to another, whilst throwing in the odd twist of the hips.

Anyway, towards the end of the lesson, they let you loose and off you go to a whole dance track, whilst the instructor shouts stomp and clap, three quarter twist or whatever it was that was intended to act as a helpful reminder to keep us all in time.

Line dancing, however, is both a step up from the wedding leagues and also a fairly solitary activity. For those as new to this activity as I was, you don't really have a partner, as in traditional dancing. Instead, a line of you are all supposed to dance the same move at the same time. Like the name implies, I suppose. It's kind of like synchronised swimming, but on a dance floor. Now although, dancing isn't my favourite pastime, with Alison by my side everything went reasonably well. I may have slightly lagged her moves, but it didn't matter and everyone had a great time.

The lesson safely completed, I determined that we should celebrate with a drink. As it was happy hour, we should even have two. Emboldened by my success in the previous lesson – actually that should read survival – and potentially flush from the false confidence that beer can give you, I suggested we do it again when they made the call for the next lesson.

"It's alright honey, I've had enough. I'll sit this one out," said Alison. "You do it though, and I'll video it for the kids."

Perhaps it was the beer that turned my two left feet into three. Perhaps it was the pressure from the increasingly rumbustious crowd enjoying the happy hour. As most British people know, Wetherspoon venues are always a lot livelier than upscale wine bars. Maybe it was because the instructor, in an effort to add variety to her day, taught us a whole different bunch of moves than she had in the prior lesson. Maybe it was just that I didn't have my soul mate to follow. Whatever it was though, things soon started to unravel.

Suddenly teacher's instructions weren't as easy to follow. Let alone remember when you had a whole sequence to execute. Then, it all happened. In fact, I am still hanging my head as I write. The moment of truth had come, and we had to put all that we had learned into the three-minute track at the end.

I still can't remember the exact moment everything fell apart. Other than, I think it was the second or third move. I am sure I got the first one right. After that though, things turned to mush pretty quickly. I was stomping when my line was stamping. I was stamping when they were clapping. I tried taking some time outs to see if I could jump back in at a certain move and catch up, but that tactic seemed to make things even worse. The nadir was reached when everyone was supposed to take two steps to the right and then turn ninety degrees clockwise. And everyone did. Except me. I took two steps to the left and turned ninety degrees anti-clockwise.

I don't know who was more surprised. Me or the guy who I turned into. Actually I think him, judging by (a) the look on his face and (b) the fact that I had the reactions to catch him as he fell onto me. Luckily the line was quite well spaced out, or the whole thing could have gone down like a set of dominoes.

In my defence, I would like to say that I am left-handed and always doing things backwards. True. I even write my sentences in the wrong order and spend forever correcting them, something you may also have noticed by this stage. It's like writing with Yoda.

If that was my low point, I ran it a close second a few moments later when for some inexplicable reason, with the line doing a step over and clap, I started spinning in circles. Whilst they all looked as slick as the Jackson Five, I was busy imitating Rudolph Nureyev in cowboy boots.

The song finished, I knew things hadn't gone as well as they might have done. Something that was confirmed when I looked up to see the crowd at the bar and all those seated around divided into two camps. Half were gaping open-mouthed, as frozen as those on the porch in Asheville. Some even had their pint still, in mid-air, unable to complete the journey to mouth or put it back down again. They looked shell shocked. They were either in disbelief or denial.

The other half were delirious with laughter. Roaring. They were having their MOMA moment. The trouble was there was a bar sized quantity of people pissing themselves. I was hoping it wasn't me that was the joke, but in my heart I knew. I was a broken man.

Slinking back to where Alison was seated, things seemed to be even worse than I thought, as she had tears streaming down her face. How badly had I embarrassed her this time? I'd certainly not seen tears of shame before.

"Are you ok love?" I asked, putting an arm out to console her.

"I'll be fine. I just need a few moments."

"I understand. I'm sorry if I ruined your bucket list day."

"Ruined it? Ruined it? You've made it."

"Really?"

"For sure. I have never laughed as much."

They say God moves in mysterious ways. I am starting to wonder if his plans for me aren't quite what I had originally hoped.

Anyway, after that, there was only one thing left to do. Hit the strip and party!

What else is there to say about Nashville? Well, whilst not plenty, there are a few things to see and do – particularly if you are a hardcore country music fan. It's also a nice enough city to visit, but it's a long way to go just for that. Put it this way, if you want sightseeing, there are many better places, much nearer. Well, for us anyway – it depends where you start from, of course. But when it comes to beer, bands and boogieing, I don't think you'll find it beaten. If you go, you'll have a blast.

Just don't forget to take your cowboy boots.

Memphis - Thank God for Elvis!

Actually, that should read thank God for Elvis and Sun Studios.

Memphis is not what you expect. Particularly if you're coming from Britain. Your mind's eye tells you it will be a laid back, hip place, filled with funky blues bars and places serving the most exquisite BBQ food. It is home to the blues and Elvis and will be cool.

Well, it is home to Elvis and Graceland, and that is beyond excellent. Don't bank on the rest.

Memphis is one of the poorest, roughest cities in America. At the time of writing, it was the second most dangerous city in the USA for violent crime, based on information gleaned from the FBI's Universal Crime Reporting Program. Only Detroit was worse. Beale Street, which is its version of Nashville's Broadway, is a small strip in the centre where you'll find the bands and blues bars. But it's an enclave, outside there isn't that much around. There are odd exceptions, like Gus's Fried Chicken and Central BBQ, not far from the Civil Rights Museum, but they are odd bright spots.

Even Beale Street is nothing compared to Nashville. It's a handful of bars where bands play, and it screams tourist trap the moment you walk down it. Sure, Nashville is also full of out-of-towners, but at least its quality. There people are laughing, cavorting, having a great time. Here, it feels that people are huddled together, killing time before they move onto their next city or leave to go home. Maybe they call it the blues for a reason.

The place is full of attitude, and not in a good way. Most bands play for tips. If they're good, you don't mind chucking in a bit. In Nashville they'll sing several songs before reminding you to tip, some will practically play a set. In Memphis, it seems after every song you get the hard squeeze. They might as well just scream, "Give us your money." At least when Bob Geldof did that, it was for a good cause. You start to wonder whether these guys are bands or professional beggars. After a while it kills the mood. Unless you want the blues, of course.

They'll tell you Memphis is the birthplace of the blues and "home of the blues." It is the birthplace of the blues, that is indisputable, but isn't home to the blues. Not anymore. This is a city living in its past. Just because you were once its birthplace, doesn't automatically mean you are still it's home. Children grow up and move on.

It's a city that relies on the lure of Elvis to bring people in and see its other facets. What will become of it if Elvis's shine ever fades, heaven only knows. And I don't invoke the reference to God there lightly. Elvis is the King, and it is inconceivable today that he won't always be, but fans age and you can't guarantee that future generations will always feel the same.

If not the biggest hype job in history, Memphis is certainly living on its former fame. And living in the past seldom guarantees living successfully in the future.

We had done our research and I tried to work out how the reality could be so different from the expectation. The only thing I can conclude was that these days people are reticent about speaking out when the news is not so good for fear of the on-line flaming they'll get. It's always easier to be happy, clappy about a place and keep your head down if things ain't so great. There's always some loon out there after all. The trouble is, that's how myths perpetuate.

The last few paragraphs have been the hardest to write. Not many people want to put the boot into places, needlessly or deservedly, but I wouldn't have been true to myself or those reading if I hadn't said it how we experienced it. There's not one British person I have ever spoken to – who has actually been there – who thinks different. Even an Australian couple of our age, who we met and shared some drinks with whilst there, felt the same. As you walk around the downtown area – which is usually not too far in case you stray into the wrong neighbourhood – you can see disbelief etched on every visitor's face.

Officially, Detroit is poorer than Memphis. At present. But whilst remaining alert, we were happy to walk around downtown Detroit. It also had lots more going for it. To be fair, it is also a lot bigger. Physically, if not necessarily in terms of population. But it's Detroit, the city everyone in America uses as the poster child for inner-city decay.

One of the things that you only realise after a while is how little life there is in Memphis's city centre. You can see the degradation; you can feel the attitude; but there is something else always gnawing away at you and you can't put your finger on it to start with. Then you realise it. There aren't many people around. Not for a city of 650,000. (Roughly the same size as Detroit incidentally, although the population of Memphis's metropolitan area is a little under a third of Detroit's equivalent).

There is also not much traffic, even when you get away from the pedestrian zoned part of Beale Street. Certainly not the level of traffic and economic activity you would normally associate with a city of this scale.

We went to the Civil Rights Museum. It was closed. The place where Dr. Martin Luther King was killed. Closed on Tuesdays. That would never happen in Washington. The other thing that struck us, as we paid our respects outside the balcony where he was shot, was how poor the grade of hotel was where he stayed. In Washington he wrote his "I Have a Dream" speech in one of the finest hotels in the city. A hotel regularly used by Presidents of the United States. In Memphis, even five years later, he hadn't been allowed to stay in the finer hotels because of the colour of his skin. That was in our lifetime. Just, but nevertheless in living memory. Shameful. At least those days are behind us.

To be fair, the fried chicken at Gus's, along with its ambience, was great. Hot, crunchy and juicy. Cheap and cheerful. The queues out the door are testament to that. We even met a couple from Arkansas who came over for a monthly treat.

Central BBQ also had rustic surroundings and was also class. Top quality Southern BBQ food, they had every option you could think of catered for. Wet, dry, pork, beef, chicken, you name it – they did it. Smoky, melt in the mouth, tasty. It was quality.

As was our trip to Sun Studios. You got to learn all about the history of the recording studio Sam Smith founded and realise just how important its contribution to modern music was. You find out how it was actually his assistant, Marion Keisker, who discovered and first recorded Elvis, when *he* came in and *paid* $3.25 to record two songs to a demo acetate. It was she who saw his potential and kept pushing and recommending him to the studio, despite their initial reluctance, until his first single was cut. Something Elvis recognised and credited publicly.

Along with many items of memorabilia, the studio has also recreated, piece by piece, the original radio booth from which local disc jockey Dewey Phillips first played Elvis's original single "That's All Right" on the 8th July, 1954. Dewey's shows were very popular and, following an unprecedented number of phone calls, he played the record over a dozen times that evening. In fact, he was so overwhelmed by the number of calls coming in, he even invited Elvis into the studio for a live on-air interview. The song became an instant hit, and the rest as they say is history.

As well as viewing rare guitars, photographs and other artefacts, you actually get to enter the studio where Elvis recorded his original hits. A studio also home to stars such as Johnny Cash, Carl Perkins, Roy Orbison, B.B. King, Howlin' Wolf, and where Jerry Lee Lewis recorded "Great Balls of Fire". U2 even used it to record some tracks for their 1988 album *Rattle and Hum.*

Elvis's microphone is still there, and the studio has helpfully marked the exact spot where he stood whilst recording his debut single. They even allow you to grab the mic and sing into it, all whilst standing on the X that marks the spot. Even if it is unplugged, for a brief interlude, you are there. You are the next Elvis. You can sing in the footsteps of the King.

And all included within the $15 ticket for entry to the studios. To be fair to Memphis, if that was Manhattan or any other major city in the US, they would have monetised that experience beyond belief. In some, they would have even created a VIP premium express line.

Maybe Memphis isn't so bad after all.

After Sun Studios, we went to the Peabody Hotel. It's possibly Memphis's finest hotel, but is probably best known for its resident ducks. Boy, have these birds got it made. They live in a $200,000 Duck Palace on the rooftop of the hotel and then every day at eleven a.m. get to come down via a red carpet and spend the day in an ornate marble fountain in the centre of the hotel. At five p.m. their march is reversed and they leave the fountain and toddle along their red route into the main elevators to spend the night in their penthouse palace. All whilst accompanied by a Duckmaster resplendent in a red jacket and red tie to match the colour of the carpet they parade down.

It's quite a sight. A little bit off the wall and certainly popular with the kids, but quite a sight nevertheless. Actually it's not just popular with kids, everyone seemed enthralled. The hotel was crammed with onlookers – all smiling, chirruping and generally having a good time. Alison was in her element.

"Aren't they so cute?" she cooed.

I thought I could do with watching these guys and learning a thing or two. I mean, not only had they wrapped all the women in the room around their little feet, they had also managed to blag a pretty good lifestyle if you ask me.

One other thing that strikes you as you watch the Peabody Parade and that is how well trained the ducks are. There's no messing, no fighting and no flying off. Mind you, if you were on a number as good as theirs I don't suppose you'd be tempted to toss it away and fly off into the wild.

From the Peabody we went to Graceland. It is hard to find the words to do this place justice. It is more than the Palace of the King.

You start in a small auditorium with a film giving background information about Elvis and his life. As the lights went up for us to catch the bus that would then take us across the busy Elvis Presley Boulevard to the mansion itself, I noticed that Alison was crying. As for many others, Elvis is her idol. It was for her and the opportunity to visit Graceland that we came to Memphis, and she was overcome with emotion. That, and as she said, the sad reflection on a life that ended too soon.

His house is amazing. Not just because you can walk around most parts of it, including the gardens and outbuildings. Not just because of its variety, with each room being so different from any other. But because it is relatively normal.

Whilst the upstairs is understandably reserved for family reasons, your visit takes you within touching distance of his kitchen units, where his legendary peanut butter and fried banana sandwiches were prepared; the dining table, where he and his family ate; the pool table in his games room; the piano in the racquetball building – at which he sang and played "Unchained Melody" the last day he was alive. The list goes on and on. Everything is set up as it was in the days when Elvis was still alive. You half expect him to walk through the door at any moment.

What is remarkable though is that mansion is too strong a word for Graceland. It is more like a very big house. The rooms, whilst containing nice furniture and decorations, are not palatial. The house reflects the original farm Elvis bought in 1957, which he then added to over the years. Whilst it is would be wrong to say it is normal (any house that contains a Jungle Room is a little unusual after all), it is nothing like you would expect from someone of his fame and wealth. Today's top sports and music stars practically live in castles after all. Whereas Graceland appears a nice, albeit large, family house.

As well as the differences between each room, you are struck by how Elvis must have loved striking colours. After walking past a nice cream coloured lounge, through the white and cream hallway with blue curtains at the top and then the tastefully decorated dining room you descend a staircase with fully mirrored walls and ceilings until you land in a TV room of the brightest yellow you could imagine. If that weren't stimulation enough, in there are three televisions.

The games room is like entering a Bedouin tent, complete with ceiling and walls covered in an ornate pleated fabric. And as for the jungle room – aside from the deep green carpet, 1970s style stone wall (in Elvis's case from floor to ceiling) and dark wood furniture, even its ceiling was covered in the same deep green carpet of the floor. Something that inadvertently produced a nice dampening of sound which lead to Elvis recording his last two studio albums *From Elvis Presley Boulevard, Memphis, Tennessee* and *Moody Blue* in it.

After a while, as you tour the house and museum afterwards, one of the key things that also comes across is what a family guy Elvis was. Clearly, being Elvis, he can never be considered regular in the usual sense, but as you absorb everything around you it seems he was quite a shy guy, and someone who adored his entire family.

A guy who also had a strong sense of right and wrong. He willingly undertook his national service, even though it came at a critical time, as his career was exploding. Two years is a long time in a musician's life and there was no guarantee that tastes wouldn't have moved on when he returned from the services. Not only that, but despite pressures on him to go into a special unit, a softer option which could be used for such things as recruitment drives, he chose to serve as a regular G.I. He also opted for all regular duties, including cleaning the latrines when his turn.

Back in Memphis, he even became an honorary member of the Memphis Police department, complete with badge and flashing lights for the dashboard of his car. Something that extended to pulling people over that were speeding and giving them a ticking off. It's also clear that he was immensely proud of his city and never once considered moving. Never once considered Graceland as anything other than home.

In the garden, behind the modest sized swimming pool, is the garden of meditation. Something Elvis had installed to help him reflect and contemplate when at home, and away from his frenetic work schedule. It is also where he is buried, along with his parents and his maternal grandmother. It completes the tour of the house and is where we paid our respects. Although open to the public, it still manages to be a private place. Enhanced by the running water of the fountain a few steps away, it is tranquil. There is a serenity. Everyone is lost in their own thoughts.

In a process that takes less than two minutes, you are then bussed back across the boulevard to the visitor centre. There you can tour the various galleries that house all sorts of memorabilia and information about Elvis. From his extensive collection of cars – yes including the iconic Pink Cadillac – to his golden discs; from his private jets to the legendary jumpsuits. Everyone loves the jumpsuits.

To say it is comprehensive would be an understatement. You even get to see the television that RCA gave Elvis to commemorate his sale of fifty million records between 1956 and 1960. It was one of those clunky old-fashioned types wedged into a sideboard to look like a piece of furniture. I doubt if it had much more than a twenty inch screen. Talk about times changing, can you imagine the stars of today being delighted to accept something like that after selling fifty million records?

It also makes you realise just how much this one man, born into abject poverty, achieved. In addition to starring in thirty-one feature films, it is believed he sold over one billion records. More than anyone else in recording industry history. The wall of golden discs and awards just blew me away. You can read on a piece of paper his achievements.

It's not the same as standing there, when you see what that means in reality. Dwarfed by a wall of golden records.

Not only was he talented, but his drive and his work ethic were immense. Even after recording all those songs, once he left films to go back into music, he still played over 1,100 shows in 130 cities between 1969 and 1977, when he died. Talent is one thing, but too often it is wasted. It is that resilience and capacity for hard work that separates the good from the great. I guess talent is a bit like electricity. Raw potential is something, but without delivery it is nothing. Elvis delivered.

He adopted the phrase "taking care of business" which he applied to all aspects of his career. Even before every concert he still reminded all those working him that, once again, it was a new audience, they may not have seen them before – and that they had to deliver as though it were still their very first time. He was the consummate professional. It made him the King.

With hindsight, rather than staying in a downtown Airbnb, we should have holidayed at the Graceland hotel and caught an Uber in when we wanted to sample the Beale Street scene and nearby offerings. It would have been the best way to approach Memphis.

As it was, Graceland made for the perfect end to our trip. Alison had knocked off the biggest item on her bucket list, and even though I wasn't particularly an Elvis fan, it would be hard to top it. Lincoln Memorial aside.

Homeward Bound

They say travel broadens the mind. It certainly broadens the stomach. Particularly in America. To start with there are the portion sizes – they're just huge. We can cope when we go Stateside by sharing meals and skipping starters until we adjust, but I wonder how Americans cope when visiting our Fair Isle? They must think it's like an enforced diet. Eating out must cost a fortune as they double up on dishes. Although, with the state of the pound these days, possibly not.

Then there's the food itself, it's just too damn tasty. These days the UK food scene is probably one of the most varied in the world, if not the most varied. But for some reason, we can't do burgers and BBQ like the Americans. Even those restaurants that claim to. That said, outside of New York, I don't think there was anywhere we went that matched the variety here. Pretty much any reasonably sized English city will give you a great choice of English, French, Spanish, Italian, Mexican, Chinese, Thai, Greek, the list just goes on and on, food. Not to mention Indian. Nowhere outside India can make a proper British curry.

Indeed, as we made our way home now, that was the thing we craved the most – there's a good reason Chicken Tikka Masala now outsells Fish and Chips as our national dish.

We'd packed a lot into our travels and had some wonderful experiences. Not everything was great – in fact that's impossible. If everything were great, nothing would seem so. Sometimes, it's the bad and indifferent things in life that make you truly appreciate the good. Nor was everything as imagined. And anyway, part of travelling is opening your mind to experience new things.

On the whole, we'd had a great time and couldn't believe the variety in the United States. No two of the cities we visited were alike. For sure you would encounter some of the same coffee chains and same hotel groups everywhere, but nevertheless each city had a very distinct and different identity. It definitely wasn't the case of seen one city, seen them all. And that was before you got out into the wider countryside, which given the vast size of the country also varied immensely from region to region.

On our trails we had seen a lot of America. From the marvels of Manhattan to the wonders of Washington. From the President's Palace to the Palace of the King. From its Great Lakes to its great seats of learning. From Mackinac Island, less than fifty miles from the Canadian Border to Key West, its most southerly point. From nearly being mugged (or worse) in Miami to the kindness of a stranger at Detroit airport. It had been wonderful.

We had also started to appreciate its evolution over time. In Washington, we had learned about the history that created this country, from the hated Stamp Act through to today. Whilst in New York, the city that never stops, we saw the buildings of tomorrow rising in front of us.

You get good and bad everywhere you go, but by and large this is a great country with great people.

All we needed to do now was hit the West Coast.

Postscript

I realise readers will be wondering by now what the hell do the sunburnt penguins have to do with anything?

Well, rather bizarrely it's a moniker we've had for more years than I can remember now. It started out early in our married life as a play on words, the penguins representing our living in a cold northern climate and the sunburn our love of travel to hot places. There was also the double entendre in that as Newcastle fans (a team that plays in black and white) exiled in the North West we longed one day to be all over the reds of England's most successful team, Manchester United. Black and white and all over the reds, where of course a sunburnt penguin is black and white and red all over. In fact thinking back it might even have arisen one night after a bottle of wine too many with our friends and a bit of football banter.

A bit odd? Probably, but as I've said before my (left handed) brain doesn't always think straight. Anyway, it was something that stuck so long ago that even many of our friends now refer to us as the sunburnt penguins. As a result, I used it as my moniker on Tripadvisor and given the positive feedback the trip report got it made sense somewhere in the left handed brain to continue the theming.

I hope that helps.

Talking of helping, if you could also do something to help future readers and leave a review on Amazon that would be wonderful – it helps so many readers decide whether a book is right for them.

I truly hope that you have enjoyed reading about our experiences of America so far. Thank you.

Jim

Acknowledgements

This book would not have been possible without the support of Alex, Aron, Delma, Geordie Paul, James, Josh, Lisa, Mel, Mike, Rhiannon, Veronica and most importantly Alison who critiqued, cajoled and above all cared. Thank you.

About the Author

Jim is someone who embraces life and the world with enthusiasm. Unfortunately, life and the world don't always seem to see things the same way.

He puts it down to his left handedness. Those that know him put it down to always being left behind.

His writing career started when posting a trip report on Tripadvisor which was remarkably well received. The feedback he got spurred him onto write this book. Sadly, this has not diminished his ardour and he is now working on his next assignment.

Printed in Great Britain
by Amazon

49277721R00170